THE
TRIUMPHANT
CHURCH

Kenneth E. Hagin

Unless otherwise indicated, all Scripture quotations in this volume are from the *King James Version* of the Bible.

Cover photograph of throne chair used by permission:
Philbrook Museum of Art
Tulsa, Oklahoma

Eighth Printing 2000

ISBN 0-89276-520-8

In the U.S. write:
Kenneth Hagin Ministries
P.O. Box 50126
Tulsa, OK 74150-0126

In Canada write:
Kenneth Hagin Ministries
P.O. Box 335, Station D
Etobicoke (Toronto), Ontario
Canada, M9A 4X3

Contents

1. Origins: Satan and His Kingdom 1

2. Rightly Dividing Man: Spirit, Soul, and Body 21

3. The Devil or the Flesh? 45

4. Distinguishing the Difference Between
   Oppression, Obsession, And Possession 71

5. Can a Christian Have a Demon? 95

6. How To Deal With Evil Spirits 115

7. The Wisdom of God 141

8. Spiritual Warfare:
   Are You Wrestling or Resting? 171

9. Pulling Down Strongholds 201

10. Praying Scripturally To Thwart
    The Kingdom of Darkness 223

11. Is the Deliverance Ministry Scriptural? 251

12. Scriptural Ways To Minister Deliverance 271

Chapter 1
Origins: Satan and His Kingdom

Believers are seated with Christ in heavenly places, far above all powers and principalities of darkness. No demon can deter the believer who is seated with Christ *far above* all the works of the enemy! Our seating and reigning with Christ in heavenly places is a position of authority, honor, and triumph — not failure, depression, and defeat.

Since the Church of the Lord Jesus Christ has the triumph and victory over the devil and his cohorts in every encounter, why does it seem so many believers are subject to Satan and his deceptions?

Whether or not believers are victorious over the devil depends on what view they have of themselves as the Church — militant, defeated, or triumphant. It all depends on how well they understand their position in Christ.

The *militant* Church depicts a body of believers who are not *yet* seated in heavenly places in Christ and are still "battling" to try to gain the victory over an enemy that hasn't been defeated yet by the Lord Jesus Christ.

The *defeated* Church also gives us a picture of a Church which is ignorant of the fact that they are seated with Christ and that they are supposed to be reigning in life through Jesus Christ. Because they are ignorant of their position in Christ or they've never used the authority they really possess, these believers are constantly ravaged by the wiles of Satan and are in a state of continual failure and defeat.

But the *triumphant Church* is the biblical perspective of the Body of Christ seated with Christ in heavenly places *far above* all powers and principalities (Eph. 1:3; 2:6). The triumphant Church scripturally portrays a Body of believers who not only *know* but *exercise* their authority in Christ and therefore reign victoriously in life through Jesus Christ over Satan, a defeated foe (Rom. 5:17).

In this age when demon activity is increasing around the world, it is vital that believers know what their redemption in Christ entitles them to. We need to be fully convinced of the authority that is ours because of the victory Jesus has *already* won for us over all the power of the enemy. The only way we can have confidence in our authority over the enemy is to *know* and *walk in the light* of the written Word of God.

With that introduction, let's go to the Book of beginnings, Genesis, and start our study by investigating the origins of Satan and his kingdom.

Hints of a Possible Pre-Adamic Kingdom

The origin and fall of Satan, or Lucifer, as he was called is made fairly clear in Scripture. He was called *Lucifer* before his expulsion and fall from Heaven, but *Satan* after his expulsion and fall. The origin of demons, devils, or evil spirits is not made so clear.

Some Bible scholars believe millions of years elapsed between Genesis 1:1 and Genesis 1:2. And some believe there could have been an original earthly kingdom *before* the creation recorded in Genesis chapter 1.

GENESIS 1:1,2
1 In the beginning God created the heaven and the earth.
2 And the earth was without form, and void; and darkness was upon the face of the deep. And the Spirit of God moved upon the face of the waters.

The evil spirits that are here on earth now could have been part of that original pre-Adamic kingdom. Many Bible scholars agree that even before the flood, a pre-Adamic kingdom existed, because we know from archeological discoveries that dinosaurs and mammoth animals once lived on the earth.

Where did they come from? Maybe those creatures came from a different kind of creation that existed on the earth before Adam — some kind of a pre-Adamic creation. In Isaiah chapter 14, we have a hint in Scriptures of a pre-Adamic kingdom.

ISAIAH 14:12-14
12 How art thou fallen from heaven, O Lucifer, son of the morning! how art thou cut down to the ground, which didst weaken the nations!
13 For thou hast said in thine heart, I will ASCEND INTO HEAVEN, I will exalt MY THRONE ABOVE THE STARS of God: I will sit also upon the mount of the congregation, in the sides of the north:
14 I will ASCEND ABOVE the HEIGHTS of the CLOUDS; I will be like the most High.

Evidently Lucifer had some kind of a throne indicating some kind of authority. Lucifer probably reigned *below* the clouds and stars because verse 13 says, *". . . I will exalt my throne ABOVE the stars. . . ,"* implying that Lucifer's throne was *below* the stars. If Lucifer's throne was below the stars, it could have encompassed and included the realm and domain of the earth.

It's possible that Lucifer ruled a kingdom here on earth which existed before Adam but at the same time pre-historic animals roamed this earth. Maybe Satan ruled his kingdom during this pre-Adamic creation, and the evil spirits we now have on the earth were fallen spirit beings from that creation. We don't have chapter and verse for it; but on the other hand, Scripture doesn't refute it either. We do see hints of it in the Scripture.

Also, we do know that there *are* evil spirits here on the earth today. So where did they come from? The other possibility is that evil spirits include those angels that fell in Lucifer's rebellion (Rev. 12:4,9).

Man was *not* part of that pre-adamic creation, for the Bible indicates that Adam was the first man: *"And so it is written, The FIRST MAN Adam was made a living soul . . ."* (1 Cor. 15:45). But some kind of creation could have existed before Adam — even an entirely different kind of creation than we know today.

I'm not presenting this theory dogmatically because we don't have enough light on it in the Scriptures to be dogmatic. We can't be dogmatic on matters we can't support scripturally. Sometimes we wish we had more light on the origin of evil spirits, but evidently God told us in His Word what He wanted us to know.

Lucifer's Original Position and Fall

We can say with certainty that the devil and demons are fallen beings because the Bible says they are. They have fallen from whatever estate they once occupied (Rev. 12:4,9). And the Bible does shed light on the origin of Satan, or Lucifer, as he was originally called.

Where did Satan come from originally? Isaiah 14 and Ezekiel 28 give us a picture of Lucifer's existence in the beginning as God originally created him and his rebellion and fall. We know that God didn't make Satan as he is today because God made everything in the beginning and it was all good (Gen. 1:10,12,18,21,25; James 1:17).

In Ezekiel chapter 28, the Bible describes Lucifer before his expulsion and fall from Heaven.

EZEKIEL 28:12-16
12 . . . Thus saith the Lord God; Thou sealest up the sum, FULL OF WISDOM, and PERFECT IN BEAUTY.
13 Thou hast been in Eden the garden of God; EVERY PRECIOUS STONE WAS THY COVERING . . . the workmanship of thy tabrets and of thy pipes was prepared in thee in the day that THOU WAST CREATED.
14 Thou art THE ANOINTED CHERUB that covereth; and I have set thee so: THOU WAST UPON THE HOLY MOUNTAIN OF GOD; thou hast walked up and down in the midst of the stones of fire.
15 Thou was PERFECT IN THY WAYS from the day that thou wast created, TILL INIQUITY WAS FOUND IN THEE.
16 By the multitude of thy merchandise they have filled the midst of thee with violence, and THOU HAST SINNED: therefore I will cast thee AS PROFANE out of the mountain of God: and I will destroy thee, O COVERING CHERUB, from the midst of the stones of fire.

In this passage the Bible refers to Lucifer as a created being, "an anointed cherub," not as a human being: *"Thou was perfect in all thy ways from the day that THOU WAST CREATED, till iniquity was found in thee"* (v. 15).

God didn't create Lucifer as we know him now. After Lucifer's expulsion and fall from Heaven, he became the *devil*, but he was not created that way. God created Lucifer perfect in his ways (Ezek. 28:15), full of wisdom and perfect in beauty (v. 12). The Bible also says that Lucifer was ". . . *upon the holy mountain of God . . .*" (Ezek. 28:14), so we know he had some access to God.

Here is another interesting thought about Lucifer as he was originally created. Ezekiel 28:13 tells us: ". . . *the workmanship of thy tabrets and of thy pipes was prepared in thee in the day that thou wast created.*"

Evidently Lucifer had something to do with music. Perhaps he was Heaven's chief musician before his expulsion and fall from Heaven. Did you ever notice how music plays a part in the plan and program of God, as well as in Satan's plan?

The right kind of music prepares you to yield to the Spirit of God, and the wrong kind prepares you to yield to the spirit of the devil. The devil works through the flesh or unregenerated soul, but God works through your spirit by the Holy Spirit.

The Bible says iniquity was found in Lucifer (Ezek. 28:15). What was his sin?

EZEKIEL 28:17,18
17 THINE HEART WAS LIFTED UP BECAUSE OF THY
BEAUTY, thou hast corrupted thy wisdom BY REASON OF
THY BRIGHTNESS. . . .
18 Thou hast DEFILED thy sanctuaries by the multitude of
THINE INIQUITIES. . . .

Lucifer was lifted up in pride because of his great beauty. Because of his pride, he wanted to become like God and ascend into Heaven so he could usurp God's authority. The Bible talks about Lucifer's iniquity in Isaiah 14, where God tells us Lucifer's evil intentions based on his five declarations or "I wills."

ISAIAH 14:13,14
13 For thou hast said in thine heart, I WILL ascend into
heaven, I WILL exalt my throne above the stars of God: I
WILL sit also upon the mount of the congregation, in the
sides of the north:
14 I WILL ascend above the heights of the clouds; I WILL
be like the most High.

Evidently Lucifer was a free moral agent and had free exercise of his own will, for Lucifer said, "I *will*." He could choose. And he made the wrong choice; he tried to exalt his throne above God's throne. Because of that, God said to Lucifer, ". . . *thou hast sinned* . . ." (Ezek. 28:16).

Then in Ezekiel 28, notice how God responded to Lucifer's five "I wills" with five "I wills" or declarations of His own. When God declared, "I will" He decreed righteous judgment for Lucifer's rebellion, which resulted in Lucifer's expulsion and fall from Heaven.

EZEKIEL 28:16-18
16 By the multitude of thy merchandise they have filled the
midst of thee with violence, and thou hast sinned: therefore
I WILL cast thee as profane out of the mountain of God: and
I WILL destroy thee, O covering cherub, from the midst of
the stones of fire.
17 Thine heart was lifted up because of thy beauty, thou
hast corrupted thy wisdom by reason of thy brightness: I
WILL cast thee to the ground, I WILL lay thee before kings,
that they may behold thee.
18 Thou hast defiled thy sanctuaries by the multitude of
thine iniquities, by the iniquity of thy traffick; therefore
will I bring forth a fire from the midst of thee, it shall
devour thee, and I WILL bring thee to ashes upon the earth
in the sight of all them that behold thee.

We see Lucifer's expulsion and fall from Heaven in these passages in Isaiah 14 and Ezekiel 28, and Jesus also described it in Luke 10.

ISAIAH 14:12
12 How art thou FALLEN FROM HEAVEN, O Lucifer, son of the morning! how art thou CUT DOWN TO THE GROUND, which didst weaken the nations!

EZEKIEL 28:16,17
16 ... I will CAST THEE AS PROFANE OUT OF THE MOUNTAIN OF GOD. ...
17 ... I will CAST THEE TO THE GROUND. ...

LUKE 10:18
18 And he [Jesus] said unto them, I beheld Satan as lightning FALL FROM HEAVEN.

Satan's Names Reveal His Nature and Character

In the garden of Eden we get a glimpse of Lucifer, or Satan, as he was called after his expulsion and fall from Heaven. This passage also reveals Satan's nature and character after his fall. The Bible says, *"Now the SERPENT was more SUBTIL than any beast of the field which the Lord God had made"* (Gen. 3:1). Once tempted, Eve told God, *"The serpent BEGUILED me, and I did eat"* (Gen. 3:13), showing Satan's crafty and deceptive nature.

Once an anointed cherub in the mountain of God, Satan was cursed by God and took the form of a serpent: *"And the Lord God said unto THE SERPENT, Because thou hast done this, THOU ART CURSED above all cattle, and above every beast of the field; UPON THY BELLY SHALT THOU GO, and dust shalt thou eat all the days of thy life"* (Gen. 3:14).

What do the Scriptures say regarding Satan's nature and character? The biblical names given to Satan reveal his nature, character, and also show his realm of authority on this earth.

Adversary: *". . . your ADVERSARY the devil...walketh about, seeking whom he may devour"* (1 Peter 5:8).

Thief: *"The THIEF cometh...to steal, and to kill, and to destroy . . ."* (John 10:10).

Murderer and liar: *"Ye [the scribes and the Pharisees] are of your father the devil, and the lusts of your father ye will do. He was a MURDERER from the beginning ...he is a LIAR, and the father of it"* (John 8:44).

Accuser of the brethren: *". . . THE ACCUSER OF OUR BRETHREN is cast down, which accused them before our God day and night"* (Rev. 12:10).

Deceiver: *"And the great dragon was cast out, that old serpent, called the Devil, and Satan, which DECEIVETH the whole world . . ."* (Rev. 12:9).

Angel of light: *". . . for Satan himself is transformed into an ANGEL OF LIGHT"* (2 Cor. 11:4). As a deceiver, Satan transforms himself into an angel of light.

The prince of this world: *"Now is the judgment of this world: now shall THE PRINCE OF THIS WORLD be cast out"* (John 12:31; 14:30; 16:8,11).

Prince of the power of the air: *". . . in time past ye walked according to the course of this world, according to THE PRINCE OF THE POWER OF THE AIR, THE SPIRIT that now worketh in the children of DISOBEDI-ENCE"* (Eph. 2:2).

The god of this world system: *"In whom THE GOD OF THIS WORLD hath blinded the minds of them which believe not . . ."* (2 Cor. 4:4).

If people understood that Satan is the god of this world, it would clear up a lot of confusion they have about why evil exists on this earth.

Some people are so taken up with the evil in the world that they think the universe is basically evil instead of good. Some people have accused God of being the author and creator of evil. For example, I read an article some time ago written by a well-known newspaper columnist here in America. He said he was not religiously inclined, didn't belong to any church, and never had. He didn't believe the Bible was the Word of God, and he didn't know if God existed or not.

In his article he said, "Christians say there *is* a God who created everything and that God is running this universe. Logically speaking, it would seem a Supreme Being did create the universe. But if God is the Ruler of this universe and He's running everything, He surely has things in a mess. Why doesn't He put a stop to war and poverty and innocent babies dying?"

He was trying to understand why a good God who is ruling the world would allow evil to exist. But this newspaper columnist had only heard one side of the argument — he didn't know that the

Bible says *Satan* is the god of this world (2 Cor. 4:4).

If this journalist had known and believed the Bible, he would have known that God made the world in the beginning and saw that everything was good (Gen. 1:10,12,18,21,25,31; James 1:17). God made man and gave man dominion over the work of His hands.

GENESIS 1:26,28
26 And God said, Let us make man in our image, after our likeness: and let them have DOMINION over the fish of the sea, and over the fowl of the air, and over the cattle, and over ALL THE EARTH, and over every creeping thing that creepeth upon the earth. . . .
28 And God blessed them, and God said unto them, Be fruitful, and multiply, and replenish the earth, and subdue it: and HAVE DOMINION over the fish of the sea, and over the fowl of the air, and over every living thing that moveth upon the earth.

PSALM 8:4-6
4   What is man, that thou art mindful of him? and the son of man, that thou visitest him?
5   For thou hast made him a little lower than the angels, and hast crowned him with glory and honour.
6   THOU MADEST HIM TO HAVE DOMINION OVER THE WORKS OF THY HANDS: thou hast put all things under his feet.

PSALM 115:16
16 The heaven, even the heavens, are the Lord's: but the earth HATH HE GIVEN TO THE CHILDREN OF MEN.

Satan Took Possession of Man's Lost Dominion

In the beginning, Adam had the dominion over this world, and in that sense, Adam was made the "god" of this world. But when Adam and Eve ate of the forbidden fruit, their eyes were opened and they knew good and evil (Gen. 3:6,7). God had told Adam and Eve that in the day they ate of the fruit, they would die. Adam and Eve didn't die physically; they died spiritually. When they died spiritually, they were cut off or separated from God. By that act of disobedience, Adam forfeited his dominion on this earth to the devil.

The Bible substantiates the fact that Adam sold out his dominion to Satan through disobedience, and allowed Satan to become the god of this world. Look at the account of Satan tempting Jesus.

LUKE 4:1,2,5-8
1 And Jesus being full of the Holy Ghost returned from Jordan, and was led by the Spirit into the wilderness,
2 Being forty days TEMPTED OF THE DEVIL. . . .
5 And the devil, taking him up into an high mountain, shewed unto him ALL THE KINGDOMS OF THE WORLD in a moment of time.
6 And the devil said unto him, ALL THIS POWER [authority] will I give thee, and the glory of them: FOR THAT IS DELIVERED UNTO ME; and to whomsoever I will I give it.
7 If thou therefore wilt worship me, ALL shall be thine.
8 And Jesus answered and said unto him, Get thee behind me, Satan: for it is written, Thou shalt worship the Lord thy God, and him only shalt thou serve.

There are several important truths to notice here. Ministers have said to me, "Satan was just lying to Jesus by saying he would give Jesus the authority over the kingdoms of the world, because Satan didn't have authority over them." But Satan did have that authority because the kingdoms of the world had been delivered over to Satan by Adam when he sinned against God.

The Amplified Bible shows this even more clearly.

LUKE 4:5,6 *(Amplified)*
5 Then the devil took Him up to a high mountain, and showed Him ALL THE KINGDOMS OF THE HABITABLE WORLD IN A MOMENT OF TIME — in the twinkling of an eye;
6 And he said to Him, To You I will give all THIS POWER and AUTHORITY and their glory . . . FOR IT HAS BEEN TURNED OVER TO ME, and I give it to whom I will.

Who turned the kingdoms of the world over to Satan? Was it God? No, God gave them to Adam originally, but when Adam sinned and disobeyed God, he forfeited his right to them, so Satan took dominion of them.

We know Satan didn't have authority over the world before Adam gave it to him, because Satan fell from the dominion he did have (Ezek. 28:16-18; Luke 10:18).

So Adam had the dominion and authority over the earth originally, but he delivered it into Satan's hands when he disobeyed God's commandment (Rom. 5:14 *Amp.*). That's when Satan became the god of this world.

Also, if Satan didn't have the authority over the kingdoms of this world, then the Bible is lying when it says that Jesus was *tempted* by the devil (Luke 4:2). If Satan had no authority and no real dominion over the kingdoms of the earth, this wouldn't have been a real temptation to Jesus. But the Bible calls it a temptation: *"And Jesus . . . was led by the Spirit into the wilderness, Being forty days, TEMPTED OF THE DEVIL . . ."* (Luke 4:1,2). Therefore, Satan did have authority and dominion on the earth because he could tempt Jesus with it.

So Satan took Adam's place of dominion and authority on the earth. But is that the end of it? Emphatically, no! God sent Jesus to the earth to redeem mankind and to *restore* to man his lost dominion and authority on this earth. And as man exercises the authority he has been given in Christ, he fulfills God's plan and will upon the earth.

However, until Adam's lease runs out — that is, until time as we know it comes to an end and Satan receives God's final judgment — Satan has authority to be here.

Remember in the New Testament when Jesus would enter into the synagogue, many times people who were possessed with demons would cry out, *". . . What have we to do with thee, Jesus, thou Son of God? art thou come hither to torment us BEFORE THE TIME?"* (Matt. 8:29).

Satan knows his time on this earth is running out, and he knows his impending torment and doom are prophesied in the Book of Revelation (Rev. 20:10).

Satan's Dominion After His Fall Also Encompasses the Heavenlies

Ephesians 6:12 tells us that Satan's kingdom encompassed not only the realm of this *world*, but it also included the regions known in the Bible as the "high places" or "the *heavenlies*."

EPHESIANS 6:12
12 For we wrestle not against flesh and blood, but against PRINCIPALITIES, against POWERS, against the RULERS OF THE DARKNESS of this world, against SPIRITUAL WICKEDNESS [or wicked spirits] **in HIGH PLACES** [heavenlies].

Instead of "spiritual wickedness" a marginal note in my *King James Version* reads "wicked spirits in the heavenlies." So we could read this verse: "For we wrestle not against flesh and blood, but against . . . wicked spirits IN THE HEAVENLIES." Therefore, we know that Satan rules in the heavenlies.

Three Heavens

What does the Bible mean by "heavenlies"? Actually, the Bible refers to three heavens. We see a direct reference to more than one heaven in Second Corinthians 12:2. Most Bible scholars agree that the Apostle Paul was talking about himself in this passage.

2 CORINTHIANS 12:2-4
2 I knew a man in Christ above fourteen years ago, (whether in the body, I cannot tell; or whether out of the body, I cannot tell: God knoweth;) such an one caught up to THE THIRD HEAVEN.
3 And I knew such a man, (whether in the body, or out of the body, I cannot tell: God knoweth;)
4 How that he was caught up into PARADISE [Heaven], and heard unspeakable words, which it is not lawful for a man to utter.

It stands to reason if there's a *third* Heaven there also has to be a first and a second heaven, otherwise there would be no point for the Scriptures to mention a *third* Heaven.

The first of the three heavens right above us is what we call the atmospheric heavens, or the "heavenlies." Beyond that, out in space, is the region where the stars, sun, moon, and planets are — the stellar heavens or space — which can be referred to as the second heaven. [1]

Out beyond that, further than science knows about or has been able to explore, is the third Heaven — the Heaven of heavens — where God's throne is located.

We are given some information about the third Heaven in the Scriptures. For example, we know that under the New Covenant, Paradise is located in this third Heaven (Luke 23:43; 2 Cor. 12:4; Rev. 2:7). We know Jesus is in Heaven at the right hand of God (Mark 16:19; Heb. 1:3; 4:14).

And the Bible tells us that Jesus is preparing a place for believers in Heaven: *"In my Father's house [Heaven] are many mansions: if it were not so, I would have told you. I go to prepare a place for you"* (John 14:2,3).

And we know with a certainty that believers go to Heaven to be with Jesus when they die. Jesus said, *"And if I go and prepare a place for you, I will come again, and receive you unto myself; that where I am, there ye may be also"* (John 14:3).

Paul also told us believers go to Heaven when they die: *". . . to me to live is Christ, and to die is gain. . . . I am in a strait betwixt two, having a desire to depart, and TO BE WITH CHRIST . . ."* (Phil. 1:21,23).

The 'Heavenlies' or the High Places

The Bible doesn't mention just one heaven, but it talks about the "heaven*lies*." Ephesians 6:12 says that we don't wrestle against flesh and blood, but we do wrestle against principalities, powers, rulers of the darkness of this world, and spiritual wickedness in the *heavenlies* or in "high places."

In 1952 Jesus appeared to me in a vision which I relate at great length in another chapter. He talked to me for an hour and a half on the subject of Satan, demons, and demon possession. One of the things He said to me was that there were four types, classes, or categories of demons or evil spirits as Paul listed them in Ephesians 6.

Jesus said that in listing these demonic powers, Paul started at the bottom of the list with the lowest class of demon and worked up in order of their rank: principalities, powers, rulers of the darkness of this world, spiritual wickedness in high places (or as some translations read "wicked spirits in the heavenlies").

EPHESIANS 6:12
12 For we wrestle not against flesh and blood, but against PRINCIPALITIES, against POWERS, against the RULERS OF THE DARKNESS OF THIS WORLD, against SPIRITUAL WICKEDNESS IN HIGH PLACES.

Below they are listed in their order or rank from the greatest to the least in power with some explanation about their rank:

1. Wicked spirits or spiritual wickedness in high places: This highest class exists in the heavenlies, not on the earth.
2. Rulers of the darkness of this world: The highest class of demons believers have to deal with on the earth.
3. Powers: The next class or category. They are dominated by and receive their instruction from the rulers of the darkness of this world.
4. Principalities: The lowest class. They are ruled

over and dominated by the other classes and do very little thinking on their own.

I believe we have scriptural grounds for believing that the first three classes of demons and evil spirits — *principalities, powers,* and the *rulers of the darkness of this world* — exist in the first heaven, which includes the air and the atmospheric heavens right above us.

It is the dwelling place of demons because the Bible calls Satan the prince of the power of the air (Eph. 2:2). That is his domain. You can't see them, but they are there and they dominate and rule anyone on the earth who will let them.

Out beyond the atmosphere or air in the stellar heavens is the second heaven where the stars and the planets are located. I personally believe the second heaven is what the Bible refers to in Ephesians 6:12 as the "high places." And that is the domain where *wicked spirits* or *"spiritual wickedness in high places"* rule.

And out beyond that is the third Heaven, the Heaven of heavens, the realm of Paradise where God's throne is. Of course, there are no wicked spirits in God's realm.

The Double Kingdom

So we know that *the heavenlies* is the domain of principalities, powers, the rulers of the darkness of this world, and spiritual wickedness in high places. And when you understand that Adam forfeited his dominion to the devil, it makes it easier to understand something we see in the Scriptures — a double kingdom.

The double kingdom refers to a wicked kingdom reigning in the heavenlies, which affects the lives of men upon the earth. *Unseen* spiritual forces rule and dominate men who rule *seen* earthly kingdoms — if men let them.

We are told in Ephesians 6 that we are not dealing with flesh and blood — with just the natures and personalities of *men* on the earth. The Bible says we are dealing with *spiritual entities* which rule in the heavenlies. Therefore, a double kingdom refers to a kingdom ruled on earth by men who are actually dominated and influenced by spiritual rulers in the heavenlies.

We see examples of this double kingdom in the Scriptures. For example, the Bible gives us a glimpse of this double kingdom operating in Ezekiel chapter 28.

EZEKIEL 28:2
2   Son of man, say unto the PRINCE OF TYRUS, Thus saith
the Lord GOD; Because thine heart is lifted up, and thou
hast said, I am a God, I sit in the seat of God, in the midst of
the seas; yet THOU ART A MAN, and not God, though thou
set thine heart as the heart of God.

In Ezekiel 28:1-10, a prophetic message is given through the
prophet Ezekiel to the prince of Tyrus, a man, who was lifted up in
pride. We know this refers to an actual prince of Tyrus who ruled a
kingdom because God said, ". . . *yet thou art a man*" (Ezek. 28:2).
Angels and evil spirits are not men. Therefore, this *prince of Tyrus*
was a *man* who ruled a kingdom on the earth at that time.

Then in the very same chapter in Ezekiel 28:11-19, another
prophetic word is given through Ezekiel, but this one is addressed
to *the king of Tyrus*, who was *not* a man. The king of Tyrus was a
wicked spiritual power ruling in the heavenlies.

EZEKIEL 28:12,13
12   Son of man, take up a lamentation upon the KING OF
TYRUS, and say unto him, Thus saith the Lord GOD; Thou
sealest up the sum, full of wisdom, and perfect in beauty.
13   THOU HAST BEEN IN EDEN THE GARDEN OF GOD;
every precious stone was thy covering . . . : the workmanship of thy tabrets and of thy pipes was prepared in thee in
the day that thou wast created.

We already saw that this passage refers to Lucifer. The prince
of Tyrus, a man, couldn't possibly have been in Eden the garden of
God. He hadn't even been born yet. No, this "king of Tyrus" is not
referring to a man; it is referring to a created being, Lucifer, a
fallen spirit being who ruled an earthly kingdom from his position
of rulership in the heavenlies (Ezek. 28:13-15).

In these two beings — the prince of Tyrus, *a man*, and the king
of Tyrus, *a spirit being* (Lucifer himself) — the Bible gives the idea
of a double kingdom. A natural kingdom on the earth is ruled by
men, but it is dominated by a spiritual kingdom ruled by spiritual
wickedness in the heavenlies.

Double Kingdom in the Book of Daniel

In the Book of Daniel, we find another example of the double
kingdom. Daniel had been fasting and seeking God. An angel
appeared to him and gave him a revelation from God.

DANIEL 10:12,13
12 Then said he [the angel] **unto me, Fear not, Daniel: for from the first day that thou didst set thine heart to understand, and to chasten thyself before thy God, THY WORDS WERE HEARD, and I AM COME FOR THY WORDS.**
13 But THE PRINCE OF THE KINGDOM OF PERSIA withstood me one and twenty days: but, lo, Michael, one of the chief princes, came to help me; and I remained there with the kings of Persia.

The prince of Persia — a wicked ruler in the heavenlies — withstood the angel of God in the heavenlies to prevent him from getting through to Daniel with God's message. Although the angel came with the answer the very first day Daniel began to make supplication, the angel said, *". . . the prince of the kingdom of Persia withstood me . . ."* (Dan. 10:13).

The angel was talking about a battle that took place out in the spirit world, in the heavenlies. The angel was not referring to a man living upon the earth who opposed him, but to a wicked ruler in the heavenlies.

On earth there was the physical, earthly kingdom of Persia with a human prince heading up that kingdom. But right above that kingdom in the heavenlies was a spiritual kingdom of darkness, also called the kingdom of Persia.

The *spiritual kingdom* was ruled by a wicked spirit called the prince of Persia, and that evil spirit dominated the *earthly government* of Persia. So this scripture is referring to a spirit being in the heavenlies that ruled a region on earth through men who yielded to him.

Why didn't this wicked spirit in the heavenlies want the angel to get through to Daniel with God's message? For the same reason evil spirits don't want God's message to get through to people today. Satan and his hosts don't want God's will to be known upon the earth, and that's why Satan blinds men's minds from seeing the truth of the gospel (2 Cor. 4:4).

In Daniel's case, Satan wanted to keep the angel from revealing God's plans and purposes to Daniel about the future. When the prince of Persia withstood the angel of God, God sent reinforcement by sending another angel, Michael, to assist in the battle: *". . . lo, Michael, one of the chief princes* [an angel of God], *came to help me"* (Dan. 10:13).

Finally, on the twenty-first day, the angel got through the heavenlies to Daniel with God's message in answer to his prayer. God wanted to reveal to Daniel what was about to take place on the earth and what would take place in the future.

So we see that wicked spirits can dominate earthly kingdoms and governments. Now let's look at the influence of demons on individual people's lives on the earth.

The Rulers of Darkness

Let's look specifically at one class of evil spirits Jesus talked to me about called the rulers of the darkness of this world (Eph. 6:12). Jesus explained, "The highest class of demons you will have to deal with upon the earth are the *rulers of the darkness of this world.* They are just exactly what the Word says they are — they are *rulers.* They rule the darkness of this world, and they rule over those who are in the darkness."

Jesus explained that rulers of darkness also try to rule over believers who are not walking in the light of their redemption, or who don't know or don't exercise their rights and privileges in Christ.

Jesus told me that according to His Word, believers are to take authority over these first three classes of demons: principalities, powers, and the rulers of the darkness of this world. He said that if we on earth will bind the operation of the first three classes of demons, according to His Word, He will deal with the fourth class of demons — spiritual wickedness in high places.

He gave me Matthew 18:18 to substantiate this.

MATTHEW 18:18
18 . . . Whatsoever ye shall BIND ON EARTH shall be bound in heaven [the heavenlies]**: and whatsoever ye shall LOOSE ON EARTH shall be loosed in heaven** [the heavenlies].

We are to bind evil spirits in their operation against us in Jesus' Name, based on the authority of God's Word (Luke 10:19; Phil. 2:9,10; Isa. 54:17; Rev. 12:11). That is what Matthew 18:18 means. As we stand in our authority in Christ and bind the operation of the first three classes of evil spirits here in the realm of earth, that stops them in their operation against us. When we do that, then Jesus said He will deal with the highest class of demons, spiritual wickedness ruling in the high places.

Jesus went on to explain that the rulers of the darkness of this world are actually the most intelligent type of evil spirit believers have to deal with.

Jesus explained, "It is always one of these rulers of the darkness of this world that possesses a person. Also, the rulers of the darkness of this world rule over the other spirits and tell them what to do.

"For example, they rule over *powers* and tell them what to do. And the powers in turn rule over the *principalities* and tell them what to do. The lowest type of demons have very little authority of their own and do very little thinking of their own; they are told what to do."

Jesus said to me that anyone who is walking in darkness can be dominated by rulers of darkness. They rule over all unsaved people and anyone walking in darkness, including believers who are walking in darkness.

That's why sometimes even saved people can yield to these spirits and let them dominate them if they are walking in darkness — if they're not in fellowship with God and walking in the light of His Word. Evil spirits will dominate believers, *if* they allow them to — by *consent, ignorance,* or *disobedience.* That's the reason people, including believers, do certain things and don't know *why* they do them.

Jesus said, "That's why sometimes people who commit acts of darkness say, 'I don't know what made me do that.' Or that's why perfectly good people say about someone else, 'I would never do anything like that,' and before long, they've done something worse."

Jesus said that's why sometimes even in someone's own family, a family member does something strange or out of character, and other family members say, "What in the world made him do that? I've never seen anything like that!"

The reason they do it is that they are being dominated by rulers of darkness — demons and evil spirits. If they're walking in darkness, they are being ruled over and motivated by those rulers of darkness.

Jesus gave me First John 5:19 to illustrate what He was talking about: *"And we know that we are of God, and the whole WORLD lieth in WICKEDNESS [darkness]"* (1 John 5:19).

Jesus said to me, "Every unsaved man and woman, regardless of who they are — whether it's your kinfolks or someone else's kinfolks, your brother, sister, mother, or father — every *unsaved* person is in the kingdom of darkness. And they are ruled or motivated more or less by these demons or evil spirits who are the rulers of the darkness of this world."

Then Jesus said, "Whether they want to admit it or not, or whether you or anyone else wants to admit it, that is absolutely the truth." Those who have not been born again and who have not come into the Body of Christ are still in the kingdom of darkness. So every person who is not in the Kingdom of light is still ruled or dominated to some extent by those demon spirits in the kingdom of darkness, although they may not know it (Eph. 2:1-3). That's the reason people do and say things they said they would never do."

We see many examples of the unsaved being motivated by evil spirits. For example, I was preaching in California one time, and I read in the newspaper that a twenty-eight-year-old young man had deliberately drowned his own four-year-old son in the bathtub.

When the authorities questioned this young man, they found he was all right mentally. He had no record of wrongdoing, had a good job, and lived in a fine home. He had no financial worries, came from a good family from whom he had inherited part of his wealth, and had worked in the family business. They couldn't find one thing wrong with him.

He told the authorities that there wasn't anything wrong with him mentally; he wasn't worried, had no problems, and the child was good. "But," he said, "while I was bathing him, I suddenly had an uncontrollable urge to harm him, and a voice told me to drown him. I yielded to it, and when I came to myself, I was holding my child under the water. I cried, 'Oh, God, why did I do that!'"

You see, he was dominated by evil spirits — rulers of the darkness of this world — because he was in darkness; he wasn't saved. But believers don't need to be dominated by evil spirits because we have been delivered out of the kingdom of darkness and translated into the Kingdom of light (Col. 1:13). We are in the light where Jesus is our Lord. He is the One who is to dominate us. He is the Ruler over us. He is our Head, not rulers of darkness.

Satan is the head of those who are unsaved. If the unsaved people of this world really knew the truth, they would run to Christians to find out how to get saved so they could come out from under Satan's dominion.

There is a spirit world that is even more real than this physical world. People need to know that. When you talk about the spirit world, you have to realize that God is a Spirit (John 4:24), and that the devil, demons, and evil spirits also exist in the spirit world, as do angels — both good and evil. But believers have authority over evil spirits; the unsaved do not, for Satan is their god.

Rulers of Darkness Can't Rule in the Light

The New Testament is a revelation of God's great plan of redemption. Colossians 1:13 tells us that Jesus came to deliver us from the power and authority of devils and evil spirits who rule in the realm of darkness: "... [Jesus] *hath delivered us FROM THE POWER* [authority] *OF DARKNESS, and hath translated us into the kingdom of His dear Son."*

The only place rulers of darkness aren't ruling is where the light has come. What light? The light of education? The light of science? No. The light of the gospel!

The Word says that believers are the children of light, not of darkness (1 Thess. 5:5) because we have been born again into God's *Kingdom of light.* That's why it's so important to walk in the light! Walking in the light of God's Word ensures protection against all of Satan's evil hosts.

Jesus pointed out to me that because believers are children of God or children of the light, they are *in* the world but not *of* the world (John 17:14-16), so they don't have to be ruled by the devil. However, they allow the devil to rule over them if they walk in darkness rather than in the light.

The devil can also rule over us if we *unknowingly* through ignorance of God's Word or *willingly* give him permission to rule over us. That's one reason the Bible exhorts believers to walk in the *light!* Rulers of darkness can't rule in the light, so they can't rule those who walk in the light!

Look at the contrast between the kingdom of darkness and God's Kingdom of light.

JOHN 8:12
12 Then spake Jesus again unto them, saying, I am the LIGHT of the world: he that followeth me shall not walk in DARKNESS, but shall have the LIGHT of life [zoe, the life of God].

JOHN 12:35,36,46
35 ... Yet a little while is the LIGHT with you. Walk while ye have the LIGHT, lest DARKNESS come upon you: for he that walketh in DARKNESS knoweth not whither he goeth.
36 While ye have LIGHT, believe in the LIGHT, that ye may be THE CHILDREN OF LIGHT. ...
46 I am come a LIGHT into the world, that whosoever believeth on me should not abide in DARKNESS.

EPHESIANS 5:14
14 Wherefore he saith, Awake thou that sleepest, and arise from the **DEAD** [SPIRITUAL DARKNESS], and Christ shall give thee **LIGHT.**

ROMANS 13:12
12 The night is far spent, the day is at hand: let us therefore cast off the **WORKS OF DARKNESS,** and let us put on the **ARMOUR OF LIGHT.**

2 CORINTHIANS 6:14
14 Be ye not unequally yoked together with unbelievers: for what fellowship hath righteousness with unrighteousness? and what communion hath **LIGHT** with **DARKNESS?**

1 JOHN 1:5-7
5 This then is the message which we have heard of him, and declare unto you, that God is **LIGHT,** and **IN HIM** is **NO DARKNESS** at all.
6 If we say that we have fellowship with him, and walk **IN DARKNESS,** we lie, and do not the **TRUTH** [LIGHT]:
7 But **IF WE WALK IN THE LIGHT,** as he is in the light, we have fellowship one with another, and the blood of Jesus Christ his Son cleanseth us from all **SIN** [DARKNESS].

Glory to God! Demon powers have no authority to rule over believers who walk in the light of God's Word and give Satan no access. Believers can walk in the light so they won't fall prey to Satan.

In fact, as believers gain knowledge of God's Word, light and liberty come. The knowledge of God's Word brings light (Ps. 119:130), and it is the knowledge of God's Word which sets us free in every area.

---

[1] Merrill F. Unger, Unger's Bible Dictionary (Chicago, Illinois: Moody Press, 1957), p. 463.

Chapter 2

Rightly Dividing Man: Spirit, Soul, and Body

Evil spirits are fallen beings or disembodied spirits. As disembodied spirits, they seek to inhabit man in order to have a greater range of expression. As fallen beings, evil spirits seek to *oppress*, *obsess*, and if possible, to *possess* mankind.

In order to understand how demons and evil spirits can affect mankind, you need to understand the difference between the *spirit*, *soul*, and *body* of man. And you need to understand the difference between demonic *oppression*, *obsession*, and *possession*.

Let's begin by looking at the difference between the spirit, soul, and body of man. When we understand that man is a spirit, he has a soul, and he lives in a body — we can understand how believers can give place to the devil in their *souls* and *bodies* (Eph. 4:27).

Man Is a Spirit Being

Someone has said that man is a three-part being: part is spirit, part is soul, and part is body. But I don't like to say it that way because it's misleading. Actually, man *is* a spirit; he's not *part* spirit. He's a spirit being. He *has* a soul — mind, will, and emotions — and he *lives* in a body.

When expressed like that, the true nature of man takes on a different significance than just saying "part" of him is spirit, "part" of him is soul, and "part" of him is body.

In the Bible we see the way *God* divides man. God distinguishes the difference between the spirit, soul, and body of man. If a person's spirit, soul, and body are one, why does the Bible divide them?

1 THESSALONIANS 5:23
23 And the very God of peace sanctify you wholly; and I pray God your whole SPIRIT and SOUL and BODY be preserved blameless unto the coming of our Lord Jesus Christ.

HEBREWS 4:12
12 For the word of God is quick, and powerful, and sharper than any twoedged sword, piercing even to the dividing

**asunder of SOUL and SPIRIT, and of the JOINTS and MAR-
ROW** [the body]**, and is a discerner of the thoughts and
intents of the heart.**

We need to understand man's nature because the devil works
through man's five physical senses and his unredeemed soul and
body to try to defeat him. When a believer understands that, he can
close the door to the devil by renewing his mind — his soul — and
keeping his body — his flesh — under the dominion of his recreated
spirit. That's essential in standing victorious against the devil.

Believers must learn *how* to let the real man — the spirit man
on the inside — dominate their soul and body. That will solve many
problems as far as the devil is concerned. As believers let their
recreated spirits dominate, they will learn how *not* to give the devil
any access — spirit, soul, *or* body.

You see, much of what is being called the "devil" or demonic
activity in the church world today is not demon activity at all. It's
man's unregenerated soul and flesh dominating his recreated
spirit. When the believer understands that, he will readily be able
to determine what *is* and what is *not* demonic activity and undergird his soul to stand strong against the enemy's attacks.

2 CORINTHIANS 5:17
17 Therefore if any man be in Christ, HE [his spirit — the
man on the inside] **is A NEW CREATURE: old things are
passed away; behold, all things are become new.**

You need to understand that it's *not* the outward man — man's
body — that becomes a new creature. It's the inward man — man's
spirit — that becomes a new creature in Christ. If you had red hair
before you were born again, you have red hair after you are born again.
If you were baldheaded before you were saved, you are still baldheaded.

The outward man doesn't change in the new birth, and neither
does the soul of man — his mind, will, and emotions. Only the man
on the inside changes. Old things are passed away and all things
are become new in man's recreated *spirit* when he's born again, not
in his soul or body.

Because all things have *not* become new in your body or soul in
the new birth, that means you still have your outward man to deal
with. As long as you are in your body, you will have the desires of
the fleshly carnal nature and the unredeemed soul to control. And
that is the realm where Satan tries to gain access to man.

Dividing the Soul and Spirit

It is easy to distinguish between the *body* and *soul* of man because that difference is obvious. But it is more difficult to divide or distinguish between man's *soul* and *spirit*. The Bible does not say that man's soul and spirit are the same thing (1 Thess. 5:23).

It will help your spiritual growth immeasurably to know the difference between your spirit and soul, because to stand strong against the devil you will need to learn how to renew your mind and feed your spirit.

To gain a better understanding of your nature, it would help you to go through this process in your thinking:

With my spirit, I contact the spiritual realm.
With my soul, I contact the intellectual and emotional realm.
With my body, I contact the physical realm.

Hebrews 4:12 tells us that only the Word of God can divide between the *soul* and the *spirit* of man: *"For the WORD OF GOD is quick, and powerful, and sharper than any twoedged sword, piercing even to the dividing asunder of SOUL and SPIRIT, and of the JOINTS and MARROW* [body]. . . ."

There has not been much sound, biblical teaching about how to distinguish the difference between the *spirit* and *soul* of man. I've read textbooks used in theological seminaries, and the way they present this subject is confusing. Some Bible teachers say that the soul and the spirit are the same. But the Bible divides them so it stands to reason they aren't the same thing. It would be just as unscriptural to say that the *spirit* and *soul* are the same as it would be to say that the *body* and *soul* are the same.

The Soul of Man

JAMES 1:21
21 Wherefore lay apart all filthiness and superfluity of naughtiness, and receive with meekness the engrafted word, which is able to SAVE YOUR SOULS.

The Book of James also makes a distinction between the soul and the spirit of man. Also, notice that our *spirits* are saved or recreated, but in this verse we see that our *souls* are *not* saved in the new birth.

You see, James wrote this epistle to Christians — to people

whose *spirits* had already been recreated when they were born again. But here James told these born-again believers that their *souls* weren't born again yet.

Why aren't our souls saved when we are born again? Because the new birth is a *spiritual* birth. It's not an intellectual birth — a rebirth of man's *mind*. It's not a soulish birth — a rebirth of man's *soul* and emotions. And it's not a physical birth — a rebirth of man's body.

The new birth is only a rebirth of man's *spirit*; it's not a mental or a physical experience. The baptism in the Holy Spirit isn't a physical or a mental experience either. They are both *spiritual* experiences which eventually affect the physical and mental realms of man.

Although the believer's *spirit* is recreated in the new birth, he will have to do something about his soul himself. If he doesn't do something with his soul, he will give the enemy access to his life.

The Saving of the Soul

James is saying that the Word of God is the only thing that will save the believer's soul — his mind, will, and emotions. Then James goes on to tell believers *how* to get their souls saved or renewed.

James told believers that receiving the engrafted word will *save* their *souls*. What does the Bible mean by the "engrafted" Word?

According to *Vine's Expository Dictionary of Biblical Words,* the word "engrafted" means *to implant.*[1] The word "engrafted" carries the idea of a seed rooting itself and causing growth. So the Word of God implanted or engrafted into the soul of man has the ability and the power to change or "save" man's soul.

That scripture used to bother me because I thought man's soul was already saved in the new birth. But then I found out that there is a difference between man's spirit and his soul and that the soul isn't recreated — only the spirit is. Actually, the saving of man's soul is an ongoing process throughout a person's life.

In studying demons and their influence on mankind, why is it important for the believer to know that his soul isn't saved yet? Because what many Christians are attributing to Satan is really a problem of their souls not being saved — their minds and emotions not being renewed with the Word of God.

An unrenewed mind is a major area where believers can give Satan access to them. Therefore, the believer needs to understand how to receive the engrafted Word to save his soul, so he can close the door to the devil.

The word "save" in James 1:21 is the Greek word *sozo. Sozo* is defined as *to save, deliver, protect, heal, preserve, make well,* and *make whole.* So we could read James 1:21, ". . . receive with meekness the engrafted Word, which is able to save, heal, deliver, protect, preserve, make well, and make your soul whole."

That means as you actively feed on God's Word, it *saves, delivers, protects, heals, preserves,* and *makes whole* your soul, which is one of your greatest defenses against Satan.

You see, if renewing or restoration needs to be done on the inside of the believer it would have to be in his soul — in his mind and emotions — not in his *recreated* spirit. If a person's spirit has been recreated in Christ, he doesn't need any restoration in his spirit.

Is receiving the engrafted Word the only thing the believer has to do to get his soul saved? No, look at the next verse: *"But BE YE DOERS OF THE WORD, and not hearers only, deceiving your own selves"* (James 1:22). You not only have to *hear* and *receive* the Word, you also have to *act* on it before it will do you any good.

Hearing the Word and acting on it is a powerful defense against Satan, because the Bible says, *"Submit yourselves therefore to God. Resist the devil, and he will flee from you"* (James 4:7). When you are submitted to God's Word, you are submitted to God. And as you keep your soul strong and renewed, it's easier to resist the devil on every front.

1 PETER 1:22
22 Seeing ye have PURIFIED YOUR SOULS in OBEYING THE TRUTH [the Word] **through the Spirit. . . .**

You'll have to be a *doer* of the Word before it will profit your soul. Your soul will be saved, delivered, protected, healed, preserved, made well and whole by receiving *and* by doing the Word.

That puts the responsibility on the believer if anything is going to be done to his soul, doesn't it? And it puts the responsibility on the believer if Satan is going to have an inroad to him through his own soul.

That's exactly what the Bible is saying. Believers *themselves* have to do something about the saving of their own souls. As they undergird their souls with the Word, Satan won't have an open door of access to them.

The major way believers close the door to the devil is to get their minds renewed with the Word and by practicing the Word. Many people are trying to cast the devil out of believers, when the problem is not demonic. The believer has just never learned to renew his mind, so he keeps on thinking like he did before he was redeemed when he was under Satan's dominion. Then eventually he will start acting in line with his unredeemed thinking, and soon he'll be dominated by the devil instead of standing in his authority against him.

Actually, the "saving" or the renewing of the soul is the greatest need of the Church today — not casting devils out of believers. Since the believer's spirit is the only part of him that is born again or recreated, his soul and his body are unchanged and still have to be dealt with if he is to successfully withstand the devil's attacks.

If the believer doesn't deal with his soul and body, he will continually be opening a door to the enemy. Only the believer himself can do something about renewing his soul and bringing his body into subjection to his spirit. And this is where the believer's major "battle" is fought.

There are many Christians who have been saved and filled with the Holy Spirit for many years, whose souls are not yet saved. Some Christians have lived and died and their souls have never been saved, and they've been tossed to and fro by the devil because of it. That's absolutely the truth! Their souls weren't renewed, restored, or made whole by the Word of God, so they couldn't stand successfully against the attacks of the devil.

Now don't misunderstand me. Just because Christians haven't renewed their minds doesn't mean they won't go to Heaven when they die. Of course they will go to Heaven because their spirits are born of God — they're children of God. But Christians who have failed to renew their minds forfeit the privilege to enter into all that belongs to them in Christ while they are here on earth. And even though they have victory over the devil in Christ, they never understand how to successfully stand in that victory because of an unrenewed mind.

'He Restores My Soul'

Let's look at another verse in connection with the saving of the soul. We've all read Psalm 23 many times. The psalmist said, *"He restoreth my soul . . ."* (Ps. 23:3). Psalm 23 is a prophetic psalm that belongs to the Church. It was written in King David's day for the Church of the Lord Jesus Christ. We are living in Psalm 23 right now because it says, *"The Lord is my shepherd. . . ,"* and in the New

Testament Jesus called Himself the good shepherd (John 10:11).

Actually, the word "restoreth" in Psalm 23 and the Greek word translated "renew" in Romans 12:2 have about the same meaning. To "restore" carries the connotation *to recover, rescue, restore, reverse.* To "renew" means to *renovate* or to *restore* or to *make like new.*

If you had a valuable antique chair, you'd probably want it restored. It might not even look like it's worth much. But after it is restored, it is still the same chair, but it's *renewed* or made like new, and it looks like a brand-new chair.

Man's spirit is *not* restored or renewed; it is actually *born again* or *recreated.* But man's emotional and mental realms need to be *restored* with the Word of God. The greatest need of the Church today is for believers' minds and emotions to be renewed or *restored* with the Word. The Word, which is spirit and life (John 6:63), has the ability to *restore, renew, save, protect, deliver,* and *heal* the soul of man.

'Inner Healing'

At times, different members of the Body of Christ get off into spiritual "fads" just like they get off into fads in other areas. For example, several years ago the Church got off into the teaching on "inner healing." That teaching has about run its course now because folks found out it didn't have long-lasting effects.

The term "inner healing" is really a misnomer if it's used to refer to healing in your *spirit* because your spirit doesn't need *healing* — it's been *recreated.* If you needed healing or deliverance from hurts on the inside, it wouldn't be in your born-again spirit because it's been made brand new. No, it's your soul that needs the help. How are you going to get all of those hurts in your soul from the past healed? By *thinking* in line with the Word.

Find Scriptures that pertain to your need. Meditate on the Word regarding your specific need. Say about yourself what the Word says, for the Word has the power to transform your mind and emotions. You talk about deliverance! That's how you get healed and delivered! Really, true biblical "deliverance" or restoration in its fullest sense includes much more than just deliverance from demonic activity, and it begins in man's soul.

Some inner healing was probably the result of some folks trying to mix psychology with the things of God. The dictionary defines "psychology" as *the science and study of mind and behavior.* But the things of God and the spirit of man are *spiritual* — not mental.

For the natural man, there may be some truth to what psychologists are saying. But for the born-again man, what they are saying is not necessarily Bible truth. For example, in psychology, people dug down into man and found out that he had something else in him below the mental consciousness, and they called it the subconscious mind. But, really, the Bible doesn't mention a subconscious *mind*. What people discovered and tapped into was man's spirit, but they didn't know what it was.

Now psychology is fine in its place if the psychologist is a believer who understands the true nature of man and takes into account man's *spirit*, not just his *mind*. Actually, in dealing with the natural man — *unsaved* people — psychology may have its place because those folks are still in the natural realm since their spirits haven't been recreated. Therefore, they can be dealt with by natural means, such as psychology.

But you can't deal with the *spirit man* the same as you would the *natural man*. The believer isn't just a natural, carnal being because his spirit has been recreated in the likeness and image of God. For the believer, God's highest and best is for his soul to be restored and made whole and sound with the Word of God by the power of the Holy Spirit. And since the believer is not just a soul or a mind, to deal only with the believer's *mind* alone isn't sufficient.

> **1 CORINTHIANS 2:14** *(Amplified)*
> **14 But the NATURAL, NONSPIRITUAL MAN does not accept or welcome or admit into his heart the gifts and teachings and revelations of the Spirit of God, for they are folly (meaningless nonsense) to him; and he is incapable of knowing them — of progressively recognizing, understanding and becoming better acquainted with them — because they are SPIRITUALLY DISCERNED and ESTIMATED and APPRECIATED.**

The Word of God says the natural man cannot comprehend the things of the Spirit of God. Because the believer is no longer a mere natural man, it makes no sense to try to apply teachings of the natural man to the born-again believer who is a spiritual man.

That is why the believer shouldn't be dealt with in the same way the natural man of the world is dealt with — only by natural reasonings and human intellect. Psychology alone is not adequate to deal with the mind of the spiritual man, nor with the recreated human *spirit* which has been created in the image and likeness of God.

Therefore, because man is a spirit, has a soul, and lives in a body the teaching of "spiritology" is more important to the believer. I call spiritology the study of the spirit of man and the things of the Spirit of God.

Since man is a spirit being, the Body of Christ needs to know what the Word has to say about man's *spirit*. The Word of God is spirit food for recreated spirit beings — believers.

I once held a meeting in California, and the pastor and his wife were busy overseeing the planning and construction of a beautiful, new church building. But the pastor's wife became overworked and nervous and finally had a physical and nervous breakdown. She went to a doctor, and he suggested she go to a psychiatrist.

This pastor's wife had been brought up in a Pentecostal home where they didn't drink, smoke, or dance. This psychiatrist decided that the woman's problem was that she'd never done any of those things, so he suggested that she start smoking, drinking, and going to dances. This was *his* cure for this pastor's wife!

She took his advice and in the end she lost her mind completely and had to be institutionalized. Actually, this woman opened a door to the devil by dealing with her problems as the world does when she was a new creature in Christ.

That particular psychiatrist wasn't born again and knew nothing about the spiritual realm. He didn't even know that man is a spirit being. In that sense he knew nothing about his own nature, so he couldn't help himself, let alone this poor pastor's wife!

We need to be careful about mixing the wisdom of man with the things of God. God told us what to do with our natural mind and with our physical bodies. He said to get our minds and emotions renewed with the Word and to present our bodies as a living sacrifice to Him. That's God way to keep the door closed to the devil.

That means you will have to keep your body — your flesh with its appetites — under subjection to the recreated spirit man on the inside.

Keeping your body subject to your spirit is one of the primary ways you protect yourself against the enemy, and actually it is one of your *greatest* defenses against Satan.

Then what is man to do about his spirit? How is the believer going to keep his spirit strong against the attacks of the enemy? He has to feed his recreated spirit on God's Word. God's Word is spirit "food" for a spirit being.

LUKE 4:4
4 . . . man shall not live by bread alone, but by EVERY
WORD OF GOD.

JOHN 6:63
63 It is the spirit that quickeneth; the flesh profiteth nothing: the WORDS that I speak unto you, THEY ARE SPIRIT,
and THEY ARE LIFE.

Jesus is using a human term — *bread* — to convey a spiritual
thought. He's saying that what bread or food is to the body or to the
natural man, the Word of God is to the spirit man on the inside.
The believer is to *feed* his spirit on the Word to keep it strong.

Then you need to charge your recreated spirit by getting built
up in the Holy Ghost: *"But ye, beloved, building up yourselves on
your most holy faith, praying in the Holy Ghost"* (Jude 1:20). Praying in tongues charges your spirit like a battery charger charges a
battery. It provides a rest and refreshing even in the midst of any
test or trial the devil would try to bring against you so you can stay
strong against his attacks.

This is how you keep your spirit strong as a powerful defense
against Satan. Well, how are you going to get help for your mind,
will, and emotions then? By digging up your past? By getting someone to pray for you? By getting someone to cast the devil out of you?
No, that's not going to help when the real problem is that your
mind and emotions just need to be renewed with the Word of God.

It is a waste of time to try to cast the devil out of someone whose
real problem is an unrenewed mind. Let's get back to the Word!
Let's find out what the Word has to say about the soul of man,
especially the mind of man where the attacks of Satan are most
prevalent.

The Mind of Man

Actually, the Bible has a great deal to say about man's mind. You
begin to talk about the mind, and some people think you're talking
about Christian Science. But God has given us specific instructions
about the mind and what man is supposed to do to keep his mind
strong so he can stand against Satan, the enemy of his soul.

ISAIAH 26:3
3 Thou wilt keep him in perfect peace, whose MIND is
stayed on thee: because he trusteth in thee.

PHILIPPIANS 2:5
5 Let this **MIND** [attitude] be in you, which was also in Christ Jesus.

PHILIPPIANS 4:6-8
6 Be careful for nothing; but in every thing by prayer and supplication with thanksgiving let your requests be made known unto God.
7 And the peace of God, which passeth all understanding, shall keep your hearts and **MINDS** through Christ Jesus.
8 Finally brethren, whatsoever things are true, whatsoever things are honest, whatsoever things are just, whatsoever things are pure, whatsoever things are lovely, whatsoever things are of good report; if there be any virtue, and if there be any praise, **THINK ON THESE THINGS.**

In other words, God is telling us exactly what we ought to be doing with our minds. We are to keep our minds and our thoughts "stayed" or focused on God.

To do that we have to put the Word of God into our minds by meditating on it. Then our thinking will be in line with the Word of God, and Satan won't be able to get a foothold in our thinking.

The Bible tells us exactly what kind of thoughts we should be thinking — thoughts that are true, honest, just, pure, lovely, and of a good report. Think thoughts in line with the Word, not the enemy's thoughts of doubt, worry, and discouragement.

Did you ever stop to think about it? The first thing God requires of you after you're born again is to change your thinking.

God knows that if you are going to keep on *thinking* like you did before you were redeemed, you'll open a door to the devil. And soon you'll be *acting* just like you acted when you were still being dominated by the devil before you were born again.

The reason God tells us to change our thinking is that man's mind is the first place where Satan tries to gain access — even the minds of Christians if they let him.

A Renewed Mind
Transforms You!

ROMANS 12:1
1 I beseech you therefore, brethren, by the mercies of God, that ye **PRESENT YOUR BODIES A LIVING SACRIFICE,** holy, acceptable unto God, which is your reasonable service.

**2 And be not conformed to this world: but be ye TRANS-
FORMED by the RENEWING OF YOUR MIND, that ye may
prove what is that good, and acceptable, and perfect, will of
God.**

You see, God wants *submitted* bodies, and He wants *transformed* minds. There's a reason for that. He knows that is your
greatest defense against Satan.

When your mind is renewed with the Word, your *thinking* is
transformed. When your thinking is transformed, your *acting* is
transformed. You no longer *think* and *act* like you used to when you
were under Satan's dominion. When your thinking and acting are
transformed — *you* are transformed.

Paul was writing to born-again, Spirit-filled Christians when he
told them that they would have to do something with their *bodies*
and *minds* or souls. He was telling believers they will have to present their bodies as a living sacrifice to God, and see to it that their
minds are renewed with the Word of God.

EPHESIANS 4:23
23 And be RENEWED in the spirit of your MIND.

The Bible says when your mind is renewed, you will know what
the good, the acceptable, and the perfect will of God is for your life
(Rom. 12:2). To renew your mind, you'll have to meditate on the
Word of God because the Word is "spirit and life" which has the
ability to renew the mind of man.

To meditate on the Word of God means to actively read, think
on, speak, and dwell upon the Word. We are to meditate on the
Word of God, not just with our spirits, but also with our minds. We
are to fill our minds and our thinking with the Word of God. In the
Old Testament, God told Joshua how to be prosperous in everything he did, and it was to just stay filled up with the Word. The
Word will work for us too, and we won't have to spend so much
time dealing with the devil.

JOSHUA 1:8
**8 This book of the law shall not depart out of thy mouth;
but thou shalt meditate therein day and night, that thou
mayest observe to do according to all that is written
therein: for THEN thou shalt MAKE THY WAY PROSPER-
OUS, and THEN thou shalt have good SUCCESS.**

One translation says, "You'll be able to deal wisely in the affairs of life." How is success going to come? By meditating on the Word. How is victory over the devil going to come? By meditating upon the Word of God.

Success and victory come in every circumstance by the Word of God being continually in your mouth and by acting on the Word. Talk and dwell on the Word, not on your problems, and the devil won't have much to work with in your life.

Unless your soul has been renewed with the Word, your outward man will rule or dominate your spirit through your soul. Satan has access to your outward man through your five physical senses. That's why you need to get your mind renewed with the Word of God so your spirit, the real you, working with your mind, can govern your body.

Success in life over the devil doesn't come by trying to cast out some kind of an evil spirit all the time. It comes from getting your mind so filled with the Word of God that your mind will side in with your spirit. And your spirit directed by the Holy Spirit will lead you in all the affairs of life — including out of the traps and snares of the devil.

You are to actively meditate on the Word of God with your mind so your thinking can be changed or transformed (Ps. 1:1-3). Unless your thinking is transformed, you can think the devil's thoughts and begin acting just like unsaved people do. But Romans 12:2 says that renewing your mind transforms *you*! That is the way the Bible says *you* will be transformed, not by trying to cast a devil out of you.

Much of what is called "demonic" activity is not caused by demons at all. It is actually the fruit of a believer's unredeemed, unrenewed mind — thinking and acting like the world does. An unredeemed, unrenewed mind gives access to the devil because the mind is the doorway through which the devil gains access to people.

Wrong Thinking
Opens the Door to the Devil

Have you ever noticed that one reason people get depressed is that they think wrong thoughts? Thinking wrong thoughts can give evil spirits access into the realm of their souls. For example, sometimes believers get to thinking about the past and how So-and-so treated them. Yes, born-again, Spirit-filled people can get depressed. Of course, the devil tries to help them get depressed by bringing oppression against them.

But believers can get depressed simply by allowing themselves to think on wrong thoughts. That gives Satan something to work with, and it gives him access to their minds. Satan operates in the realm of the five senses by using wrong suggestions, thoughts, and feelings to try to influence people to wrongdoing.

But the Bible says, *"Neither give place to the devil"* (Eph. 4:27). We are not to let the devil into our thinking. Thinking wrong thoughts is one way believers give the devil a place in them — through their minds, thoughts, and emotions. Thoughts of guilt and condemnation and worry and anxiety are the devil's thoughts, and he will accommodate believers to think on the negative side of life.

Thinking thoughts of guilt and condemnation allow Satan to take advantage of believers and keep them in bondage to his lies. Bondage to wrong thoughts hinders believers from standing in their place of authority in Christ and exercising their rightful authority over the devil. In reality, believers are triumphant over the devil and his weapons of accusation because Jesus triumphed over Satan in the Cross (Col. 2:15). But if believers don't stand in that authority, the devil will dominate them.

Christians who continually think wrong thoughts can even get to the point in their thinking that they want to commit suicide. Yes, believers! Then some well-meaning folks say, "Let's cast the devil out of them!" Actually, it's not a devil problem at all. It's the result of wrong thinking.

Certainly Satan will try to accommodate believers to do things that are wrong. But if Christians who think wrong thoughts would get their minds renewed with the Word of God, they wouldn't have trouble with depression in the first place because their minds would be closed to the devil.

Actually, if believers would only train themselves in every instance to ask, "What does the Word say?" they wouldn't fall prey to the devil's bondage of depression, guilt, and condemnation in the first place. They would be triumphant in Christ — victorious over Satan's wiles and tactics.

It would answer so many problems, even regarding the devil, for Christians just to ask, "What does the Word say about my situation?" Believers need to train their minds to think on the Word, not on the devil's thoughts. A *renewed* mind thinks on the Word of God. That's how you stand strong against the devil. An *unrenewed* mind thinks on the devil's thoughts. And that's how you become weak and give way to thoughts of doubt, worry, fear, guilt, condemnation, and the like.

Another area where believers can open a door to the devil is by harboring unforgiveness in their hearts. Believers need to learn not to dwell on their past mistakes or on the past mistakes of others because the enemy of their souls, Satan, will use it to gain an inroad into their lives.

ISAIAH 43:25
25 I, even I, am he that BLOTTETH OUT THY TRANS-GRESSIONS for mine own sake, and WILL NOT REMEM-BER THY SINS.

Thinking about your past sins, failures, or mistakes gives the devil access to your thinking and emotions. If you've made mistakes but have asked God's forgiveness, God doesn't remember that you've done anything wrong (1 John 1:9). So why should you?

Get your mind renewed about God's lovingkindness and forgiveness, otherwise, Satan will take advantage of you. Actually, if Satan can get you thinking negative thoughts, he'll try to take more and more ground in your mind and soul. That's why you can't afford to give him any ground at all in you! When Satan comes to tempt you to think his negative thoughts, remind him what God's Word says. You don't need to fall prey to depression or any other kind of negative thinking.

Get your mind renewed with the Word! Don't go back in the past and try to dig up the things you've done by dwelling on them. The Word says to forget the past and to strive for your high calling in Christ (Phil. 3:13,14).

The devil will always try to bring a picture of past sins to your *mind.* But when your mind is renewed to God's love and forgiveness, you'll just laugh at him, and say, "Mr. Devil, the Word says I've been forgiven. Isaiah 43:25 says God has blotted out my transgressions! You're just showing me a photo of past failure, but it doesn't exist anymore." And then you can walk on in victory.

When you put the devil in his place with the Word of God, you're being a doer of the Word (James 1:22)! The Bible says it's the doer of the Word that is blessed (James 1:25). God made and fashioned you, so just follow the instructions He gave in His Word about how to keep the door closed to the devil. Then you can become successful in every area of life.

How Evil Spirits
Can Effect the Soulish Realm

You know my testimony about how I was raised up from the bed of sickness. But my own mother's life was a tragedy. Demons of worry, depression, and oppression got into her emotional or soulish realm and held her in bondage. Yes, she was saved, but she did not know her rights and privileges in Christ. She did not know how to renew her mind in order to shut the door on the devil. Sad to say that as a child of God, she lived below her privileges in Christ.

My daddy left us when I was about six years old, leaving my mother with four little children to raise by herself any way she could. All the trouble my mother had in life began to eventually affect her physically, mentally, and emotionally.

Finally she even began to lose her sight until she became totally blind. Doctors couldn't find anything physically wrong with her, but they said it was evidently a nervous disorder. She eventually had a complete physical, nervous, and mental breakdown. For several years she had mental problems and even tried to kill herself.

My mother was a Christian, but she didn't know how to believe God and appropriate His promises. It was so sad. Someone might ask, "If she had succeeded and killed herself, would she have been saved?" Certainly, she would have been saved! She was born again, but she had just allowed evil spirits of worry and fear to affect her mentally, physically, and emotionally. She was sick in her mind just like a person can be sick in his body.

And after these incidents were over, she didn't have any remembrance of attempting suicide. Through her ignorance of not knowing who she was in Christ and how to appropriate God's Word, she had allowed demons of worry and oppression to get into her mind and emotional realm.

Deliverance in the Realm of the Soul

You see, evil spirits can cause problems in the emotional realm of man. We sometimes act as though problems don't exist. But the Holy Spirit working in line with the Word of God always has an answer to every problem when the natural man does not.

I was holding a meeting in a certain place, and for three nights in a row after the service, a young married woman cried pathetically at the altar. I asked the Lord to show me how to help her.

Suddenly I had a vision. I saw this young woman when she was nine years old coming home from school one day. And when she came into the house, she found her mother in bed with a man who wasn't her husband. You can understand what that would do to the emotions of a nine-year-old child.

This woman was in her twenties at the time of my meeting. I saw in the Spirit that her trouble was in her marriage. I saw that she had been married two years but because of this emotional block, she was unable to consummate the marriage, and it was finally breaking up the marriage.

I went to the pastor of the church and asked him if he knew what was wrong with her. He asked if I did, and I told him the Lord had shown me her problem. He told me to go ahead and minister to her. I told the young woman what the Lord had shown me, and she said it was exactly what had happened. She loved her husband but had never been able to be a wife to him. I told her that it was wrong for her mother to be in bed with a man she wasn't married to, but that *marriage* wasn't wrong.

After giving her Scripture and talking to her about the sanctity of marriage, I laid hands on her and cast the evil spirit out of her soulish realm that had been holding her in bondage to the past. Then I taught her how to get into the Word of God and get her mind renewed, so Satan wouldn't have an entrance back into her mind and emotions.

The next year I went back to preach a meeting in that same church, and she and her husband had a bouncing baby boy whom they had named after me. They were happily married. You see, she didn't have an evil spirit in her *spirit*. But the evil spirit had gotten into her emotional realm when she was nine years old and was still dominating and afflicting her and had to be dealt with.

Christians shouldn't need to go to the unsaved for counsel and help. There is help in God. But there is more to the study of demonology than just telling people to cast demons out of everyone they meet. The believer has his part to play in standing strong against the devil.

The Body of Man

It's important to realize that since your body isn't born again, it is with your body — your five physical senses — that you contact this world where Satan is god (2 Cor. 4:4). That's why *you*, the man on the inside, must do something with your own body. If you let your body do whatever it wants to do and let your mind think anything it wants to think, the devil can get into your mind and body and dominate you.

Think about it. Doesn't your body want to do things that are wrong? Of course it does. Everyone's body does, no matter how long he's been saved, or how spiritual he is, because the body hasn't been redeemed. We have a promissory note on the redemption of our bodies (1 Cor. 15:53). But in this life, *we* will have to do something with our own bodies or Satan will take advantage of us through our flesh.

The Scripture instructs you what to do with your body:

1. *You* must present your body as a living sacrifice to God (Rom. 12:1).
2. *You* must crucify or mortify the deeds of the body (Col. 3:5).
3. *You* must keep your body under subjection to your spirit man — the inward man — the real man on the inside (1 Cor. 9:27).

You have control of your body, so you can keep your body from doing what it wants to do. God said you could. You don't have to allow Satan to use your body as an instrument of unrighteousness (Rom. 6:13).

Remember in Colossians 1:12, it says that God made us "meet" or *able* to be partakers of the inheritance of the saints in light. That means we *can* walk in the Spirit and not after the flesh. That means we don't have to yield to the devil's temptations through our carnal nature.

To understand how to obey God's Word about your body, you'll have to recognize that the Scripture makes a distinction between man's *body* — the outward man — and the real man on the inside — his *spirit*.

Man's Body Referred to as a 'House'

Many times in the Scripture, man's body is referred to as a "house." You need to know that because evil spirits can be in a person's *house* — his body — and yet not actually in the fullest sense be in the person — in his spirit. That's because man is a *spirit*, not a *body*.

For example, if you lived in a house that had termites, that doesn't mean *you* have termites in you. The house is just where you live, but you *yourself* don't have termites. Well, an evil spirit can try to afflict your body, but that doesn't mean *you* have an evil spirit in *you* — in your spirit.

Scripture bears out the fact that man's body is often referred to as his "house." When man dies physically, his *body* dies, but *he* still lives.

Paul refers to the body as "the earthly HOUSE of this tabernacle."

2 CORINTHIANS 5:1,2,4
1   For we know that if our EARTHLY HOUSE OF THIS TABERNACLE [man's body] **were dissolved, we have a building of God, AN HOUSE not made with hands, ETERNAL in the heavens** [man's spirit].
2   For in this we groan, earnestly desiring to be clothed upon with our HOUSE which is from heaven. . . .
4   For we that are in THIS TABERNACLE [the body] **do groan, being burdened: not for that we would be unclothed, but clothed upon, that mortality might be swallowed up of life.**

The Bible is talking about the *inward man* and the *outward man* here. The *outward man* is our earthly house, *the body*. But there is also an *inward man*, a house not made with hands, man's *spirit*, and that is eternal. Paul talks about the difference between the outward man and the inward man.

2 CORINTHIANS 4:16
16   For which cause we faint not; but though our OUTWARD MAN perish, yet the INWARD MAN is renewed day by day.

The spirit man or the inward man is the same as "the hidden man of the heart."

1 PETER 3:3,4
3   Whose adorning let it not be that OUTWARD adorning [the adorning of the outward man or the body] **of plaiting the hair, and of wearing of gold, or of putting on of apparel;**
4   But let it be THE HIDDEN MAN OF THE HEART [the inward man], **in that which is not corruptible, even the ornament of a meek and quiet spirit, which is in the sight of God of great price.**

By something Paul said, you can see that man's body is different from the man on the inside.

1 CORINTHIANS 9:27
27 But I keep under my body, and bring IT [my body] **into subjection: lest that by any means, when I have preached to others, I myself should be a castaway.**

Paul called his body "it." Then who is the "I" that brought his body into subjection? It's the man on the inside that has become a new creature in Christ! Paul made a definite distinction between *"it"* — his body — and *"I"* — the real man on the inside.

Paul wasn't saying he had to bring himself — the man on the inside — into subjection. No, he said the man on the inside had to bring *his body* into subjection.

Not obeying this scripture is one of the major areas where believers unknowingly give Satan access into their lives. Satan is given a foothold in people's lives when they allow their bodies or flesh to dominate them, instead of allowing their recreated spirits to rule and dominate their flesh.

Keeping Your Body Subject to Your Spirit

In First Corinthians 9:27, Paul was saying, "I keep my body under the subjection of my spirit." That means Paul didn't let his body do everything it wanted to do. If the Apostle Paul, this great man of God who wrote much of the New Testament, had to keep his body under the dominion of his spirit, evidently his body must have wanted to do things that weren't right. Paul had to keep his body under the control and dominion of his spirit just as we do.

Too many times believers want to try to cast a demon out when it's the flesh! You can't cast the flesh out! Or too many times folks want God to do something with their bodies. God is not going to do anything with *your* body. After all, it's not *His* body; it's *yours*, and you are the one who has dominion over it.

When you're born again, your inward man belongs to God. But then *you* must make the decision to keep your body subject to your spirit, which is only possible as you present your body to God as a living sacrifice.

In Romans 12:1, Paul talks about the importance of believers' presenting their bodies to God.

ROMANS 12:1
1 I beseech you therefore, brethren, by the mercies of God, that YE present your BODIES a living SACRIFICE,

holy, acceptable unto God, which is your reasonable service.

It astounded me when I fully realized what these verses were actually saying. Paul wasn't writing to sinners. He was writing to saints — believers. He was telling Christians that even though they are born again, their bodies are not born again, and they will have to do something with their own bodies.

If you don't present your body to God as a "living sacrifice," your body is going to want to do everything it did before you got saved when you were still under the dominion of Satan, the god of this world (Eph. 2:2). In other words, if your inward man, which is a new creature in Christ, isn't in control of your body, you leave the door open for evil spirits to have access, because demons try to dominate man through the soul and the body.

I saw this happen in a minister's life. He was a wonderful Christian — a kind and good man who had been a pioneer in Pentecost. He had enjoyed excellent health for years, but in later years he began to have trouble physically. He eventually had three strokes, which affected his mind.

He was partially paralyzed, and at times he wasn't himself. He would cuss at his wife and knock her around. This woman and her daughter would pray and pray about his condition. When he would pray in tongues, he would be all right for a while, but he never got delivered.

His wife said that after hearing me teach on the believer's authority, she realized what she should have done. The stroke had affected her husband's brain, so he couldn't oversee his own mind and body anymore. Because of that, the devil took advantage of him.

He became a different person, partially because of the stroke, of course, but in his case an evil spirit was also involved. Saved or unsaved, man can be *oppressed* in mind or body by evil spirits. His wife didn't know to stand against it in the Name of Jesus and take authority over it.

After her husband had gone to be with the Lord, his wife realized she should have stood against Satan and commanded him to take his hands off God's property. I assured her that Satan had to obey the Word!

Protection Against the Enemy

Keeping your body under subjection to your recreated spirit is a major defense against Satan. The Bible says, *"Submit yourselves therefore to God. Resist the devil, and he will flee from you"* (James 4:7). When you submit your body to God and don't allow it to do things that are wrong, it's going to be a lot easier for you to resist the devil.

God knows without submitted bodies and transformed minds, believers won't be able to follow the leading of the Holy Spirit as they should. The Bible says, *"For as many as are led by the Spirit of God, they are the sons of God"* (Rom. 8:14).

It doesn't say, "For as many as are led by the body or the five physical senses, they are the sons of God." Or "As many as are led by the soul, they are the sons of God." *Spirit*-ruled, Word-based believers have a strong defense against Satan. Body-ruled and sense-ruled believers are an open target for Satan and his wiles.

And if a believer hasn't been taught correctly, when his body wants to do things that aren't right, the devil will take advantage of him and mislead him to think he isn't even saved. Then once the devil gets a believer under condemnation, he can cheat him out of walking in his inheritance in Christ, which includes exercising authority over him.

But if Christians understand that their body is not born again and that *they* must do something about their own body, they can learn to present it to God as a living sacrifice by bringing it into subjection to their recreated spirit. This is one of the most important ways a Christian takes his place in Christ so he can stand strong against the devil.

If we don't get our minds renewed with the Word of God, our *mind* will side in with our *body* against our *spirit*. That provides no strong defense against Satan!

Don't Blame the Devil for Carnality

What does the word "carnal" mean? According to *Vine's Expository Dictionary of New Testament Words*, the word "carnal" signifies *the flesh that is sensual, controlled by animal appetites, and governed by human nature instead of by the Spirit of God.*[2]

Christians are to walk by faith in God's Word and to be led by the Holy Spirit — not by their senses. A person can have all the gifts of the Spirit operating in his life and still be carnal if he doesn't learn how to keep his body and soul under the dominion of his spirit.

The Corinthians were like that. Those believers were even filled with the Spirit, yet they were held in a babyhood state of Christianity because they were carnal or body-ruled and sense-ruled (1 Cor. 3:1,3). They allowed their five senses to dominate them, rather than the Holy Spirit.

Paul said to the Corinthians, ". . . *ye are yet carnal: for whereas there is among you envying, and strife, and divisions, are ye not carnal, and walk as* [mere natural] *men?*" (1 Cor. 3:1-3). And the Bible says, *"For where envying and strife is, there is confusion and every evil work"* (James 3:16).

If Christians don't develop their spirits but allow their bodies, minds, and emotions to rule them, they will remain in a carnal or babyhood state of spirituality. Carnal Christians easily fall prey to the devil's wiles through envy, strife, and division.

Then some Christians think they continually need evil spirits cast out of them because they are so easily tossed about by Satan. But, really, they just need to grow and develop and learn how not to yield to envy, strife, and division.

As you learn to yield to the Spirit of God and base your life on the Word of God rather than on your feelings or flesh, you grow out of the carnal state of Christianity where Satan can dominate you.

Satan doesn't have access to you in the arena of faith in God's Word, but he does in the realm of the senses when you are sense-ruled and led by your body and soul.

Man is always trying to come up with excuses rather than relying on what God has already laid down in His Word. For example, in His Word, God gave us instructions about what to do with our *spirit, soul,* and *body* as a strong protection against the enemy.

But man is always trying to find some other way than *God's* way to arrive at spiritual maturity, success, and victory over the devil in every circumstance.

If he can find an easy way to do things, like blaming everything on the devil, he'll do it, rather than to live by the principles in God's Word.

It is much easier to try to cast a devil out than it is to take the responsibility to consistently renew your mind with the Word and keep your flesh under subjection to your spirit!

A preacher I once knew understood man's carnal nature. He saw a title on a billboard that said, "The Beast and I." That inspired a title for a sermon he was preaching called, "The Beast That Is in All of Us."

Did you know there is a beast in all of us? The "beast" is your flesh — your carnal unregenerated human nature, and you will have that carnal nature to subdue as long as you are on earth.

In that sense, we could say there is a "beast" in all of us. There is a carnal nature in the unregenerated human nature — in the flesh of man.

However, the carnal nature is not in your spirit if you're born again. And, thank God, one day you will also have a new glorified body (1 Cor. 15:42, 50-54). Until that day, God tells you in His Word how to stand strong against your enemy, Satan.

---

[1] W. E. Vine, Vine's Expository Dictionary of Biblical Words (Nashville, Tennessee: Thomas Nelson, Inc., 1985), pp. 200,201.

[2] Ibid., pp. 89,90.

Chapter 3
The Devil or the Flesh?

Some things that folks attribute to the devil are really nothing more than works of the flesh. It is important to realize that everything that's wrong in life is not directly the work of an evil spirit.

When the Bible talks about keeping the flesh under the dominion of the spirit, too many times folks think that only refers to keeping sexual desires under control. Well, it's true you'll have to keep your body under subjection in that area. But right on the other hand, did you ever notice what else the Bible lists as works of the flesh or the old man nature?

The Works of the Flesh

Galatians chapter 5 lists the works of the flesh.

GALATIANS 5:17,19-21
17 For the flesh lusteth against the Spirit, and the Spirit against the flesh: and these are contrary the one to the other: so that ye cannot do the things that ye would. . . .
19 Now the WORKS OF THE FLESH are manifest, which are these; Adultery, fornication, uncleanness, lasciviousness,
20 Idolatry, witchcraft, hatred, variance, emulations, wrath, strife, seditions, heresies,
21 Envyings, murders, drunkenness, revellings, and such like. . . .

What many folks call works of "the devil," the Bible calls the works of the flesh. In Ephesians 4:25-32, Paul lists some of the traits of the "old man" — the flesh or man's unregenerated nature: lying, stealing, corrupt communication, bitterness, wrath, anger, clamour, evil speaking, and malice. And he also describes some of the traits of the new man in Christ: truthfulness, tenderheartedness, and forgiveness.

You can see that keeping the flesh under control or under the dominion of the new man in Christ involves more than just keeping sexual desires under control. It involves keeping *all* the evil tendencies of the flesh in check and under the dominion of the recreated spirit.

'Put Off' the Flesh

The Bible tells us how to deal with the body and soul — man's carnal, fleshly nature. We are to "put off" the old man with his fleshly lusts. And we are to "put on" the new man in Christ.

EPHESIANS 4:22-24
22 THAT YE PUT OFF concerning the former conversation [lifestyle] THE OLD MAN, which is corrupt according to the DECEITFUL LUSTS;
23 And [you] be RENEWED in the spirit of your MIND;
24 And that YE PUT ON THE NEW MAN, which after God is created in righteousness and true holiness.

Who is to put off the nature of the old man or the works of the flesh? *You* are! "You" is the subject of verse 22. God is not going to "put off the old man" for you. You will have to *put off* the old man with his envy, bitterness, wrath, anger, clamor, and evil speaking. You aren't dealing with evil spirits when you put off those evil tendencies; you are just dealing with your *flesh*.

All too often believers try to take the easy way out and call these evil tendencies of the flesh a "demon" or an "evil spirit." That way they don't have any responsibility; they can blame everything on Satan. But the Bible just calls these evil tendencies man's fleshly nature, and the believer has to do something about that *himself*.

The only way you can put on "the new man" is to renew your mind with the Word of God. Putting off the old man and putting on the new man is part of your "reasonable service" or your "spiritual worship" (Rom. 12:1,2).

You've got to keep those evil tendencies and attitudes under the dominion of your spirit — the man on the inside — and let the new creature in Christ dominate. As you "put on" Christ you'll be able to walk in the Spirit of God and not in the flesh where you are an easy prey for Satan.

If you didn't have your flesh and its carnal nature to deal with, you wouldn't be human. And as long as you're in your body, you will have your fleshly, carnal nature to contend with. For example, if someone hits you and your flesh isn't in subjection to your spirit, it will want to retaliate and hit him back. That's the way the carnal nature acts apart from God. If someone hurts you, your flesh wants to get even and retaliate and hold bitterness and resentment against the person.

That's the old "get-even" nature of the flesh. It's not a devil or demonic activity. It's just the carnal nature of man left unchecked. "You hurt me and I'll get even with you." Have you ever heard Christians talk that way? Flesh is just that way, and that's why you've got to keep it under the dominion of the man on the inside ". . . *which after God is created in righteousness and true holiness"* (Eph. 4:24).

Put On the God-kind of Love

Let's look in Colossians chapter 3, to see how the new creature in Christ acts and to see what we are commanded to "put on."

COLOSSIANS 3:12-14
12 PUT ON therefore, as the elect of God, holy and beloved, BOWELS OF MERCIES, KINDNESS, HUMBLENESS OF MIND, MEEKNESS, LONGSUFFERING;
13 FORBEARING ONE ANOTHER, and FORGIVING ONE ANOTHER, if any man have a quarrel against any: even as Christ forgave you, so also do ye.
14 And above all these things PUT ON CHARITY, which is the bond of perfectness.

In verse 13, the phrase "forbearing one another" means putting up with one another. When we begin to get agitated and impatient with one another, it isn't necessarily a devil at work. We just need to exercise forbearance and forgive one another, even as Christ forgave us (v. 13).

The word translated in verse 14 as "charity" is the Greek word, "agape" — the God-kind of love. We are to put on love. Putting on love is a protection against the enemy because then we don't give the devil any place in us (Eph. 4:27).

When we're born again, the love of God has been shed abroad in our hearts by the Holy Ghost (Rom. 5:5). But we're going to have to take the love that's in our hearts and put it on our *outward* man because the love of God hasn't been shed abroad in our *flesh*. If we don't put on the love of God on our outward man, Satan can have a heyday in our lives through our flesh.

Anger — Flesh, Not 'the Irish,' And Not the Devil

I heard one fellow talking about his grandpa. With the least little provocation, his grandpa would fly off the handle and go into a rage. This man's grandfather always used the excuse, "Well, that's just the Irish in me." No, it wasn't "the Irish" in him. It was *the flesh!*

EPHESIANS 4:26
26 Be ye angry, and sin not: let not the sun go down upon your wrath.

According to Ephesians 4:26, putting off the old man and putting on the new man is a choice: *"Be ye angry, and sin not. . . ."* That means if you get angry about something, you don't have to let your flesh take over. You don't have to lose control of your temper. *You* have a choice. You don't have to give in to the dictates of your fleshly, carnal nature.

If you let the flesh dominate you, you can get out of control and do and say things you'll regret later on. Many people want to blame the devil when they lose control and go into a rage or a fit of anger. But they're just giving in to their flesh and letting it dominate them. And by not keeping their flesh in check, they are opening a door to the devil.

Some folks think you can get so "sanctified" that you won't ever have any more problems with the flesh or Satan. But the only way you won't have problems with the flesh or Satan is to die and leave this world!

A fellow came to me one time after one of my morning meetings. He said, "Brother Hagin, I want you to pray that I won't ever have any more trouble with the devil." I asked, "Do you want me to pray that you'll die?" He said, "No, I don't want to die." I said, "The only way you'll never have any more trouble with the devil is to die and get out of this world!"

Much of the trouble this man thought was coming from the devil was really nothing more than his flesh, but he hadn't learned to distinguish the difference. To be perfectly honest with you, I'm persuaded that Christians have more trouble with their flesh than they do with the devil.

Often Christians who are having problems with the flesh think if they could just "get away" from it all, or move to another state, or change jobs or churches, things would be different. But you can't get away from the flesh; moving or changing churches isn't going to solve the problem if it's your unredeemed flesh you're dealing with. Wherever you go, your flesh is still going to be there. You might just as well go ahead and stay right where you are and learn to bring it in subjection to your recreated spirit.

The Flesh Has Its Own Lusts
And It's Not the Devil

You need to realize something else about the flesh. It has its *own* lusts and appetites, and it's not a devil at work or even demonic activity. Look again at Ephesians 4:22.

EPHESIANS 4:22
22 That ye put off concerning the former conversation [lifestyle] THE OLD MAN, which is CORRUPT according to the DECEITFUL LUSTS.

We can learn something else about the lusts of the flesh from the Book of Romans.

ROMANS 1:24-28
24 Wherefore God also gave them up to uncleanness through the LUSTS OF THEIR OWN HEARTS, to dishonour their own bodies between themselves:
25 Who changed the truth of God into a lie, and worshipped and served the creature more than the Creator, who is blessed for ever. Amen.
26 For this cause God gave them up unto vile affections: for even their women did change the natural use into that which is against nature:
27 And likewise also the men, leaving the natural use of the woman, BURNED IN THEIR LUST one toward another; men with men working that which is unseemly, and receiving in themselves that recompence of their error which was meet.
28 And even as they did not like to retain God in their knowledge, God gave them over to a reprobate mind, to do those things which are not convenient.

In the margin of my Bible, the word "reprobate" is defined as *a mind void of judgment*. The Bible isn't talking about a *spirit* of lust here. Notice in verse 27, the Bible doesn't call this a "spirit of lust." It just says those in disobedience burned in *their* lust toward one another.

Verse 24 says, *"Wherefore God also gave them up to uncleanness through the LUSTS OF THEIR OWN HEARTS. . . ."* It's the lust of their own hearts — the unredeemed thoughts and feelings of man — that caused those walking in darkness to finally be turned over to a reprobate mind.

Then in verse 27 it says they "burned in their lust" toward one another. That's man's unregenerated nature apart from God. The Bible doesn't call that a devil; it calls it the "lusts of their own hearts." The flesh — the unredeemed nature of man — has its own lusts because it is degenerate; it's never been born again. The lusts of the flesh have nothing to do with a "spirit" of lust. The flesh has its own appetites or "fleshly cravings."

1 PETER 2:11
11 Dearly beloved, I beseech you as strangers and pilgrims, abstain from FLESHLY LUSTS, which WAR AGAINST THE SOUL.

As long as you allow your fleshly lusts to dominate you, you will always have trouble in your soul — your mind, will, and emotions. And that will give Satan an open door.

JAMES 1:13-15
13 Let no man say when he is tempted, I am tempted of God: for God cannot be tempted with evil, neither tempteth he any man:
14 But every man is tempted, when he is drawn away of HIS OWN LUST, and ENTICED.
15 Then when LUST hath conceived, it bringeth forth SIN: and sin, when it is finished, bringeth forth DEATH.

According to this Scripture, it's the lust of a person's own unredeemed nature that draws him into error. Some people mistake the corruption that lust, sin, and death produce, and think it's demonic activity at work. But it isn't. It's the fruit of the flesh left unchecked.

Ephesians also talks about the *lusts* of the *flesh* and of the *mind* or *soul*.

EPHESIANS 2:3
3 Among whom also we all had our conversation [lifestyle] in times past in the LUSTS OF OUR FLESH, fulfilling the DESIRES OF THE FLESH and OF THE MIND; and were by nature the children of wrath, even as others.

Crucify the Flesh

If an evil spirit is involved trying to work through your flesh, you have authority over it. The devil and evil spirits have no dominion over you, as long as you're walking in line with the Word and doing what you're supposed to with your flesh. Stand against Satan and his wiles, because the Bible says he has to flee (James 4:7).

But if it's just the flesh you're dealing with, you won't be able to cast it out like you could an evil spirit. No, you have to *crucify* or *mortify* the deeds of the body (Gal. 5:24; Col. 3:5). Everyone — preacher and layperson alike — must crucify the lusts of his own flesh and the cravings of his own carnal nature.

In Paul's epistles, he talks about "mortifying" the deeds of the body.

COLOSSIANS 3:5
5   MORTIFY therefore YOUR MEMBERS [your body] which are upon the earth; fornication, uncleanness, inordinate affection, evil concupiscence, and covetousness, which is idolatry.

ROMANS 8:5-8,12-14
5   For they that are after the FLESH do mind the things of the FLESH; but they that are after the SPIRIT the things of the SPIRIT.
6   For to be CARNALLY MINDED IS DEATH; but to be spiritually minded is life and peace.
7   Because the CARNAL MIND IS ENMITY AGAINST GOD: for it is not subject to the law of God, neither indeed can be.
8   So then they that are in the FLESH [those who are domi-nated by their fleshly carnal nature] CANNOT PLEASE GOD....
12   ... brethren, we are debtors, not to the flesh, to live after the flesh.
13   For if ye live after the FLESH, ye shall die: but if ye through the Spirit do MORTIFY the DEEDS OF THE BODY, ye shall live.
14   For as many as are LED BY THE SPIRIT OF GOD, they are the sons of God.

To "mortify" means *to kill, become dead, cause to be dead, put to death*, or *subdue*. Mortifying or crucifying the flesh is something each believer must do for himself; God can't do that for him.

Your husband, your wife, or your pastor can't mortify the deeds of your flesh for you. *You* must "kill," "put to death," and subdue the lust of your own carnal, fleshly nature. That is part of your "spiritual worship" (Rom. 12:1,2) in presenting your body as a living sacrifice to God. It's part of submitting to God so you can resist the devil.

Those who continually practice putting to death the deeds of their unregenerate nature won't have the problems with the devil that carnal Christians do. That doesn't mean the devil won't try to attack them, but they will know how to keep from giving the devil any place in them.

GALATIANS 5:24
24 And they that are Christ's have CRUCIFIED the FLESH with the AFFECTIONS and LUSTS.

Crucifying the flesh is not pleasurable. Every Christian has the same way of escape from falling prey to the devil through the lusts of his own flesh. But not every Christian takes the way of escape provided for him by crucifying his own flesh. Why? Because it hurts to deny the flesh.

We don't have much teaching on crucifying the flesh in the Charismatic Movement. That's one reason some people have taken the teaching on demons to the extreme and thought that everything bad that happens is the devil at work. No, not everything bad is the direct result of the devil or a demon. Much of what believers call the devil is just the work of the flesh. And no one can do anything about your flesh for you; *you* have to crucify it yourself (Col. 3:5).

These folks who are always trying to cast out a devil want the easy way out. It's easier for a believer to get someone *else* to try to cast a demon out of him than it is to crucify and mortify his own flesh with its lusts and affections because it hurts to do that.

Years ago a woman came up to me after one of my meetings wanting deliverance from a devil. She said, "Brother Hagin, I wish you would cast this ole unforgiving spirit out of me." She explained that another Christian woman had offended her. "Sister So-and-so did me wrong. God knows I want to forgive her, but I *can't*. Please cast this ole unforgiving spirit out of me!"

I asked her, "Have you ever forgiven your husband?"

She said, "Yes, of course."

I said, "I thought you said you *couldn't* forgive because you have an unforgiving spirit in you. No, if you can forgive one person, you can forgive another person. The real problem is you don't *want* to forgive this sister. You want to hold a grudge against her.

"You don't need a devil cast out of you. That unforgiveness is just your flesh, and you're going to have to deal with that yourself. You just need to do what the Word of God says in Ephesians 4:32: '*And be kind one to another, tenderhearted, forgiving one another, even as God for Christ's sake hath forgiven you.'"*

If God told us to be kind and forgive each other as He's forgiven us, that means we can do it. But you won't be able to forgive if you allow your flesh to control you. But God wouldn't tell you to do something you couldn't do, because He would be unjust if He did. And God is not unjust.

We *can* forgive just as God forgives because the love of God has been shed abroad in our hearts (Rom. 5:5). So most of the time it's not a matter of casting out an evil spirit; it's a matter of crucifying the flesh so the love of God in our hearts can be manifested in the outward man.

God doesn't have any "quick fixes," and He isn't running any fast-food joints or ninety-nine cent sales! If you want to experience a triumphant Christian walk over the devil, the flesh, and the world, then it costs the same price as it always has.

You'll have to be thoroughly Word-based, living by the principles in God's Word. And you start by crucifying your own flesh and learning to walk in the God-kind of love! You're not going to solve all your problems by just trying to deal with the devil all the time. Yes, there are times to deal with the devil, but much of the time it's your own flesh causing you the problems!

Jesus' Remedy for 'Flesh' Problems

MATTHEW 5:29,30
29 And if thy right eye offend thee, PLUCK IT OUT, and cast it from thee: for it is profitable for thee that one of thy MEMBERS should perish, and not that thy whole body should be cast into hell.
30 And if thy right hand offend thee, CUT IT OFF, and cast it from thee: for it is profitable for thee that one of thy MEMBERS should perish, and not that thy whole body should be cast into hell.

Jesus' instructions about how to deal with the flesh were just as direct as Paul's. In these scriptures, Jesus wasn't saying to literally pull your eye out or cut your hand off. That's symbolic. He was saying that sometimes it will hurt you to deal with your fleshly lusts and appetites just about as much as it would be to cut off one of your bodily members.

It will be painful to your flesh to put these cravings away from you. That's why the Bible uses the words *"crucify"* and *"mortify"*;

it's not pleasant. It hurts the flesh.

Just as Paul did, Jesus also emphasized that *you* are the one who has to pluck out the evil tendencies, lusts, appetites, and cravings of your own flesh and put them away from you. God is not going to do that for you.

God will strengthen and encourage you, of course, but He won't do it for you. It won't be pleasant, but this is one way you become Spirit-ruled and Spirit-led instead of body-ruled, body-conscious, body-led and open prey to the devil. Actually, this is one way you submit to God and resist the devil (James 4:7).

'God, Take the Snuff!'

There was a woman down in Texas who came to one of my meetings. After everyone else left, this woman prayed at the altar, just bawling and squalling. Every now and then, she'd yell, "Take it away from me, Lord! You know I don't want it!" And then she'd get to screaming like a freight train going through a tunnel.

I finally said to her, "Sister! What is it you don't want?"

She said, "Why, that old snuff."

I said, "God isn't going to take snuff away from you. What would He do with it if He had it? He doesn't dip snuff. You're going to have to do something about it yourself. You're going to have to crucify your own flesh."

She said, "Oh, but *I* couldn't give up good ole snuff!"

Remember, Jesus said if your hand offends you — *you* cut it off. He didn't mean to get an axe and cut your hand off. But when you put away the lusts and the cravings of your own flesh, it's going to "crucify," "kill," and "put to death" your flesh. Most folks today would have wanted to cast a "snuff" devil out of that woman! That's what she wanted too — the easy way out.

You will have to crucify your own flesh and bring your fleshly appetites, lusts, and carnal cravings into subjection. The devil will try to gain access to you any way he can, and he will use the cravings of your own flesh to do it if you allow him to. *But you don't have to allow him to.*

When the devil tries to use your flesh to gain access to you, it doesn't mean you're demon possessed. The devil will always work through the flesh because your body isn't redeemed and your five physical senses contact this world where Satan is god (2 Cor. 4:4). But if you don't furnish the devil anything to work with — if you don't give him any place in you — he won't have any access to you.

So the Bible says there are lusts of the human carnal nature which have nothing to do with evil spirits. You can't cast the flesh out; you have to *crucify* or *mortify* the deeds of the flesh. However, if you continue to give place to the lusts of your flesh, you will eventually open the door to an evil spirit.

The devil will accommodate believers and help them fulfill the lust of their own fleshly desires. And eventually an evil spirit can get ahold of believers who continually indulge in the lust of their carnal, sensual nature. That is one way Satan gains access, even to believers.

Put the Responsibility Where It Belongs

Have you ever thought about it? The Holy Spirit helps and encourages believers to do what's right. And if we yield to the Holy Spirit, we can do what is right. But even though He *helps* us do what is right, we can't really say it is the *Holy Spirit* who does right — *we* do. *We* ultimately make the choice to yield to the Holy Spirit and walk in line with the Word and do what's right. The Holy Spirit assists us, of course, but we have to *yield* to His gentle promptings.

It's the same way with the devil. The devil will help and encourage people — saved and unsaved alike if they will allow him — to do what's *wrong* in every way he possibly can. The Christian is not under his dominion, but Satan will still try to work through a Christian's flesh to get him to do wrong *if the person allows it.*

Satan has dominion over those who walk in darkness, so he can greatly assist them in wrongdoing. But in one respect, you can't say that all the evil committed by those in darkness is entirely the work of the devil either.

According to the Scriptures, the lust of their own fleshly nature is also involved in wrongdoing. Just as the Holy Spirit *assists* us to do right, the devil *assists* anyone walking in darkness to do wrong. But it's still the person's responsibility what they do because people have free choice.

EPHESIANS 2:1-3
1 And you hath he quickened [made alive], **who were dead in trespasses and sins;**
2 Wherein in time past ye walked according to the course of this world, according to the prince of the power of the air, the spirit that now WORKETH in the children of disobe-

dience:
3 Among whom also we all had our conversation [lifestyle]
in times past in THE LUSTS OF OUR FLESH, fulfilling the
DESIRES of the FLESH and of the MIND; and were by
nature the children of wrath, even as others.

The Scriptures tell us that the devil, or "the prince of the power
of the air," *works* in people for evil, just as the Holy Spirit *works* in
God's people for good.

PHILIPPIANS 2:13
13 For it is God which WORKETH IN YOU both to will and
to do of his GOOD pleasure.

People can't lay everything off on the devil and blame him for all
the bad things that happen to them. Not all evil is directly the work
of a demon. Indirectly, of course, everything that is evil originated
with the devil. But the point I'm trying to make is that people still
have their own part to play in wrongdoing — the choice is theirs.

On one side of the ditch, just as believers try to lay everything
off on the devil, on the other side of the ditch, they can't lay everything off on the Holy Spirit either. In other words, they cannot put
all the responsibility for their actions on the Holy Spirit.

The Holy Spirit prompts us and gently leads us, but we have to
yield to Him and respond to His instructions. We still have to
choose to do what is right or *choose* to do what is wrong. When you
choose to do wrong, that's not the *devil* making the choice — it's
you. He may tempt you, of course, but you ultimately make the
choice to whom you are going to yield — Satan or the Holy Spirit.

The Pleasures of the Flesh

This passage in James, which was written to Christians, also
addresses the subject of the works of the flesh, or "pleasures of the
flesh."

JAMES 4:1-3
1 From whence come wars and fightings among you? come
they not hence, even of YOUR LUSTS that war in YOUR
MEMBERS?
2 YE LUST, and have not: ye kill, and desire to have, and
cannot obtain: ye fight and war, yet ye have not, because ye
ask not.
3 Ye ask, and receive not, because ye ask amiss, that ye

may consume it upon YOUR LUSTS.

According to Vine's *Expository Dictionary of New Testament Words*, the word "lust" is also translated *pleasures*. Lusts are "pleasures" of the flesh. Pleasures of the flesh aren't demons or evil spirits.

The *Holy Spirit* uses the believer and his personality and body to work acts of righteousness (Phil. 2:13). The *devil* can also use the believer and his fleshly, carnal nature and the pleasures of his flesh to influence him to work acts of unrighteousness and disobedience.

That's why you can't just call all lusts of the flesh "an evil spirit" or "a devil." Lusts can *also* be the "pleasures" of the flesh. When a person gets saved, even though his *spirit* is recreated, his body still wants to go right on fulfilling the pleasures of the flesh just as it did before he got saved.

For example, if a young man got saved and he was used to having sexual relationships with women before he was saved, his flesh will want to keep right on doing that. That doesn't necessarily mean he needs to have a devil cast out of him. He just needs to learn to keep his flesh under subjection to his spirit and walk in line with God's Word because God does not condone sin.

Every new believer needs to get into the Word of God for himself to renew his mind and learn how to present his body to God as a living sacrifice. As a born-again new creature, he will have to learn how to let his inward man dominate his flesh.

So not every act of wrongdoing is directly the result of a *devil*. Sometimes you hear preachers who want to cast *this demon* and *that demon* out of believers when demons aren't the cause of the trouble at all — it's just the unregenerate flesh at work.

For example, I've heard of ministers trying to cast a demon of gluttony out of a person. But overeating is a lust or a *pleasure* of the flesh. There is pleasure in eating. When pushed to the extreme, eating is gluttony and it's wrong, and I'm sure the devil can get involved with overeating and encourage people in wrongdoing, just like he can with any extreme. But overeating is not necessarily a devil at work. It can be a lack of the fruit of the spirit of temperance or self-control (Gal. 5:23; Phil. 4:5).

Although the devil can sometimes get involved in overeating, on the other hand, it's simply pleasant to eat. It's not pleasant to fast; the flesh doesn't like to be denied or crucified. But we are admonished in the Word to keep the flesh under and fasting helps us do that.

Extremes and Excesses

We see some of the same extremes and excesses in this day about demons as we did in the days of *The Voice of Healing*. *The Voice of Healing* was a magazine published by Gordon Lindsay, but it was also an organization of evangelists and ministers. In the days of *The Voice of Healing*, some ministers were always trying to cast demons out of believers.

For example, when believers came forward for prayer to be delivered from cigarettes or from some other addiction, some ministers were always trying to cast a demon of nicotine or alcohol out of them.

I don't know that nicotine is a *spirit*. It is a *substance*, and it does damage to the human body. The devil can get ahold of substance abuse, of course, just as he can get ahold of anything that's extreme or harmful to the body.

But the point is, carnal desires or "pleasures" of the flesh — including physical addictions — will always try to dominate you if you don't do something about them yourself.

ROMANS 6:6,7,11-16
6 Knowing this, that our OLD MAN is CRUCIFIED with him [Christ], that the BODY OF SIN might be destroyed, that henceforth WE SHOULD NOT SERVE SIN.
7 For he that is dead is FREED FROM SIN. . . .
11 Likewise RECKON ye also yourselves TO BE DEAD INDEED UNTO SIN, but alive unto God through Jesus Christ our Lord.
12 Let not sin therefore reign in your MORTAL BODY, that ye should obey it in the LUSTS THEREOF.
13 Neither yield ye YOUR MEMBERS [your body] as instruments of unrighteousness unto sin: but yield yourselves unto God, as those that are alive from the dead, and your MEMBERS as instruments of righteousness unto God.
14 For SIN SHALL NOT HAVE DOMINION OVER YOU: for ye are not under the law, but under grace.
15 What then? shall we sin, because we are not under the law, but under grace? God forbid.
16 Know ye not, that TO WHOM YE YIELD YOURSELVES SERVANTS TO OBEY, HIS SERVANTS YE ARE TO WHOM YE OBEY; whether of sin unto death, or of obedience unto righteousness?

The Bible clearly says that we aren't to yield the members of our body to unrighteousness (v. 13). We don't have to serve sin, and sin isn't supposed to have dominion over us because Jesus set us free from sin's dominion.

However, you'll have to "reckon" yourself dead to sin in order to keep your bodily members from serving sin, because your body will want to keep right on serving sin if you let it. Your body and its members aren't dead; that's why you have to "reckon" or *count* them as dead to sin.

Close the Door to Satan In Your Thought Life

In order to "reckon" or "count" your physical members as dead, you'll have to learn to close the door to Satan in your thoughts. If you fail in that area, you will always have problems with the devil because you're giving him an open door to attack you.

Satan will always try to enter into a person, saved and unsaved alike, through the person's thoughts, if the person will yield and listen to him.

Thoughts may come — in fact, you can't always keep thoughts from coming. But you can keep from *entertaining* unwholesome and unedifying thoughts. It's like the old saying, "You can't keep birds from flying overhead, but you can keep them from building a nest in your hair!"

You can't help who comes by and knocks on your front door, but you have something to say about who you invite into your home. Thoughts will pop into your mind, and then the devil will come along and say, "Why, you're not even saved or you wouldn't even think that!"

At times, the most holy saint finds thoughts in his mind that his heart resents. *Thoughts may come and thoughts may persist, but thoughts that are not put into action die unborn.*

The most holy saint who is filled with the Holy Spirit and in whose life the power of God is demonstrated — still has to keep the door of his mind closed to the devil's thoughts. He still has to keep his mind strong by renewing it with the Word and subduing his own flesh so he's not open prey for the devil.

Paul had to keep his body under and bring *it* into subjection (1 Cor. 9:27). Wasn't Paul a man of God? Wasn't he an apostle? Weren't there signs and wonders and miracles following his ministry? Of course. But Paul's flesh was not born again or redeemed, just as our flesh isn't redeemed, and it will always want to do what is wrong.

If you keep your body under subjection to your recreated spirit, you won't have all the problems with the devil some folks have because Satan won't have anything to work through. And if you'll renew your mind with the Word, you won't be likely to yield to Satan's thoughts and suggestions. The Bible talks about "girding up the loins of your mind." You do that with the Word so your mind is strong, and you can successfully resist the thoughts of the enemy.

Watch what you feed your mind. Someone has said that the mind is the gateway into the soul. That's why it's vitally important what you allow your mind to dwell on. Let me show you how evil spirits can get into a believer's mind. A man came to see me who had been the head of the psychology department at a university. He and his wife came to me for help because he was having problems with demons.

He told me, "I majored in psychology and specialized on the behavior of the sexual criminal." He had many books in his personal library at home on the sexual criminal. He wasn't a Christian at the time he began studying these books.

In the course of time, he and his wife were saved and baptized in the Holy Spirit, and he retired as the head of the psychology department. When he first retired, he didn't read those books anymore. For two years he didn't have any problems. But he still kept those books, and eventually, he started reading them again.

When he and his wife came to me for help, he told me, "I don't know why, but I got all these books down on the sexual criminal, and I began to read case histories of child molestation again." He kept feeding that into his mind and studying about people motivated by the devil to commit sexual crimes, and an evil spirit got into his mind. He began having a strong desire to molest little girls. Finally, he began acting on that desire.

You need to be careful what you read. You ought to be as careful about what you read as you are about what you eat. You wouldn't think about eating poison, would you? If someone told you, "Don't eat that! It's poisonous and it will kill you," would you just go ahead and eat it anyway? No!

Well, you need to be as careful about what goes into your mind as you do about what goes into your stomach. The devil can gain access to your soul through a book, television, and so forth — by what you put into your mind.

This man's wife eventually discovered what he was doing and

filed for divorce. But when he finally came to see me for help, she came along with him. He told me, "It just seemed like I couldn't help myself." The devil got in because he yielded to his flesh. He allowed an evil spirit into his mind by reading those books. He had opened the door to the devil, and the devil accommodated him. Evil spirits were working with his flesh to drive him to commit these acts.

He told me, "I know about this subject. I've studied it and I've taught it. What happens is that the sexual criminal usually ends up killing one of the little girls he molests and goes to the electric chair. Brother Hagin, that thing just got ahold of me. I didn't want to molest those little girls. Can you help me?"

As he was talking, the Holy Spirit showed me that in his case three demons were involved. I knew that by the word of knowledge. You have to depend on the Holy Spirit in these areas. You won't know what's operating against a person unless the Holy Spirit shows you.

I answered him, "I can help you. I perceive that there's not just one spirit driving you, but there are really three spirits involved. First, there is a spirit of deception that's gotten ahold of you. Then there's a spirit of lying. And there is also an unclean spirit involved. I can cast all three of these spirits out of you, but it won't do a bit of good unless you do something yourself about the situation."

When people sin, they have to repent and completely turn away from wrongdoing before you can help them. Anyone can be set free from an evil spirit *if he's willing*. But what a person does after he's delivered of evil spirits is of the utmost importance.

Is he going to feed his mind on the Word of God? Is he going to get filled with the Holy Spirit and give the devil no more access to him? Or will he be like the scripture says: ". . . *EMPTY, swept, and garnished*" (Matt. 12:44)? If a person is delivered from an evil spirit and isn't taught the Word of God, evil spirits can enter back into him.

Also, you can't cast an evil spirit out of someone who doesn't want to be delivered. If a person wants to keep an evil spirit, he can. You won't be able to go against someone else's will and get him delivered if he wants to keep an evil spirit. That's why you don't just indiscriminately try to cast devils out of people.

If a person really has a demon, you would do him an injustice to cast the demon out of him unless you teach him to get filled with the Word and the Holy Spirit. It's the Word dwelling in him that will enable him to resist Satan's attacks. If he doesn't get himself filled up with the Word and if he isn't taught how *not* to give place to the devil, the Bible says he can end up worse than he was before (Matt. 12:43-45).

So I told this retired professor, "If you give me permission, I can exercise my authority over these three evil spirits for you. But as soon as you leave here, you'll have to take a stand against the devil for yourself.

"You see, there's no use casting evil spirits out of you and getting you delivered unless you are going to do something about this situation yourself. Otherwise, the devil will come back and find your house *empty*, and you'll end up worse off than you were before," and I showed him Matthew 12:43-45.

I told him, "In this scripture it says the man's house was *clean* — swept and garnished — but it was *empty*. It hadn't been filled with anything."

What do you fill a house with after it's been cleaned? The Word first, and prayer second. Never put prayer before the Word. And prayer must always be in line with the Word of God.

2 PETER 1:4
4   Whereby are given unto us EXCEEDING GREAT AND PRECIOUS PROMISES: that BY THESE YE MIGHT BE PARTAKERS OF THE DIVINE NATURE, having escaped the corruption that is in the world through LUST.

God's Word, His exceeding great and precious promises, are given to us so we can escape the corruption of worldly lust. One way we partake of the divine nature is by feeding on God's Word.

I told this retired professor, "I'm not going to do a thing for you — I'm not even going to pray for you unless you promise me *you* will do three things."

He said, "I'll do whatever you say."

I said, "First, burn those books. Second, don't ever read books like that again because that's how you let the devil in. You opened your mind to evil spirits. Third, read the Word of God and pray in other tongues every day. Keep full of the Word and full of the Holy Spirit."

A person can get saved, but if he's not going to walk with God, read the Bible, go to church, and fellowship with other Christians, he'll never amount to anything spiritually. He'll always be open to the attacks of the devil, and he'll backslide. It's what a person does *after* he's saved and filled with the Holy Spirit that determines how successfully he can stand against the devil.

I taught this man how to keep from giving the devil access to him. Then I cast those evil spirits out of him. I never even got out of my chair. I just pointed my finger toward him and said very calmly, "I command all three of you evil spirits to come out of the man in the Name of the Lord Jesus Christ."

In the spirit realm through the discerning of spirits, I saw those three spirits leave, just like birds flying away. It is not necessary to see anything in order to effectively deal with evil spirits. The man didn't see anything, nor did his wife or my wife. But I was seeing into the realm of the spirit because the gift of discerning of spirits was in operation. However, in the natural *there was no physical manifestation in the man whatsoever.*

About a year later, this man and his wife came to one of our meetings. They were back together, smiling and holding hands. He told me, "Brother Hagin, I haven't had a bit of trouble, praise God! I did just what you said to do. I burned every single one of those books. I've stayed in the Word and prayed in tongues every day, and I've never had another bit of trouble or even been tempted in that area. It's all gone."

If this man had been taught to present his body as a living sacrifice to God, he wouldn't have had that trouble with evil spirits in the first place, because he wouldn't have been reading those kinds of books.

If he had presented his body to God, he wouldn't have given the devil a place in him — in his *thinking* or in his *body.* But he didn't know his carnal nature wasn't redeemed and that the devil would accommodate his flesh, so he indulged his flesh and those spirits were able to get ahold of him. Actually, if he'd known his authority in Christ, he could have dealt with those evil spirits himself.

In some of these cases, nothing but the flesh is involved, so there's nothing to "cast out." In other cases, especially in *un*natural cases like this one, evil spirits are involved. And in some cases it is a combination of the two, the flesh and the devil working together.

For example, you can understand how a man might get physically involved with a woman because a man has a natural desire for a woman. Of course, all sexual relations outside of marriage are expressly forbidden by Scripture (1 Cor. 6:18). But when it comes to a grown man molesting little children, that's *unnatural.* That's beyond just a work of the flesh; an evil spirit is involved in that kind of unnatural sexual desire, and it will have to be dealt with for deliverance to be complete.

A 'Spirit' of Gluttony?

Once a woman approached my wife after one of our meetings. She was a young woman, about twenty-eight years old and obese. She said, "In our prayer group, they cast the spirit of gluttony out of me, but I've gained fifty-eight pounds since then."

My wife asked her, "Well, did they say anything to you about your diet and about developing good eating habits?"

She said, "Oh, no. They just said, 'That spirit is gone now. You can eat anything you want.'"

That's pushing the demon issue too far! Wouldn't that be wonderful if that were true! Go back to the Bible. What does the Bible say? It says, ". . . *put a knife to thy throat, if thou be a man given to appetite"* (Prov. 23:2). In other words, *you* do something about overeating. *You* cut off eating so much. I don't care how many diets you're on, in the final analysis, the only way to control your weight is for *you* to control your own eating habits.

In some cases, people may need a medical checkup to see if a chemical imbalance is causing the problem. But it's too easy to blame overeating and other fleshly weaknesses on a devil and remove the responsibility from believers to do something about overeating.

People are too often looking for a quick fix. "Let's just cast that demon of gluttony out!" But God doesn't always provide an "easy" way out because He's not in the "quick-fix" business. It will cost you a price to curb your own appetite and deny your own flesh.

These are some of the extremes that are being taught and practiced in the Body of Christ today. People can be gullible by following extreme teaching and practices in any area. We need to maintain scriptural balance and go down the middle of the road in every area and not get in the ditch on one side of the road or the other.

Sanctification

There's very little teaching about sanctification in Charismatic circles. As a result, there are some ungodly practices going on in the Church today. Basically, you need to understand that sanctification is an ongoing process. You're not just going to get sanctified one day, once for all, so that you can never sin again. I don't care how much of the Word you know, you'll still have to do your part by setting yourself apart unto godliness.

In old-time Pentecost, some "holiness" groups taught about sanctification. Their teaching was probably extreme in some areas, but they did endeavor to teach people to live a sanctified lifestyle. Living a sanctified lifestyle helps keep your flesh under the dominion of your spirit so Satan can't dominate you. Satan can't dominate you if he can't find a place in you and if you exercise your authority in Christ.

What does the Word say about sanctification?

> **1 THESSALONIANS 4:1,3-5,7**
> **1 Furthermore then we beseech you, brethren, and exhort you by the Lord Jesus, that as ye have received of us HOW YE OUGHT TO WALK and TO PLEASE GOD, so ye would abound more and more. . . .**
> **3 For this is the will of God, even your SANCTIFICATION, that ye should abstain from FORNICATION:**
> **4 THAT EVERY ONE OF YOU SHOULD KNOW HOW TO POSSESS HIS VESSEL IN SANCTIFICATION AND HONOR;**
> **5 Not in the LUST of concupiscence, even as the Gentiles which know not God. . . .**
> **7 For God hath not called us unto UNCLEANNESS, but UNTO HOLINESS.**

Those two words, "uncleanness" and "holiness," in verse 7 have to do with the believers' spiritual walk with the Lord mentioned in verse 1. Believers can't walk in *uncleanness* and please God. They'll have to walk in *holiness* to please Him.

Paul used the word "uncleanness" in verse 7. He just mentioned fornication and the lust of concupiscence in verses 3 and 5. "Concupiscence" means *a desire for what is forbidden*. Let's see how Paul uses this word "uncleanness" in his epistles, because if you walk in *sanctification* and *holiness* you won't give place to the devil.

> **ROMANS 1:24-28**
> **24 Wherefore God also gave them up to UNCLEANNESS through the LUSTS OF THEIR OWN HEARTS, to dishonour their own bodies between themselves:**
> **25 Who changed the truth of God into a lie, and worshipped and served the creature more than the Creator, who is blessed for ever. Amen.**
> **26 For this cause God gave them up unto VILE AFFECTIONS: for even their women did change the natural use into that which is against nature:**
> **27 And likewise also the men, leaving the natural use of the woman, burned in their LUST one toward another; men**

with men working that which is unseemly, and receiving in themselves that recompence of their error which was meet.

28 And even as they did not like to retain God in their knowledge, God gave them over to a REPROBATE MIND, to do those things which are not convenient.

Remember "reprobate" means *a mind void of judgment.* The Bible is referring here to homosexuality, which includes lesbianism. The Bible calls homosexuality *uncleanness.* Homosexuality is certainly not practicing sanctification or holiness, is it? God has called us not unto uncleanness, but unto holiness!

Then in Romans 6, we see that sanctification has to do with one's body.

ROMANS 6:19
19 I speak after the manner of men because of the infirmity of your FLESH: for as ye have yielded your [bodily] MEMBERS servants to UNCLEANNESS and to iniquity unto iniquity; even so now YIELD YOUR [bodily] MEMBERS servants to righteousness unto HOLINESS.

The Bible speaks of uncleanness in relation to sins of the flesh.

2 CORINTHIANS 12:21
21 And lest, when I come again, my God will humble me among you, and that I shall bewail many which have SINNED already, and have not repented of the UNCLEANNESS and FORNICATION and LASCIVIOUSNESS which they have committed.

Notice the word "uncleanness" is linked with the words "fornication" and "lasciviousness." Another translation reads "impurity, sexual vice, and sensuality."

There hasn't been much teaching on how believers are to possess their "vessels" or bodies in sanctification and honor. The Holy Spirit, abiding in the inward man, dwells within the believer's vessel, his body. And God has not called your vessel unto uncleanness, but unto holiness.

Paul is preaching the same message to every believer about sanctification. He uses different words as he wrote to the various churches, but he's basically teaching believers how to possess their bodies in sanctification and honor so they can close the door to the enemy.

COLOSSIANS 3:5
5 MORTIFY therefore your members which are upon the earth; fornication, uncleanness, inordinate affection, evil concupiscence, and covetousness, which is idolatry.

What does Paul tell believers to "mortify" or make dead? The list sounds familiar: fornication, uncleanness, inordinate affection, and so forth.

In Romans chapter 1, the Bible talked about women having unnatural affection toward women, and men toward men. Paul called it *vile affections*. Here he calls it *inordinate affection*. That means affection that is *not ordinary*, clean, or wholesome. It's not ordinary for a man to leave the natural use of a woman and to lust after another man. It's not natural for a woman to want another woman.

God made man and woman to desire a member of the opposite sex within the confines of marriage. Sex is not wrong in marriage, but it is wrong outside of marriage. Fornication, adultery, and uncleanness are wrong. Practicing those things will give Satan great inroads into your life.

Believers are to mortify those unclean deeds of the body, so they can possess their vessels with sanctification and honor. Some Christians say "I can't do that." But God said we can. Either He is lying about it or they are!

The truth is many people don't want to mortify their flesh. They just want that old stinking flesh to dominate them. They want to live in the flesh with its pleasures and lusts instead of in the Spirit because it's easier.

Actually, the greatest "war" the believer will ever wage is not with the devil, but it is between the flesh and the spirit.

GALATIANS 5:16,17
16 This I say then, Walk in the Spirit, and ye shall not fulfil THE LUST OF THE FLESH.
17 For the FLESH lusteth against the SPIRIT, and the SPIRIT against the FLESH: and these are contrary the one to the other: so that ye cannot do the things that ye would.

Paul is writing to Spirit-filled Christians in this passage. He says, ". . . the flesh lusteth against the Spirit. . . ." *The King James Version* capitalizes the letter "s" in the word "Spirit," making the passage refer to the Holy Spirit. But Paul isn't talking about the Holy Spirit in this verse; he's talking about the human spirit.

As W. E. Vine points out in his *Expository Dictionary of New Testament Words*, there is only one word translated "spirit" from the Greek and that is "pneuma." Therefore, we have to determine by the context of the passage whether "pneuma" is referring to the human spirit or to the Holy Spirit.

Galatians 5:17 is saying that the flesh "lusteth against," "wars," or "fights" against the recreated human spirit. Another translation says, "the flesh *fights* against the spirit."

People are talking a lot about spiritual warfare in Christian circles today. But the biggest warfare in the Christian walk is between the flesh and the spirit. Yes, we have to deal with the spiritual forces of darkness, all right. But if you get this war between your flesh and your spirit settled, you won't have to contend with Satan as much, because you won't be leaving a door open to the enemy.

You need to understand the conflict between the flesh and the recreated human spirit and how to crucify the flesh so you can possess your vessel in sanctification and honour (1 Thess. 4:3,4,7). Then you won't be giving access to the devil.

The Spirit of the World in the Church

If folks do *not* mortify these evil deeds of the flesh listed in Colossians 3:5, are they going to get by with it?

COLOSSIANS 3:6
6   For which things' sake the wrath of God cometh on the children of disobedience.

Paul is writing here to children of God, saying that the wrath of God comes on the children of disobedience. You see, we are living in a world where Satan is god, and the same spirits that are in the world will try to get into the Church if we let them. That's why it's so important for believers to stay holy and separate from sins and lusts of the world where Satan is god.

The Bible makes a strong statement about believers living holy lives separated from the world.

JAMES 4:4
4   Ye adulterers and adulteresses, know ye not that the FRIENDSHIP OF THE WORLD is ENMITY WITH GOD? whosoever therefore will be a FRIEND OF THE WORLD is the ENEMY OF GOD.

This verse doesn't mean we aren't supposed to love sinners or want to help them. But we're not to become entangled in worldly practices. Friendship with the world and indulging in worldly practices and pleasures will open wide the door to the devil in our lives.

We need to understand that the Bible teaches *separation*, not *segregation* (2 Cor. 6:16,17). That is where some Christians miss it. Some folks think they are practicing separation by segregating themselves and practically isolating themselves from the unsaved.

But Jesus said we need to be *in* the world, but not *of* the world (John 17:16-18). He meant that we don't have to abide by the world's standards and act like the world. Our lives should reflect a *separation* from the world and a sanctification and separation unto God in holiness. We need to be very careful that we don't allow the spirit of the world to get into the Church — the Body of Christ.

The spirit of the world got into the Church at Corinth (1 Cor. 5:1-5). Paul wrote to the Church about the sexual sin that was being tolerated within that local body of believers (1 Cor. 5:1). A man was cohabiting with his stepmother. If you are a student of history, you know that Corinth was one of the most licentious and immoral cities of that day. And that immoral spirit had gotten into the Church.

In this day, we are living in a time of lightness and looseness. You can see it in many realms of life. That same trend is happening in the spiritual realm. There is such lightness and looseness in the world, as we've entered into this age of "sexual liberation," as some people call it. Sin is now considered acceptable by some as long as you are an adult and your sin doesn't hurt anyone else. That same spirit has gotten into the Church.

In Colossians we can also see another area where the spirit of the world has gotten into the Church today.

COLOSSIANS 3:8
8 . . . PUT OFF ALL THESE: anger, wrath, malice, blasphemy, FILTHY COMMUNICATION out of your mouth.

We hear so much filthy communication in this day by unsaved people who are subject to the spirit of the world. But I am appalled sometimes at the way some Christians talk. Some of them use filthy communication too! If they would listen to their spirit, their conscience would condemn them. But they are not living in the spirit realm; then they wonder how the devil is getting into their lives! They open the door themselves with their own mouths!

When I was born again, I had never heard anyone preach on this subject. Although my tongue still wanted to say some words I'd said before I was saved, after I was born again, I began listening to my spirit, and I couldn't talk like that.

But we are living in a time of looseness and lightness. You can hear people using these words, but worse than that, you hear Charismatic people talking like that too.

If you are a believer and you are guilty of filthy communication, you need to straighten up. You need to obey what God said in His Word: *". . . put off . . . filthy communication out of your mouth"* (Col. 3:8). Otherwise, you are on dangerous ground. And when you're on Satan's territory, he has access to you.

Thank God, as believers we know what to do about Satan, and we know our authority in Christ. We know how to put off the old man nature with its lusts and pleasures, and we know how to put on Christ. We can possess our vessels in sanctification and honor and learn how to stand strong against all the wiles of the devil.

---

[1] W. E. Vine, Vine's Expository Dictionary of Biblical Words (Nashville, Tennessee: Thomas Nelson, Inc., 1985), p. 384.

[2] Ibid., p. 593.

Chapter 4
Distinguishing the Difference Between Oppression, Obsession, And Possession

The primary way Satan tries to gain access to people is through their mind and body. The degree to which a person yields to Satan in these areas determines how much Satan is able to influence him. Since man is a spirit, he has a soul, and he lives in a body, demons can affect and influence man in his *body* and *soul* (mind, will, and emotions), yet not be present in his *spirit*.

To really understand how demons affect people, it's also important to understand the difference between *oppression, obsession*, and *possession*. Many people use these terms interchangeably when they are actually referring to three separate degrees of demonic influence.

Oppression

Evil spirits can exert a certain amount of influence as they seek to oppress mankind. Evil spirits can oppress anyone, even Christians if they allow it, from within or without their body or soul.

Of course, evil spirits have their widest range of influence if they can embody a human because then they can express themselves in the natural realm. If evil spirits can't embody people, they try to exert influence round about people in the spiritual realm. Many times believers, even Spirit-filled believers, can be oppressed by demons from the outside. Satan tries to oppress us by putting all kinds of pressure on us until we are keenly aware of that pressure.

And we need to realize that there are degrees of oppression. In other words, a person can be more oppressed or less oppressed. We've probably all experienced oppression in our lives at one time or another. For example, sometimes oppression can be manifested as a bad "mood" that tries to come over us. That can be the direct result of satanic oppression. People have also said to me, "Please pray for me. It just seems like there's a big black cloud hanging over my head."

That's satanic oppression. And people are more oppressed at certain times than they are at other times. But as we rebuke that oppression in the Name of Jesus, stand against it and resist it, the devil will flee from us (Matt. 18:18; Luke 10:19; Phil. 2:9-11; James 4:7). Believers don't need to live under the oppression of the enemy. And sometimes when oppression leaves a person, it feels just like a weight has lifted off his shoulders.

Fear is a form of oppression that comes against many Christians and holds them in bondage and causes them to stumble again and again. Fear can take ahold of believers' minds and cause their spirit not to function as they should — that is, not to be in dominion over their soul and body.

Fear can also take ahold of a believer's body and cause his stomach to tighten up as though some power had gripped it. That can open the door to despair and despondency. But the Bible says God has not given us the spirit of fear (2 Tim. 1:7) so that means we have authority over it. We have a right to stand against fear and rebuke it.

Learn to stand in the power of God's might and use His glory and power, which is His Word, to fight against the enemy. God never said *you* had to fight the enemy (2 Chron. 20:17). You are to fight the good fight of faith, which is standing against the enemy by faith in God's Word (1 Tim. 6:12). When you stand against the enemy with the Word, fear has to depart from you.

Fear isn't a friend; fear is an enemy. It isn't to be accepted, nurtured, or endured. Stand against it and avoid it like you would avoid sickness and disease. Speak God's Word to fear and take your authority over it in the Name of Jesus, and it must depart.

Anyone's body, even that of a Christian, can be oppressed by an evil spirit from within or without. Let me give you an illustration of physical oppression. Physical oppression can be the direct result of an evil spirit afflicting a person's body.

I was ministering in a church once, and a Christian man came forward in the healing line for prayer. He said, "The doctors told me that I have a cluster of ulcers in my stomach as big as a wasps' nest." The doctors were fearful that his condition might worsen, but the man wouldn't let them operate on him.

I said to this man, "Matthew 8:17 says, '. . . *Himself took our infirmities, and bare our sicknesses.*'" Then I laid hands on him and prayed. The minute I laid hands on him, I had a manifestation of the word of knowledge — a supernatural revelation by the Holy Spirit (1 Cor. 12:8). I knew this man's body was being *oppressed* by an evil spirit, and I knew that I had to cast the evil spirit out of his body before he could be set free from this stomach condition.

But I also knew if I didn't explain to the congregation what I was about to do, it would cause more harm than good. When ministering in public, if you just cast an evil spirit out of someone without explaining it to the congregation, people can think, *That person is saved, filled with the Holy Spirit, and a member of this church. If he has a devil in him, maybe I have a devil in me.*

And if people start thinking and talking like that, they can unknowingly open a door to the devil and an evil spirit will accommodate them. That's why people need to exercise wisdom when ministering in public.

So before I ministered to this man, I explained to the congregation, "Satan, not God, is the author of sickness and disease. Satan is indirectly the cause of all sin, sickness, and disease. Sometimes there can even be the literal presence of a demon in a person's body that enforces sickness and disease. When that's the case, the evil spirit must be dealt with by the power of the Holy Spirit.

"In this man's case, an evil spirit is present and oppressing this man's *body* and causing these ulcers. I'm going to cast that evil spirit out of his *body*. It's not in his soul or in his spirit."

I went on to explain, "If you lived in an old house that had termites in it, that doesn't mean *you* have termites in *you*. Well, your body is just the house you live in. Your body isn't the real *you*. The real *you* is the spirit man on the inside. And if you're born again, the spirit man can't have a devil in him. But your body — the house of your spirit — can have an evil spirit afflicting it."

After I explained that to the congregation, I laid hands on the man again. When I did, the Holy Spirit also revealed something else to me by a word of knowledge. I knew by an inward revelation or word of knowledge what had happened to him that let the evil spirit into his body in the first place. The man had opened the door to the devil.

I had what I call a "mini-vision." I knew that what I was seeing in the Spirit had occurred two nights before. I saw this man in bed in the front bedroom of his house. It was midnight, but he couldn't sleep. I saw him get up and walk through his house.

The back porch was screened in. There was a bed out there, and I saw him just fall across that bed and roll from side to side holding his stomach because it was burning like fire. Then I knew by the Spirit of God that something else was also troubling him, and I knew exactly what it was. I knew all of this in just a moment of time through the word of knowledge.

I said to the man, "Two nights ago at midnight you were in the front bedroom of your house and you couldn't sleep, so you finally got up and walked through your house. You went back to the sleeping porch, and you fell across the bed, rolling and groaning in pain. You were holding your stomach because it was burning like fire.

"But something else was bothering you too. Your conscience was bothering you. Now I don't want to embarrass you. But you are saved, baptized with the Holy Spirit, and you have been a member of this church for a number of years. Yet the Lord shows me that you've never paid your tithes. You don't pay tithes, and you never have paid tithes."

He answered, "No, no, I haven't."

I said, "That's one thing that's bothering you. Not only was your stomach burning like fire, but your conscience was hurting you. I can't minister to you until you get this cleared up with the Lord. What are you going to do about paying your tithes? Are you going to obey God or are you *not* going to obey God?"

He said, "I'm going to obey God. I'm going to pay my tithes."

You see, people can open a door to the devil through disobedience. Once this man repented and got in line with God, then I could minister to him. I laid hands on him and cast out the evil spirit that was oppressing and afflicting his body and causing the ulcers.

After I cast the evil spirit out of him, I told him, "On the way home from the meeting tonight, go buy yourself a T-bone steak and eat it when you get home." He hadn't eaten anything except baby food for two years, and he hadn't worked for two years. He did just that. Later he went back to the doctors and they x-rayed his stomach. That cluster of ulcers had completely disappeared, and he was back on the job the very next week.

Now let me give you an example of mental oppression — of an instance when an evil spirit got ahold of a Christian's mind. I was ministering in a meeting and a man came forward for prayer. He had a nervous condition and couldn't sleep. I laid hands on him and prayed for him, and he went back to his seat. I kept on ministering to other people.

I happened to look over to where this man was seated. I had my eyes wide open, and God gave me a manifestation of the gift of discerning of spirits; I saw into the realm of spirits. I saw what looked like a little spirit being sitting on this man's shoulder. It looked a lot like a little monkey, although its face was different.

This little creature had its arms around the man's head in a vice-like headlock. I didn't know until afterwards, but this man had already been committed to a mental asylum. He was just waiting for the authorities to come and get him to be institutionalized.

I said to him, "Brother, come back up here, please." He came back to the front. I spoke to the evil spirit that was oppressing his mind. (You deal with the *evil spirit*, not the *person*.) I didn't tell anyone I had seen anything, because it's not always wise to do that in a public meeting. I just said to this evil spirit, "You foul spirit that has oppressed and bound this man, I command you to loose him in the Name of Jesus. Take your hands off his mind now in Jesus' Name."

When I said that, that little monkey-like creature turned loose of the man's head and fell off his shoulder, and lay at his feet just whimpering and whining. Then the little creature spoke up and said, "Well, I sure don't want to. But if you tell me to, I know I have to."

I replied, "Not only leave him, but leave these premises in the Name of Jesus," and the little creature got up and ran out the door. This man lifted both hands and began to praise God. He told me, "It's like an iron band snapped from around my head." He had been mentally oppressed, but he was completely delivered.

Just because this man's nervousness was caused by a demon, doesn't mean *every* case of nervousness is caused by a demon. You'll have to rely on the Holy Spirit to know when the literal presence of a demon is causing the affliction. In your own human knowledge or wisdom you won't know whether or not an evil spirit is present. But in this case, I knew by the Holy Spirit that this man's mental oppression was a direct result of the presence of an evil spirit.

That man never did go to the asylum. In fact, years later he was still doing fine. Thank God for God's power and the supernatural manifestations of the Holy Spirit. *We are powerless and helpless without the Word of God and the leading and guidance of the Holy Spirit.*

Christians Can Yield to the Devil

We've seen how an evil spirit can oppress the body or the mind of a person — saved and unsaved alike. It's also possible for a Christian to *yield* to an evil spirit when he is being oppressed by one and to give it place.

Scripture bears out the fact that a person can yield to God and then turn right around and yield to the devil. Peter did. Although

Peter wasn't born again yet because Jesus hadn't gone to the Cross yet to pay for our redemption, Peter was used by God to bring forth a revelation of the Holy Spirit. But then almost immediately afterwards, he yielded to the devil (Matt. 16:20-23).

But there's a vast difference between *yielding* to an evil spirit and being *possessed* by an evil spirit. It's also possible to only partially yield to evil spirits. But the more a person yields to them, the more those spirits will influence and try to control him (Rom. 6:16). The good news is that Christians don't have to yield to the devil *or* to the flesh. They can learn how to yield to the Holy Spirit.

ROMANS 6:16
16 Know ye not, that to whom ye yield yourselves servants to obey, his servants ye are to whom ye obey; whether of sin unto death, or of obedience unto righteousness?

The Bible teaches that when you yield or submit yourself to someone, you will eventually become his servant. Sometimes we only partially yield to the Holy Spirit, and at other times we are more fully yielded to Him. I don't know anyone who is totally yielded to the Holy Spirit. We're all working on it, but we haven't gotten there yet.

The same thing is true on the negative side that's true on the positive side. Just as a person can partially yield to the Holy Spirit, he can partially yield to evil spirits, or he can fully yield to them. The more a person yields to evil spirits, the more ground those spirits will take in him and eventually try to possess him.

I'll give you an illustration of a Christian yielding to the devil. I sometimes tell about my son-in-law, Buddy Harrison, who at one time had a problem with yielding to evil spirits. Today Reverend Harrison is the founding pastor of Faith Christian Fellowship in Tulsa, Oklahoma, and he is also president of Harrison House Publishers. But in 1963, he had problems.

Back then, Buddy was unable to stick with anything for any length of time. He couldn't keep a job; he'd just quit and walk off. He wouldn't stay in church. One time we'd see him in church leading the choir, and everything would be fine. The next time we'd see him, he would be out of church. And sometimes he'd walk up to me and blow cigar smoke in my face. I never said anything to him. I just loved him. I knew in his case it was the devil influencing him; it wasn't just his flesh dominating him. He was a "roller-coaster" or "yo-yo" Christian, up and down and in and out.

I was praying one afternoon about my evening service. Suddenly, the Spirit of God spoke to me about Buddy. He said, "There are three demons that follow Buddy around." Immediately I had a spiritual vision — a "mini-vision." I saw Buddy walking down the sidewalk. I saw three spirits following him like little dogs, except they didn't look like little dogs. They were monkey-like and wiry looking. One was on the right edge of the sidewalk, one on the left edge, and one in the middle of the sidewalk following after Buddy.

The Spirit of God said, "These three spirits follow Buddy. Buddy will turn to the right and yield to the demon on the right for a while. Then he'll turn back around and straighten up and act right. Then he'll turn and yield to the demon on the left for a while. Then he'll turn back and start acting like a Christian again. Then he'll yield to the demon that's in back of him for a while.

"At times Buddy yields to these three evil spirits, yet at other times he also yields to the Holy Spirit. That's why it seems like he almost has a split personality."

Buddy would begin acting like whichever demon he was yielding to. Relatives had even remarked, "I don't understand Buddy. Is he schizophrenic?" Buddy was a born-again, Spirit-filled Christian. But just because a person is filled with the Holy Spirit doesn't mean he's incapable of yielding to the devil. Believers still have a will of their own; they have free choice.

When the Lord showed me these three demons tagging after Buddy like little puppy dogs, I said to the Lord, "Lord, what do You want me to do about it? Do You want me to pray about it?"

"No," He said, "don't pray about it."

"Well," I said, "what do You want me to do about it then?"

The Lord said to me, "You speak to those evil spirits. Command them in My Name, in the Name of Jesus, to desist in their maneuvers and stop in their operations against Buddy."

I said, "But I'm in Oklahoma. Buddy is in Texas."

Jesus said, "There is no distance in the spirit realm. You can speak to spirits where you are that are operating against someone who is in another location, and in the Name of Jesus, they have to obey you. You don't have to be there in person."

I said, "Tell me how to do that."

He said, "You simply say, 'In the Name of the Lord Jesus Christ, I command all three of you foul spirits that are following Buddy around to desist in your maneuvers and stop in your operations against him.'"

I simply spoke out those exact words that Jesus told me to say.

And in the spirit realm, I saw those three spirits disappear. Then the Word of the Lord came unto me, saying, "Buddy will have a job within ten days. He will stay with that job until he does something else I have for him." I wrote that down on a piece of paper, dated it, and put it in my billfold.

The next time I saw Buddy, he said to me, "Dad, I got a job."

I said, "I know it."

I pulled that piece of paper out of my billfold and handed it to him. He said, "That's exactly right! I got the job on the tenth day." He stayed with that job and made a success of it. The owner of the business made him an assistant manager, and later God called him into the full-time ministry. He's been walking with God ever since.

The Devil, the Flesh, and the World

Believers can yield to the *devil* and his wiles and let the devil dominate them any time they want. Believers can also yield to the *flesh* with its lusts and appetites and let the flesh dominate them. And believers can yield to the influence of the *world* and let the world dominate them.

Many people would try to cast the devil out of a believer when he's yielding to the world, the flesh, or the devil. But the Bible teaches that believers have to deal with the *world*, the *flesh*, and the *devil* because we will never be free from these influences until we go to be with Jesus in Heaven (1 John 4:3,4; 1 John 2:15-17). But just because believers yield to the world, the flesh, or the devil, doesn't mean they are demon possessed or have a demon in them.

Thank God, the Bible teaches that the believer does *not* have to yield to the world, the flesh, *or* the devil. The Bible says, if we are born again, through Jesus we have overcome the world (1 John 5:4,5; John 16:33; 1 John 4:4) Because we are *in* Christ and Jesus has overcome the world for us, we don't have to yield to the influence of the world, nor to the lusts and cravings of our own physical nature. And we don't have to be defeated by the devil, because Jesus' triumph over Satan is our triumph.

If a Christian opens the door to the devil, the devil will come in and can eventually possess his body or soul if given free access to them over a period of time. However, in the case of a Christian, a demon cannot inhabit his *spirit* unless the believer meets the conditions stated in Hebrews 10:26,27 and Hebrews 6:4-6. I'll talk about these passages in greater detail later.

For now I'll simply say that the majority of Christians never reach a level of spiritual maturity which would put them in a position to commit the sin unto death. The sin unto death can only be committed by a mature Christian by willfully denying Christ with deliberate forethought (1 John 5:16). So Christians don't need to be preoccupied with wondering whether or not they are possessed by the devil in their spirit. If they are concerned that they might be, it's a sure sign they aren't! However, Christians can open a door to the devil in other areas of their lives.

I'll give an example that shows how a Christian can unknowingly open a door to the devil. Many years ago I read about Dr. Lilian Yeomans who was a medical doctor in a large New York City hospital. She became hopelessly addicted to drugs and was given up to die by medical science. Then someone told her about divine healing, and she was saved and healed by the power of God and spent the rest of her life teaching about divine healing.

Near the end of World War II, Dr. Yeomans became desperately ill to the point of death, even though she had taught and ministered on divine healing for more than forty years. At that time, she was probably about eighty years old.

Later I read that Dr. Yeomans had been healed. In an article she wrote, she explained how she had gotten sick by unknowingly opening the door to the devil. It was during World War II, and she had begun to worry because some of her kinfolk were in those countries where Hitler dominated.

Dr. Yeomans said that the worry over her kinfolk began to bear on her mind, and worry and fear opened the door to the enemy. Finally, she became desperately ill. She ran a high fever, lost all her hair, and was at death's door. She said she repented and asked God to forgive her for worrying. She said, "God not only restored my health, but He also restored my hair. Only my hair didn't grow back white as it was before. I have a full head of solid black hair!"

Dr. Yeomans became sick by opening a door to the enemy through worry and fear. It doesn't make any difference how long a Christian has been saved or if he's been preaching or teaching the Word for years. Mature Christians have to make sure they keep the door shut on the devil just as much as baby Christians do.

In Dr. Yeomans' case, she'd walked in what she called "divine health" for more than forty years and had never been sick. Dr. Yeomans was a strong Christian and knew about God's covenant of health. But, you see, no matter how strong you are in the Lord or how many years you've preached the Word, the devil will never leave you alone. And if you yield to him, you can open the door to him.

A Christian Whose Mind Was Possessed by an Evil Spirit

I'm going to go into quite a bit of detail in relating an account of a Spirit-filled minister who became *obsessed* in her thinking with worry and fear, until she finally allowed the devil to possess her thinking, and she went totally insane.

In other words, first she was *oppressed* by the devil's thoughts. But as she *yielded* to Satan's thoughts of worry and fear, she became *obsessed* with those thoughts, until finally she opened a door to the enemy and allowed her mind to become *possessed* with an evil spirit.

This minister's sister told us the following story. When the woman minister had gone through menopause, she began to be oppressed with worry. She allowed herself to brood and became emotionally upset and increasingly disturbed. She either consciously or unconsciously *yielded* to a demon in her mind and emotions.

This minister didn't keep her mind focused on the Word; she became *obsessed* with worry. She allowed an evil spirit to gain more and more ground in her thinking until her mind was taken over by an evil spirit. Finally, she entirely lost her mind and was *possessed* in her mind by that evil spirit and became violently insane. She tried to kill herself and others.

She was institutionalized and spent more than two years in a padded cell for her own protection because she was violent. She would try to kill herself by butting her head against the walls. She ate with her fingers like an animal because she tried to use a knife or a fork to kill herself.

The sister of this insane woman wanted my wife and me to minister to the woman, even though no one was allowed in her cell. I said I would turn the matter over to my prayer group so they could begin praying for the woman. We had a group of women in that Farmersville church where I was pastoring at that time who could pray Heaven and earth together. They got answers to their prayers!

About ten days after we began praying, the authorities said this insane woman could come home. They sent a letter to her family saying she was no longer violent, but that she would always need institutional care. Her general health, however, had deteriorated, and the authorities felt that if the change in environment didn't help her, she probably wouldn't live much longer. Now here's a minister of the gospel who had gone insane! Imagine that! People just said, "Oh, the poor dear. Something happened to her, but we don't know what it was." But we need to understand what can happen to people, and how Christians can open a door to the devil and give him access in their minds and bodies.

That's one reason believers need to know how important it is for them to renew their minds with the Word of God and to think God's thoughts instead of thinking on the enemy's thoughts of worry and fear. If they think the wrong thoughts, they can unknowingly open a door to the devil. Believers are not subject to the devil; *they* have authority over him in Jesus' Name. They *can* resist him, and they are not under his dominion in any way, unless *they* allow him to take dominion over them.

This Full Gospel minister was not subject to the devil either. She didn't have to give place to Satan in her thinking. If she would have stood her ground against worry and oppression with the Word of God and kept her mind renewed, Satan wouldn't have had access to her mind. If she had rebuked Satan's oppression and resisted him, he would have fled from her (Matt. 18:18; James 4:7).

On the first Saturday of May 1943, this Full Gospel minister was brought to our parsonage by her sister. My wife and I didn't know they were coming. But here's something I want you to see.

That morning after breakfast, my wife and I went about our usual morning chores. I always washed the dishes and cleaned up the kitchen; it was a habit of mine. I expected my wife to help me in the ministry, so it was only right that I help her around the house. All the time I was cleaning up the kitchen, I was praying in other tongues, not loudly, but just to myself. I had an inward urge or leading to do so.

Then I went over to the church next door and checked to see that everything was in order for the service the next day, and as I did, I was continually praying in tongues. It seemed like I had a divine urge to pray in other tongues. Don't misunderstand me; the Holy Spirit wasn't forcing me to pray, for He is a Gentleman, and He doesn't *force* us to do anything. He gently leads. The devil pushes, but the Holy Spirit gently leads and urges.

For the rest of the morning I just went about my business, but I yielded to that urge on the inside to pray in tongues. When people were around, I just prayed on the inside, quietly to myself and to the Lord. Then I walked to the post office to get the mail, because they didn't deliver mail in those days. The entire time, I followed that divine urging to pray in other tongues. My spirit was communicating with God (1 Cor. 14:2,14).

I would say from eight o'clock in the morning until about two o'clock in the afternoon, I spent the majority of the time praying in other tongues as I went about my daily business. And every now and then I'd think to myself, *The Lord must be preparing me for my service tomorrow. It's going to be a "stem-winder"!*

You see, the Bible says, *"For if I pray in an unknown tongue, my spirit prayeth . . ."* (1 Cor. 14:14). And in Jude 20 it says, *". . . building up yourselves on your most holy faith, praying in the Holy Ghost."* So I knew God was preparing me and getting me ready for something, but I thought it was for my Sunday service. Then about two o'clock, that insane woman was brought to our parsonage by her sister. She acted like a robot; she just stared straight ahead like she was in another world, except that her mouth was continually moving, almost involuntarily.

When her sister mentioned that I was a preacher, immediately the insane woman began to quote scriptures; the Word just started running out of her mouth like water out of a faucet, her eyes just blazing the entire time. The Word wasn't coming out of her mind, because she was mentally incompetent; scriptures were coming up out of her recreated, born-again spirit.

I'd never seen anyone like this before, and I didn't know what to do. I made the comment, "Anyone who can quote Scripture like that must really know the Lord."

When I said that, her eyes looked like they flashed fire. I was standing right in front of her, and, eyes blazing, she reached up and grabbed her hair and began pulling it, screaming, "Oh, no, no! No! No! I couldn't know God! No! No! No! I've committed the unpardonable sin! No! No!" And her sister had to get ahold of her and shake her to try to get her calmed down.

Her sister finally made her sit down in a chair, but she just sat staring straight ahead like she was in another world. I kept watching her, but she didn't blink or even bat an eye. Her eyes were wide open and she looked like she was in a trance. No matter what went on around her, she sat there and never moved a muscle or batted an eye.

The sister said to us, "I asked the head of the institution, 'Is her condition unusual? Is it peculiar to my sister that she thinks she's committed the unpardonable sin?' And he said, 'Oh, no. About ninety percent of the people in the asylum think they've committed the unpardonable sin.'" That tells you the devil has something to do with tormenting people in this area, telling them that they've committed the unpardonable sin — the sin unto death. In this case, this minister had allowed an evil spirit to get into her soul, and it had convinced her that she had committed the sin unto death. You see, if you get sick in your mind through wrong thinking, that opens a door for the devil to come in. Devils, demons, and evil spirits have more to do with these things than we sometimes realize.

I knew that the woman could be sick in her head or mind, just as someone could be sick in his stomach. If a person is sick in his stomach, it just means his stomach isn't working right. If a person is sick in his mind, it means his mind isn't working right. So I knew this woman's mind could just be sick. But I also knew that a demon could have come in and gotten ahold of her mind, and it could be the cause of her insanity.

The demon didn't possess this woman's spirit; it only possessed her mind because *she* had opened the door to it through worry and fear. Satan can't just move in and occupy a Christian's mind or body unless the person gives him permission by opening the door to him either through ignorance or disobedience. In full demon possession, the demon would have possessed her — spirit, soul, and body. But she was a Christian, so the devil couldn't take over her spirit unless she had willfully denied Christ, which she hadn't.

How are you going to deal with someone in that condition, particularly when you can't get through to the person's mind? At that time, I didn't know. I'd never dealt with anyone like that. So I said to my wife, "Let's go get Sister Sylvia."

Sister Sylvia was a layperson in our church, but she could pray Heaven and earth together. While we were waiting in the car for Sister Sylvia to get ready, I began to talk to the Lord about what had just happened. I knew if the woman were just sick in her mind, I could pray for her, anoint her with oil and lay hands on her, and she could be healed.

However, I knew if an evil spirit was the cause of her insanity, it would have to be dealt with by the power and leading of the Holy Spirit. I told the Lord He was going to have to help me. I didn't know what to do. I spent my time praying this way until Sister Sylvia was ready, and then we all went back to the parsonage.

We all started praying, and soon we were praying in the Spirit. We prayed to God for direction for more than two hours. We weren't praying against the devil; we weren't combating evil spirits. We were just seeking God for His direction and about how to minister to this woman.

Here's something else you need to understand. The prayer of faith won't work in every situation. This was an instance where the prayer of faith wouldn't work because this woman was not in a position mentally to agree with us and use her own faith.

Now don't misunderstand me; the prayer of faith will work in those situations where it is supposed to work. But when another person's will is involved, you won't always be able to pray the prayer of faith unless the person is in agreement with you (Matt. 18:19).

Before I could pray the prayer of faith for this woman, I needed her participation and agreement, but she couldn't give that because of her mental condition. Therefore, her deliverance couldn't come about through the operation of *her* own faith.

Some people have tried to make the prayer of faith work in every situation and in every circumstance. And in some cases, it's sort of like trying to put a square peg in a round hole; it won't work. In other words, there are different kinds of prayer, and they each have their own rules for their successful operation.

So we were seeking God for His direction; we weren't yelling at the devil or trying to drive out a demon. We needed to get the leading of the Holy Spirit so we would know how to deal with this insane woman.

We have to rely on the Holy Spirit in situations like this. How often we read the scripture, ". . . *Not by might, nor by power, but by my spirit, saith the Lord of hosts"* (Zech. 4:6), and yet we go right ahead and try to do something in our own strength, power, and might, and nothing happens. No, we will have to learn to rely on God's Word, His power and might, and His Spirit in order to be successful in life.

Actually, when we rely on our own power and might, we labor and labor, and very little is accomplished. But if we'll put the Greater One on the inside to work for us, He will rise up big in us and give illumination to our minds and direction to our spirits, which we can't get from any other source. And He always leads us in line with the holy written Word of God.

So as we were all seeking God's direction, I prayed, "Lord, show me how to minister to this woman." When I said that, the anointing of the Holy Spirit came upon me, and the Holy Spirit said to me,

"Go stand in front of her and say, 'Come out, you unclean spirit in the Name of Jesus.'"

I was reluctant to do that because I'd never been in a situation quite like that before. When I didn't obey God, the anointing lifted and left me, and then there was nothing I *could* do. You see, casting out a demon in a situation like this has to be done under the anointing and power of the Holy Spirit.

Then the Holy Spirit rebuked me for disobeying. I said to the Lord, "Lord, let that anointing come on me again, and I'll obey." I knew there was no use standing there saying, "Come out!" without the anointing of the Holy Spirit. If it were just me in the flesh trying to cast that demon out, I knew nothing would happen. But the anointing of the Holy Spirit came upon me again, and I obeyed God and said to the evil spirit, "Come out, thou unclean spirit in the Name of Jesus."

The woman didn't look any different afterwards; she looked and acted just as mentally insane as she had before. Nothing happened as far as I could tell. Her sister bundled her up and took her home. But even though there was no perceptible difference in her, I knew she was delivered; no one could have told me differently.

That's where we miss it sometimes. I knew that the command of faith had been spoken by the direction and unction of the Holy Spirit and that the woman was set free. You see, when the gift of faith is in operation, the Holy Ghost gives you faith to do whatever He says to do and it will always work.

When it comes to dealing with devils in other people's lives, such as in this woman's situation where she was unable to give her consent or cooperation, you must be led by the Holy Spirit in what to do. If the Holy Spirit doesn't tell you to do something, then you're just doing it on your own, and you'll fall flat on your face. However, if people ask you for help and give their permission, then you can exercise authority over the devil in their lives in the Name of Jesus (Mark 16:17).

Once a person is delivered, you need to teach him how to stand against the devil for himself. Of course, in dealing with the devil in your own life, you don't need someone else to rebuke the devil for you. If you are submitted to God, you have authority over the devil to resist him, stand against him, rebuke him, and he has to flee (Luke 9:1; Eph. 6:13; James 4:7).

This woman was set free by the command of faith on a Saturday. On the following Monday afternoon, the sister returned and said to us, "Please pray. My sister is having a violent attack just like she had when she first lost her mind." I said, "What of it?" It absolutely astounded me how calm I was. I knew exactly what was happening. I'd told that demon on Saturday afternoon he had to leave, and he knew he had to go. He was just rending or "tearing" this woman as he departed.

I explained this to the sister and showed her the scripture where Jesus rebuked an evil spirit in a person, and the devil "rent him sore" or convulsed him before he came out (Mark 9:26). I told the sister, "The devil knows he has to go, so he is just rending her as he's departing. After this spell is over, she'll be fine."

That is exactly what happened. When the attack was over, this woman's mind was completely restored. You see, when the command of faith is spoken by the unction and power of the Holy Spirit, it doesn't necessarily bring instant results, but it always brings results.

The moment this woman's mind was restored, she was just the same person she'd always been, and her spiritual walk with the Lord was just as it had always been. She had no knowledge of being insane for two and a half years, nor was she aware of trying to kill herself or others. All that was just a vacant spot in her memory. Soon afterward the woman was pronounced well and dismissed from the mental institution.

The evil spirit had taken over her *mind* and had worked through her *body*, but she didn't have a devil in her *spirit*. But at a time in her life when she was nervous and unstable, she yielded to an evil spirit and it obsessed her thoughts. She *allowed* that evil spirit to gain more and more access in her thinking, and as she kept *yielding* to it, the evil spirit finally was able to *possess* her soul — her mind, will, and emotions.

Nineteen years after she was delivered, we checked up on her. Her sister told us, "Her mind is strong. She has a good job and she teaches Sunday school."

Full Possession: Spirit, Soul, and Body

As we have seen, a person can be *oppressed* or *obsessed* in his *soul*; that is, in his *mind* or *emotional* realm, even if he is a Christian. And even a Christian can be oppressed by a demon or an evil spirit in his *body* from within or without. But that is not the same as demon *possession*.

Remember, total possession implies giving over spirit, soul, and body to an evil spirit because to possess something means *to own* it. Therefore, it's erroneous and unscriptural to say a Christian can be possessed by an evil spirit. Certainly, no Christian can have a devil in his spirit, or you couldn't call the person a Christian anymore. We need to be careful with our terminology and define what we really mean by certain expressions.

Also, we must realize that there is a vast difference between being *oppressed*, *influenced* by, *yielded* to demons, or *obsessed* by them — and in being fully *possessed* by demons. In total possession, a person has submitted his whole being to be possessed or owned by evil spirits. And because man has three dimensions to his being — he *is* a spirit, he *has* a soul, and he *lives* in a body — he is not fully possessed unless he is taken over spirit, soul, and body.

The Greek word that is translated "possessed" also carries with it the sense of being *under the power of or the influence of a demon*. It seems the biblical use of the word "demonized" has a broad meaning, and it includes being *afflicted* or even *influenced* by demons. In its widest range to be demonized includes not only *possession*, but also *oppression*, and *obsession* and can actually include any activity of the devil which influences mankind.

In other words, when people are *oppressed*, *obsessed*, or *possessed* by the devil, they are "demonized." So in its broadest sense, the word "demonized" means *to be affected by the works of the devil*.

Our thinking is not clear along this line many times because our terms and their meanings aren't clear. For example, if someone asks, "Can a Christian be possessed by a devil?" the question the person may be trying to ask is, "Can a Christian be demonized?" In other words, Can a Christian be *oppressed* or *obsessed* or *influenced by* or *yielded to* evil spirits?

Expressed that way, the answer is yes. A Christian can be "demonized" by evil spirits. But, no, a Christian cannot be fully possessed spirit, soul, and body by evil spirits. Certainly the devil could eventually possess any part of a person who continually yields to him and gives him more and more access. I'll show you how that applies to a Christian later.

Sometimes even within full possession, there can be degrees of possession. In other words, one can be more fully or less fully controlled by the devil. A person is partially possessed if only his mind or soul is possessed by an evil spirit. And even in partial possession of the mind or soul, there are degrees of possession. One can be more or less possessed and controlled by the devil. In other words, one could be more or less in control of his own faculties.

Let's look at a biblical account of full or total demon *possession.* The madman of Gadara was possessed by a demon — spirit, soul, and body. When Jesus appeared to me in the 1952 vision, He talked to me at great length about this case of demon possession He encountered when He was on the earth.

MARK 5:1-20

1 And they came over unto the other side of the sea, into the country of the Gadarenes.

2 And when he was come out of the ship, immediately there met him out of the tombs a man with AN UNCLEAN SPIRIT.

3 Who had his dwelling among the tombs; and no man could bind him, no, not with chains:

4 Because that he had been often bound with fetters and chains, and the chains had been plucked asunder by him, and the fetters broken in pieces: neither could any man tame him.

5 And always, night and day, he was in the mountains, and in the tombs, crying, and cutting himself with stones.

6 But when he saw Jesus afar off, he ran and worshipped him.

7 And cried with a loud voice, and said, What have I to do with thee, Jesus, thou Son of the most high God? I adjure thee by God, that thou torment me not.

8 For he said unto him, Come out of the man, THOU UNCLEAN SPIRIT.

9 And he asked him, What is THY NAME? And he answered, saying, MY NAME is LEGION: for we are many.

10 And he besought him much that he would not send them away out of the country.

11 Now there was there nigh unto the mountains a great herd of swine feeding.

12 And all the devils besought him, saying, Send us into the swine, that we may enter into them.

13 And forthwith Jesus gave them leave. And THE UNCLEAN SPIRITS went out, and entered into the swine: and the herd ran violently down a steep place into the sea, (they were about two thousand;) and were choked in the sea.

14 And they that fed the swine fled, and told it in the city, and in the country. And they went out to see what it was that was done.

15 And they come to Jesus, and see him that was POS-SESSED WITH THE DEVIL, AND HAD THE LEGION, sit-

ting, and clothed, and in his right mind: and they were afraid.

16 And they that saw it told them how it befell to him that was POSSESSED WITH THE DEVIL, and also concerning the swine.

17 And they began to pray him to depart out of their coasts.

18 And when he was come into the ship, he that HAD BEEN POSSESSED WITH THE DEVIL prayed him that he might be with him.

19 Howbeit Jesus suffered him not, but saith unto him, Go home to thy friends, and tell them how great things the Lord hath done for thee, and hath had compassion on thee.

20 And he departed, and began to publish in Decapolis how great things Jesus had done for him: and all men did marvel.

We have much to learn from this account, and we can make some interesting observations about the madman of Gadara. But it's important to realize that this man was not a Christian; he had never been born again because Jesus had not yet gone to the Cross to purchase mankind's redemption.

We also need to understand the difference between a case such as this madman of Gadara who evidently wanted to be set free, and a person who willingly yields to Satan time and time again and doesn't want deliverance. There is a vast difference between a person who is struggling to be free from satanic power, and one who willingly yields himself to Satan again and again and does not want to be free from Satan's dominion.

I know from experience that it is relatively easy to get those delivered who desire to be free; folks who *want* to be delivered can be. But very seldom are you ever able to help those people who continually and willingly yield to satanic power and do *not* want to be set free.

The Lord met this madman of Gadara with great compassion (Mark 5:19). By His word of command, Jesus set the man free (Mark 5:13; Luke 8:32). Immediately the man's entire appearance was changed. Before he'd been a wild maniac who tore his clothes off and cut himself with stones, but after Jesus' command, the man was normal: *"And they come to Jesus, and see him that was possessed with the devil, and had the legion, sitting, and clothed, and IN HIS RIGHT MIND: and they were afraid"* (Mark 5:15).

When the man was set free, he clung to Jesus, his Deliverer. He wanted to go with Jesus (Luke 8:38). But Jesus immediately sent this man out to tell his friends what Jesus had done for him (Luke 8:39).

Jesus knew that for the man's own benefit, he needed to begin serving the Lord. Jesus knew the man needed this discipline of confession and witnessing to grow in his new-found faith, so He sent the man to spread the glad tidings of the gospel in his own hometown: *". . . Jesus . . . saith unto him, Go home to thy friends, and tell them how great things the Lord hath done for thee, and hath had compassion on thee"* (Mark 5:19). Jesus knew that every new advance in walking toward the light would give this man assurance and strength in his new-found walk with the Lord.

We must often trust even the newest convert with the most bold and difficult service. It strengthens their Christian testimony and makes them strong in their faith. I'm not saying to put those who have been recently saved or delivered in positions of authority. However, young believers do immediately need to get involved in service and bold witnessing of what the Lord has done for them.

Anyone who has been delivered from sickness, demonic influence, or any other satanic bondage would do well to remember this principle. It is especially important for anyone who has been delivered from Satan's bondage to immediately get into the discipline of confession, testimony, and service because it will immensely strengthen him to boldly speak about the Lord's delivering power.

Jesus also knew that before long the whole region of Decapolis would be so stirred by this one man's testimony that it would prepare a way for His visit to that region: *"And he [the man] departed, and began to publish in Decapolis how great things Jesus had done for him: and all men did marvel"* (Mark 5:20).

Apparently, cases of insanity are still the same in nature and cause as they were in the days of Jesus. In Jesus' day insanity was a matter of demon activity either directly or indirectly. In this man's particular case, the literal presence of an evil spirit was the direct cause of this man's insanity.

Now let's go back and note in detail several key elements found in this passage in Mark 5. In Mark 5:13, evil spirits are called unclean spirits : *". . . And the unclean spirits . . . entered into the swine. . . ."*

There's no such thing as a "clean" evil spirit. As *fallen* spirit beings, they are all unclean in nature. So generally speaking, an "unclean spirit" indicates the nature of an evil spirit — that it is a fallen eternal spirit being. Specifically speaking, however, an unclean spirit refers to its *type* or *kind*, as in the case of the madman of Gadara.

Another key element to notice in Mark chapter 5 is that when the evil spirits could no longer oppress, embody, or possess this man, as a second choice, they sought embodiment in animals — these demons asked Jesus for permission to go into the swine (Mark 5:12).

As *eternal* evil personalities, if evil spirits do embody man, they make man what *they* are. In other words, a person will take on the character and personality of the *type* or *kind* of evil spirit that is influencing him.

I said that in its broadest sense the term "unclean spirit" refers to spirits of a fallen nature. But used in a specific sense as in Mark 5, the term "unclean spirit" refers to the *type* or *kind* of evil spirit it is: Referring to its *kind*, Jesus said, *"For he [Jesus] said unto him, Come out of the man, THOU UNCLEAN SPIRIT"* (Mark 5:8).

We know that this wasn't the spirit's *name*, because in verse 9, Jesus asked its name: *". . . What is thy name? . . ."* The evil spirit replied, *". . . My name is Legion . . ."* (Mark 5:9).

It's obvious that this man took on the characteristics of the unclean spirit. The unclean spirit caused the man to tear off his clothes, to wander around naked, and to cut himself with stones (Mark 5:5; Luke 8:27).

It's likely this evil spirit was manifested through this man in connection with the sexual appetite of man. This fellow was probably a masochist, deriving sexual pleasure from suffering physical pain.

We see that this unclean spirit made the madman of Gadara what it was, because as soon as the man was delivered and restored to his right mind, he put on clothes: *". . . they come to Jesus, and see him that was possessed with the devil . . . sitting, and clothed, and in his right mind . . ."* (Mark 5:15).

Also, when this fellow was restored to his right mind, he began sitting at the feet of Jesus to learn of Him. People who are delivered from Satan and sin are restored to their right minds and begin to sit at the feet of Jesus to learn of Him.

Another important element in this passage is found in Mark 5:2. Only one devil does the possessing. Notice the Bible says, *". . . when he [Jesus] was come out of the ship, immediately there met him out of the tombs a man with an unclean SPIRIT."* The word "spirit" is singular. That's the first evidence we have that only one spirit does the possessing.

Soon after His encounter with this man, Jesus told the unclean spirit to come out of the man, *". . . Come out of the man, thou UNCLEAN SPIRIT"* (Mark 5:8). But the unclean spirit did not come out of the man. So then Jesus asked: "What is thy name?" The unclean spirit answered, ". . . *MY NAME is Legion: for we are many"* (v. 9).

That indicated there was only one spirit that did the possessing — and it was an unclean spirit named Legion. In this case, "Legion" refers not only to the *name* of the unclean spirit but also to its *number.* This one evil spirit that was an unclean spirit was named Legion, and by its name we know that it brought in with it many other evil spirits to inhabit the man.

How else do we know that only one spirit does the possessing? In Mark 5:15 the scripture says, *"And they come to Jesus, and see him that was POSSESSED with THE DEVIL, and HAD the LEGION. . . ."* In other words, the whole legion didn't *possess* the man, although the legion of devils were *in* the man too. Only one devil did the possessing, and he brought with him a legion of other devils. This is quite typical. It's not possible to be possessed by a whole legion of devils.

Jesus said, "It's always a ruler of the darkness of this world that possesses a person, as in the case of the madman at Gadara. Some people have said that two thousand demons possessed him, but that isn't right.

"Read that passage again. Only *one* of those evil spirits possessed him, and this is always the case. The possessing one will let the others come in with him, but only one ever possesses a person."

Scriptural Insights About Evil Spirits

Matthew 12 gives us more insight about evil spirits and their operation.

> **MATTHEW 12:43-45**
> **43 When the unclean spirit is GONE OUT OF A MAN, he walketh through dry places, seeking rest, and findeth none.**
> **44 Then he saith, I will return into my HOUSE from whence I came out; and when he is come, he findeth it empty, swept, and garnished.**
> **45 Then goeth he, and taketh with himself seven other spirits more wicked than himself, and they ENTER IN and DWELL THERE. . . .**

First of all, notice what the unclean spirit said in verse 44: *"Then he SAITH, I will return into my house from whence I came out; and when he is come, he findeth it empty, swept, and garnished."*

Although we don't know the exact origin of evil spirits, we do know they are eternal fallen beings or eternal evil *personalities.*

1. As personalities, demons can talk: *"Then he* [the unclean spirit] *SAITH . . ."* (Matt. 12:44). Jesus said to me, "When a person is fully possessed, the demon can speak through the person."

2. As personalities, demons can think and they have volition: *"I WILL return to my house . . ."* (Matt. 12:44). The evil spirit made a decision to return to his former dwelling place.

3. As personalities, demons can communicate with other evil spirits: *"Then goeth he, and TAKETH WITH HIMSELF seven other spirits more wicked than himself . . ."* (Matt. 12:45).

When the evil spirit went back to what he called his "house" — the man he had originally come out of — he found it empty, swept, and garnished, so he went and got seven other spirits to inhabit the man with him.

This indicates a certain amount of intelligence in the ranks of evil spirits. And the list in Ephesians 6:12 shows us that the devil is well regimented in his work because we see rank and division in Satan's kingdom.

Matthew 12 also shows us that the devil is persistent in his attacks. The devil doesn't let up in his maneuvers against us: *"Then he* [the evil spirit] *saith, I WILL RETURN into my house from whence I came out . . ."* (Matt. 12:44). The devil will always try to return after he has been cast out of a person. He will endeavor to go right back to the "house" he has left, and he will always keep on in his attempts to entice the person to do wrong or to bring sickness and disease upon him.

We can see this principle at work in the case of an unsaved person. If he gets saved, the devil will always try to get back into his life. Satan tries to get baby Christians to do wrong just as they had done before they were saved, many times trying to influence them to return to their former lifestyle. That's why new converts must be rooted and grounded solidly on the Word of God, so they can stand against the wiles of the devil.

Also, we can see the principle in Matthew 12:43-45 at work in the life of a person who has been delivered from sickness or disease. The Bible calls sickness and disease *satanic oppression* (Acts

10:38). Many times the devil tries to put the same sickness or disease right back on someone who was healed: *"Then goeth he, and taketh with himself seven other spirits more wicked than himself, and they enter in and dwell there: and the LAST STATE of that man IS WORSE THAN THE FIRST . . ."* (Matt. 12:45).

Of course, not every case of sickness and disease is caused by the direct presence of an evil spirit. But sometimes sickness or disease *is* the result of the presence of an evil spirit that is enforcing the affliction.

That's why it is *not* enough just to cast an evil spirit out of a person who is afflicted with sickness or disease if it is the direct result of the presence of an evil spirit that is enforcing the condition. The person must be taught the *Word* so he can stand against the devil for himself, because Satan will always try to return with the same sickness, disease, condition, or sin.

So the believer must be taught not only how to *get* free by the Word of God, he must be taught how to *stay* free by appropriating the Word for himself. The Word of God is our protection against the wiles and strategies of the devil.

That is why it is so important in dealing with demonic influences in the lives of Christians, to be especially careful to get the Word into them. Christians need to know who they are in Christ and the authority they possess in that Name (John 14:13,14; Phil. 2:9,10). Otherwise, we do them an injustice in casting a spirit out of their bodies or minds, because the Bible says they can end up seven times worse than they were before.

Believers simply need to take their place of authority in Christ. Believers don't need to be continually on the run from the devil or harassed in mind or body. The believers' authority in Christ is a place of victory and triumph *far above* principalities and powers!

As Christians, we are seated in heavenly places in Christ, and therefore we look *down* on Satan and his hosts from a place of triumph, not fear or defeat (Eph. 1:3; 2:5,6). And if we're going to deal biblically with the kingdom of darkness, we need to always be mindful of that *triumphant* position as joint-heirs with Christ. It is a position of *authority in Christ* over the devil and all his works and operations against us.

Chapter 5
Can a Christian Have a Demon?

Can a Christian have a demon? This is a subject of great debate in the Christian world. I've heard some preachers make comments on this subject that made me cringe inside because what they were saying wasn't scriptural. They leave the impression that *all* Christians have demons in them that routinely need to be cast out. That statement is wrong for many reasons.

First, a Christian can't have a demon in his *spirit*. That's impossible. A *mature* believer would have to deny Christ willfully and with deliberate forethought before he could ever allow a demon to gain access into his spirit, because if he's a Christian, the *Holy Spirit*, not a demon, indwells his spirit. If a mature believer did deny Christ, he would cease to be a Christian, for the word "Christian" means *Christ-like*. It means that the life and nature of God dwells in one's spirit (2 Cor. 5:17).

The reason it's impossible for a Christian to have an evil spirit in his *spirit* is that a Christian's spirit has been recreated by the *Holy Spirit* (2 Cor. 5:17). Therefore, a Christian's spirit becomes the *dwelling place* of the Holy Spirit (John 14:23; 1 Cor. 6:17) and cannot also be the dwelling place of an evil spirit (2 Cor. 6:14-16; James 3:11,12).

Those who say that a Christian can "have" a demon don't define their terms properly; they don't divide man correctly. They don't recognize that man *is* a spirit; he *has* a soul; and he *lives* in a body. And they don't make it clear that a demon can be affecting a person's soul or body, but not be in his spirit.

If people mean a believer can be *oppressed* or *obsessed* in body or soul by a demon, that's one thing. Yes, a Christian can be oppressed or obsessed in body or soul by a demon. But it's quite another thing to say that a Christian can be *possessed* spirit, soul, and body by a demon.

Also, all Christians don't "have" demons even in the sense that they're all oppressed or obsessed with demons either. That is an extreme teaching and should be avoided. Extreme teachings in any area aren't biblical.

Actually, not one single person who had a demon cast out of him in the four Gospels was a Christian. They couldn't have been Christians, that is, born again by the blood of Jesus, because Jesus hadn't yet died and shed His blood for mankind.

Many people were Jesus' followers or disciples until the new birth became available after His death, burial, and resurrection. They had a promissory note on their salvation until the new birth became available to them. But in the Gospels, those who did have evil spirits cast out of them were not yet born again — they weren't Christians.

To get a biblical balance on demons in the lives of believers, study the Gospels to find out what Jesus instructed the disciples about casting out demons. Did Jesus ever cast demons out of His twelve disciples? No, He didn't. Did Jesus teach His disciples to cast demons out of each other? No, He didn't. Before Jesus ascended, did He give His disciples a formula for casting demons out of other believers? No, He did not!

Even in the Acts of the Apostles, those out of whom the devil was cast were not Christians. In fact, there is no record anywhere in the Bible of an evil spirit being cast out of a Christian or of a Christian being demon possessed.

That doesn't mean a Christian couldn't have an evil spirit *oppressing* him or *obsessing* him, which I've already talked about. The Bible even says sickness and disease is the result of *satanic* oppression (Acts 10:38). For example, sometimes in dealing with sickness in a person, I've found that I have to deal with demons which are afflicting and oppressing the person's body.

Sometimes, but not always, there is a literal presence of an evil spirit in the body enforcing the sickness or disease. And it must be dealt with by the power of the Holy Spirit in order to get the person healed. When the demon is cast out, the person is well.

On the other hand, there have been other people who were sick but didn't need a devil cast out of them; they only needed healing. So we can't make ironclad rules in this area. We have to rely on the Holy Spirit's leading to know whether or not sickness or disease is caused by the actual presence of an evil spirit.

A Christian, just as an unsaved person, can have anything he wants to have because all people — saved and unsaved — have free will. We don't lose our free will when we're born again. If we did, we would be robots, but God didn't create us to be robots.

Even after a person is filled with the Holy Spirit, he still makes his own choices. He can think the devil's thoughts and yield to the devil's suggestions if he wants to. The devil always works through the mind, will, and emotions of man to try to get him to do wrong so he can gain access to him. However, a Christian doesn't *have* to yield to evil spirits *or* to the flesh. He should learn how to yield to the Holy Spirit.

I am dubious of teachings and practices I don't see demonstrated in the Bible. And when some ministers teach that *all* Christians have devils *in* them that need to be cast out over and over again — that's not biblical. You won't find that extreme teaching or practice anywhere in the Bible. Stay scripturally based and stay away from extremes and excesses.

Anyone — saved and unsaved alike — can listen to the devil and yield to his suggestions. But there is a vast difference between temporarily turning and *yielding* to evil spirits and being *oppressed* by demons that are working from the outside or even inside the mind and body. There's also a vast difference from being *obsessed* and being *possessed* by evil spirits.

In more than fifty-eight years of ministry, I have never cast one devil out of a Christian's *spirit,* and no one else has either because evil spirits can't be in a believer's spirit. If evil spirits are present in the believer, they are either in the body or soul — the mind, will, or emotions. In most cases, believers haven't renewed their mind so the devil takes advantage of them in their souls and bodies. But most believers aren't having trouble with demons anyway; they're just having trouble with their flesh.

Actually, very few *unsaved* people in this country are even demon possessed, although there is higher incidence of it now with the rise in occult practices. In my years of ministry, I have only seen one person who was fully demon possessed — spirit, soul, and body.

The 1952 Vision:
Enveloped in a Cloud of Glory

When Jesus appeared to me in the 1952 vision, He talked to me extensively on the subject of demons and how they get ahold of people. There were three parts to the 1952 vision in which Jesus taught me how demons try to gain access to people.

I was holding a meeting in a church in 1952. I was staying at the parsonage, and after the meetings the pastor and I would fellowship together.

After one of the evening meetings, the pastor and I began to pray. I no more expected anything unusual to happen at that moment than I expected to be the first man to land on the moon! I never felt so *ordinary* in all my life. But as soon as I knelt down to pray, it just seemed like a white cloud came down and enveloped me, and I found myself kneeling in a cloud of glory. I couldn't see a thing; my physical senses were suspended. My eyes were wide open, but I couldn't see the stove, the table, or anything else in the kitchen.

Many times in the Old Testament the glory of God manifested in a cloud. (*See* Exod. 40:34,35; 1 Kings 8:10,11; 2 Chron. 5:13,14.) That's scriptural. I looked up to where the ceiling should have been, and I saw Jesus standing there. As I was caught up in that cloud of glory, Jesus spent an hour and a half talking to me.

He began His conversation with me by saying, "I'm going to teach you concerning the devil, demons, and demon possession. For from this night forward, what is known in My Word as discerning of spirits will operate in your life when you are *in the Spirit*."

Jesus said, "I'll show you exactly how demons and evil spirits get ahold of people and dominate them and possess them, even Christians, if Christians let them." Jesus talked to me for some time about the gift of discerning of spirits. One of the things He said to me was that discerning of spirits is supernatural insight into the realm of spirits. [1]

Then still enveloped in that cloud of glory, Jesus opened the realm of the spirit to me, and I began *seeing* into that realm. I saw a woman, and Jesus began to narrate the following scene to me. I saw this scene all in action as it unfolded. Jesus said to me, "For instance, this woman was a child of Mine. She was in the ministry with her husband, and she had a beautiful singing voice."

In the vision, I recognized the woman; I knew who she was. I did not know her personally. I knew she had left her husband, who was a pastor, for another man, (In fact, her former husband was this very pastor I was praying with in that parsonage kitchen.)

You see, unless Jesus shows us, we only see the *result* of things that happen; we don't know *why* they happen. I knew this woman had left her husband, but I didn't know any of the details. We see situations that happen in the natural, but we don't usually know what has occurred spiritually in the spirit realm to cause them to happen.

The Lord said to me, "This woman was My servant. Her husband was a pastor, and she was in the ministry with him. The devil came to her," and as Jesus narrated, I saw what looked like a little imp — it almost looked like a little monkey. I saw it come and sit on this woman's shoulder and begin to whisper in her ear.

The Lord continued speaking to me. He said, "This evil spirit whispered to this woman, 'You are a beautiful woman, and you have been robbed in life. You are being cheated. In the world you could have fame, fortune, and popularity.'"

There's no doubt in my mind that with this woman's singing ability, she could have been an outstanding singer. But here's something I want you to see. Although the devil's statement had some truth to it, "In the world you could have fame, fortune, and popularity," according to Philippians 4:8, it wasn't in line with the Word of God.

PHILIPPIANS 4:8
8 Finally, brethren, whatsoever things are TRUE, whatsoever things are HONEST, whatsoever things are JUST, whatsoever things are PURE, whatsoever things are LOVELY, whatsoever things are of GOOD REPORT; if there be any VIRTUE, and if there be any PRAISE, THINK ON THESE THINGS.

What the demon was saying didn't line up with Scripture because it wasn't *true, honest, just, pure, lovely,* or of a *good report.* It certainly didn't have any *virtue* in it. Therefore, it wasn't scripturally sound.

Some people wonder how to distinguish the voice of Satan; this is how you do it. What you hear must line up with the Word. The Bible tells us exactly what to think on: ". . . *think on these things,"* and the Bible lists the kind of thoughts we should think on. The Bible is our standard for our thought life.

Jesus continued, "This woman knew it was the devil speaking those thoughts to her, so she said, 'Get behind me, Satan.'" And I saw that little demon jump down and run off and leave her.

Jesus still narrating, said, "By and by this demon came back to her again, and sat upon her shoulder and began to whisper in her ear."

At this point, that evil spirit wasn't on the inside of her, but it was on the outside *oppressing* her mind, trying to gain access to her through her mind. But she still had *authority* over it because the Bible says, ". . . *greater is he that is in you, than he that is in the world"* (1 John 4:4). She could have *resisted* the devil because the Bible says she could (James 4:7). And she didn't have to give *any place* in her thoughts to the devil at all (Eph. 4:27).

Jesus said, "By and by this demon came back again, sat upon her shoulder, and said, 'You are a beautiful woman, but you have been cheated in life. You have been robbed in life. In the world, you could have had fame, fortune, and popularity.' But she knew that was the devil. So she said, 'Get thee behind me, Satan.' And the demon left her for a season."

Notice when this woman exercised her rightful authority over the devil in Jesus' Name, that demon had to leave her. But after a season he returned again to tempt her.

Just because you resisted Satan one time doesn't mean he won't try to come back again. The Bible doesn't teach that. Look at the temptation of Jesus. The Bible says the devil left Jesus "for a season" (Luke 4:1-13). And in the vision, I saw the devil return to this Christian woman to tempt her again.

As Jesus began narrating, I saw that little imp come again and sit on this woman's shoulder and whisper in her ear. Jesus said, "By and by, the evil spirit came again and whispered in her ear, 'You are a beautiful woman, but you have been cheated in life. In the world you could have had fame, fortune, money, and popularity.'"

Jesus explained that at this point, this woman was still just being *oppressed* by the devil. Any Christian can be oppressed by an evil spirit. No Christian is immune to Satan's suggestions and oppression, but we don't have to yield to his suggestions. And we have authority over any oppression he tries to bring against us.

Then Jesus said, "But *this time* she began to think Satan's thoughts after him. She began to think, *I am beautiful*, because she liked to think that. And she began to think, *I have been cheated in life*."

This woman didn't keep her thoughts in line with the Bible; she didn't keep her mind focused on Jesus. The Bible says, *"Thou wilt keep him in perfect peace, whose mind is stayed on thee . . ."* (Isa. 26:3). But instead of keeping her mind on the Lord, she began to dwell on and entertain Satan's thoughts.

She was a beautiful woman, but she got to thinking about her beauty instead of keeping her thoughts centered on God, His Word, and on God's will for her life. When she began thinking the devil's thoughts, she got lifted up in pride. The Bible says, *"Pride goeth before destruction, and an haughty spirit before a fall"* (Prov. 16:18)..

Suggestion: Satan's Tool

Many believers wonder how Satan is able to gain ground in their lives. The first place Satan starts to work is in their mind, and one of Satan's greatest and most powerful weapons is the weapon of suggestion. After all, that was the weapon Satan used against Eve in the garden (Gen. 3:1-7). Eve followed Satan's *suggestion*, and she was "beguiled" or *deceived* by him (Gen. 3:13). One of Satan's main strategies today is still to beguile people; he tricks and deceives them by his suggestions.

But we don't have to fall prey to Satan's suggestions because the Bible says we are to give the devil *no* place in us. That means don't give him any place in your thought life. If the devil can get a place in your *thought life*, he can get a place in *you*.

Jesus then told me that when this woman began to think Satan's thoughts and follow Satan's suggestions, she became *obsessed* with that kind of thinking. She began to like thinking those thoughts. Then in the vision, the woman changed and she became transparent, as if her body were made of glass. And I could see a black dot in her head about as big as a half-dollar.

Jesus explained to me, "At first this woman, My servant, was merely *oppressed* by this evil spirit from the outside. She rebuked him because as a child of Mine she had authority over the devil. She resisted him several times and he left. But the last time she began to listen to him and to continue to think his thoughts and listen to his suggestions, because she liked to think those thoughts. Then she became *obsessed* with the devil's thoughts."

Jesus said to me, "She became *obsessed* with that kind of thinking, *but even then it wasn't too late*. She was still My child. She knew what to do. If she had wanted to put those thoughts out of her mind, she could have. She could have said, 'I refuse to think like that. That's of the devil, and I resist you, Satan, in the Name of Jesus.' But she *wanted* to think those thoughts, so she continued to think like that until she became obsessed with that thinking."

It's possible for a believer to become obsessed in his thinking with the devil's thoughts. But I want you to understand this: That woman could have rebuked the devil *at any time* because she had authority over Satan in Jesus' Name, even in her thought life.

Jesus explained, "She *knew* what she was doing. She even knew she was obsessed with that kind of thinking. At any time she could have said, 'These thoughts are of the devil, and I refuse to think like that. I command you, Satan, to leave me. Get behind me, in the Name of Jesus,' *and Satan would have obeyed her*. But she liked to think, *I'm beautiful*. So she continued to think, *I have been cheated. In the world I could have had fame, fortune, and popularity*."

Jesus explained, "It wasn't until she began listening to what the devil was saying and to *entertain his thoughts that she began to go wrong.*

"She eventually left her husband and took up with another man. She went from that man to another man. Then she went from that man to still another man, until she'd had five different men and didn't marry any of them; she just lived with them."

Jesus said, "It still wasn't too late. If she had repented and turned back to Me and asked Me, I would have forgiven her. She didn't need anyone to put the devil on the run for her. She could have done it herself."

Jesus doesn't endorse and condone wrongdoing, but, thank God, He forgives wrongdoing if the believer is sincerely sorry, asks for forgiveness, and repents and turns from his sin (1 John 1:9). Also, notice Jesus' statement, "She didn't need anyone to put the devil on the run for her. She could have done it herself."

It's not enough just to have authority in Christ. Believers need to *exercise* the authority they have over the devil before it will do them any good.

Then in the vision, I saw a leader of a particular Full Gospel denomination go to a hotel. In the vision I was standing outside the hotel. I saw the name of the hotel.

Then it seemed as if I went right inside the hotel with this Full Gospel minister. He went up to the desk to inquire if Mr. and Mrs. So-and-so were registered there. They were. This woman was registered with a man as his wife.

The minister of this denomination went up to the door of their hotel room, and in the vision, in the Spirit, I was standing in the hallway. I saw the whole scene as it was taking place. The minister knocked on the door. This woman came to the door with almost no clothes on and opened it. When she opened the door, she recognized this man, a leader of the Full Gospel denomination.

She said, "I know what you came for." The minister had come to try to restore her and pray with her and get her back to God and to come back to her husband.

She said, "But I want to tell you as far as Jesus Christ is concerned, to hell with Him." And she slammed the door in the minister's face.

Jesus said to me, "You see, she doesn't want Me anymore."

"Now," Jesus continued, "if she had been overly tempted and in a fit of temptation or in a rage of passion and had said, 'I don't want Him,' I would have overlooked it and forgiven her. But she knew exactly what she was doing. She willfully and deliberately said, 'I don't want Him.'"

And when she said that, I saw that big black dot in her head, about as big as a half-dollar, go from her head down inside of her, into her heart and down into her spirit. Then Jesus said to me, "Now she has become *possessed* with that devil. That devil has control of her now, but only *by her permission*."

Oppression, Obsession, and Possession

You see, there's a vast difference between oppression, obsession, and possession. This woman had been in the ministry with her husband for about twenty years; she was not a baby Christian. She was *oppressed* and *obsessed* at first, but when she deliberately and willfully denied Christ as a mature Christian, she became *possessed* with that demon. But it was only *by her permission* that she became demon possessed. And the moment she denied Christ, she could no longer be called a Christian.

I said to Jesus, "Lord, why are You showing me this? Do You want me to cast that devil out of her?"

He answered, "No, you *can't* cast the devil out of her. No one can cast it out because she doesn't want it to go; she wants it. No man — not you, the church elders, other believers, nor anyone else — can exercise authority over the human spirit. When I was on the earth, I exercised authority over *evil* spirits, but not over *human* spirits. Even God the Father does not exercise authority over the human spirit.

"I did exercise authority over evil spirits and demons," Jesus said. "And believers in the Church can exercise authority over evil spirits and demons. But if any human spirit wants the condition to remain as it is, then there is nothing you can do about it; it will stay that way. If this woman wants to have this devil, that's the way it will be, and you can't cast that evil spirit out of her.

"My Word says, '. . . whosoever WILL, let him take the water of life freely,' and '. . . CHOOSE you this day whom ye will serve . . .' [Rev. 22:17; Josh. 24:15]. Man has free will to make whatever choice he will on the earth. God will *not* override man's will."

Jesus explained to me that before this woman denied Christ, if she had wanted to be free, I could have cast those spirits out of her body or soul in His Name. But *she* could have also dealt with the devil at any time and rebuked him. But because she didn't want to be free, there was nothing anyone could do to help her.

Of course, after she denied Christ as a mature Christian, it was no longer possible to cast that evil spirit out of her. She had made the choice which master she would choose, and she chose the devil (Rom. 6:16). God Himself doesn't exercise authority over people's *wills*. If people want to think Satan's thoughts and yield to him, God won't override their will, and you won't be able to either.

You can't *make* people think in line with God's Word, and you can't *make* people want what God has for them. You can't make them want more of the Holy Spirit rather than evil spirits. You can teach people what the Word says, and you can encourage them to believe God's Word and walk in line with it, but you can't *make* people do anything.

The Unpardonable Sin — The Sin Unto Death

When I asked Jesus, "Do You want me to pray for this woman?" He replied, "No, don't even pray for her." Now that came as a real jolt to me! Did you ever hear of not praying for people? I'm a stickler for the Word. If someone tells me something, I don't care who it is, I want to see it in the Word. I said to Jesus, "Why, Lord? I've never heard anything like that. Is that scriptural?"

He answered, "Didn't you ever read in My Word, *'If any man see his brother sin a sin which is not unto death, he shall ask, and he shall give him life for them that sin not unto death. THERE IS A SIN UNTO DEATH: I DO NOT SAY THAT HE SHALL PRAY FOR IT'?*" (1 John 5:16).

Jesus said, "There is a sin unto death and the Word says *not* to pray for those who commit it."

There's no way you could know whether a person has sinned the sin unto death or not unless God showed you by divine revelation. Three different times in my ministry the Lord has told me *not* to pray for a certain person because he or she had committed the sin unto death. This woman was the first person.

Jesus told me I was not to pray for this woman because she had committed the unpardonable sin — the sin unto death. I told the Lord I still wasn't satisfied. I said, "I won't accept any kind of vision or experience, even though I'm seeing You, Jesus, if what You say can't be proven by the New Testament. I won't accept a word of what You are saying to me unless You can give me another scripture to substantiate that I'm not to pray for this woman."

I reminded Him what His Word says, *". . . in the mouth of two or three witnesses every word may be established"* (Matt. 18:16). He gave me the following scriptures and began discussing them with me.

HEBREWS 6:4-6
4 For it is impossible for those who were once ENLIGHT-ENED, and have TASTED OF THE HEAVENLY GIFT, and were MADE PARTAKERS OF THE HOLY GHOST,
5 And have TASTED THE GOOD WORD OF GOD, and THE POWERS OF THE WORLD TO COME,
6 IF THEY SHALL FALL AWAY, to renew them again unto repentance; seeing they crucify to themselves the Son of God afresh, and put him to an open shame.

Jesus explained to me that before a Christian could be guilty of committing the sin unto death, all five conditions mentioned in this scripture would have to apply to the person.

First, it says, *"For it is impossible for those who were once enlightened . . ."* (Heb. 6:4). Jesus said this referred to what many of us in those days called "getting under conviction." The preaching of the Word enlightens the sinner. It's like the prodigal son when he "came to himself" (Luke 15:17). Through the preaching of God's Word, the sinner sees that he is lost. He's enlightened about the truth of God's Word and he sees his need for a Savior.

Second, Hebrews 6:4 says, *". . . and have tasted of the heavenly gift. . . ."* Jesus said a man under conviction has not yet tasted of the Heavenly Gift, because *Jesus* is the Heavenly Gift.

Jesus quoted John 3:16: *"For God so loved the world, that he gave his only begotten Son, that whosoever believeth in him should not perish, but have everlasting life."* So "tasting of the Heavenly Gift" refers to salvation — receiving Jesus Christ as his Savior.

Then, third, *". . . and were made partakers of the Holy Ghost"* (Heb. 6:4). Jesus told me that means more than being born again and becoming acquainted with the Holy Spirit through His indwelling Presence (John 14:16,17). It refers to being filled with the Holy Spirit — having received the baptism in the Holy Spirit (Acts 1:5; 2:4).

Then, fourth, *"And have tasted the good word of God . . ."* (Heb. 6:5). Jesus said this can't apply to baby Christians. They haven't tasted the good Word of God. Baby Christians are still on the "sincere milk of the Word." First Peter 2:2 tells us: *"As newborn babes, desire the sincere milk of the word, that ye may grow thereby."*

Another translation calls it "the *solid meat* of God's word." In other words, babes in Christ couldn't qualify for committing the unpardonable sin because they haven't tasted the solid meat of God's Word. They're only on the milk of the Word.

Only those who have had some degree of spiritual growth and who fully understand the seriousness of denying Christ and are experienced in the solid meat of the Word could be guilty of committing this sin.

Jesus pointed out the similarity between spiritual and physical growth. He said baby Christians can't be guilty of committing the unpardonable sin because they wouldn't be mature enough to know what they are doing.

The fifth condition for committing the unpardonable sin is that a person has ". . . *tasted . . . the powers of the world to come*" (Heb. 6:5). Jesus explained to me what this meant. He said that "the power of the world to come" are spiritual gifts.

Jesus explained, "Those who have tasted of the powers of the world to come are mature Christians who have the gifts of the Spirit operating in their lives or ministries." He explained that the baptism of the Holy Spirit with the ensuing gifts is the earnest of our inheritance in the world to come (Eph. 1:13,14; 2 Cor. 5:5).

So there are five Bible qualifications a believer would have to meet before he or she could be guilty of committing the unpardonable sin. You can readily see that very few believers could qualify to be guilty of committing this sin.

Jesus said this woman in the vision who denied Him *did* qualify to be able to commit the unpardonable sin, and He explained why. He said this woman had been enlightened; she knew her need for a Savior. She had tasted of the Heavenly Gift because she was born again. Jesus Christ had been her Savior for many years.

This woman had also been filled with the Holy Spirit and had been in the ministry for many years with her husband. She knew the Word of God. She had experienced enough spiritual growth so that she wasn't a spiritual baby anymore on the milk of the Word. She had tasted of the solid meat of God's Word. She had the gifts of the Spirit operating in her life. Therefore, this woman met every scriptural condition as one who could commit the unpardonable sin.

Jesus told me He would have forgiven her if she had just been tempted and overcome by the devil. He told me that she didn't commit the sin unto death because she went off with another man. He explained if she'd had a hundred men, but had turned back to Him and repented, He would have forgiven her. But Jesus told me that she came to the decision without being tempted or overcome, where she *willfully* and *deliberately* said she didn't want Jesus anymore. That is the sin unto death — the unpardonable sin. It's what the mature Christian does about *Jesus* that determines whether or not he commits the sin unto death. If the mature Christian willfully denies Christ with deliberate forethought, the Bible calls that committing the unpardonable sin, which is the sin unto death. The sin unto death leads to *spiritual* death — eternal separation from God.

Stop and think about it. A person gets saved by receiving Jesus Christ into his heart. The only way people can lose their salvation is by what they do about *Jesus*. Jesus is the central issue of salvation. That's why when people ask, "Can a Christian have a demon?" they need to define what they mean by that. Actually, as I said, Christians can *have* anything they want to have because they have free will.

If they keep on yielding to the devil, mature Christians could finally get to the point where they *choose* to deny Christ, as this woman did. But then they would no longer be Christians because they would no longer be "Christ-like" and endeavoring to follow Jesus. Once the Spirit of Christ departs, a person couldn't be called a Christian anymore. And only at that point can they become possessed.

So just because this woman was a Christian at one time, she didn't continue as a Christian. She ceased being Christ-like when she followed the devil and denied the Lord Jesus Christ. Jesus said, ". . . *If YE CONTINUE IN MY WORD, then are ye my disciples indeed*" (John 8:31). This woman didn't continue in God's Word; she wanted nothing more to do with Jesus.

Let me say something else here. Just because people *claim* to be Christians, is no sign they are born again. If there's no evidence of the fruit of the born-again, recreated spirit in their lives, I would seriously wonder about their salvation experience. You can put all the labels you want on people, but that doesn't make it so.

For example, a woman once told me that her husband claimed to be a Christian but that he was involved in all kinds of devilment. He didn't show any evidence of being a new creature in Christ. She wanted to know if he could really be a Christian.

I said, "No, he is not a Christian. The word *Christian* means *Christ-like*. Is he acting as Christ would act? No, he certainly isn't. Is he following Christ or walking in the light of the Word in any way? No, he's not. He's following after the devil, so don't call him a Christian."

Then in the vision, Jesus gave me Hebrews 10, and He explained more about the sin unto death.

HEBREWS 10:26-29
26 For IF WE SIN WILFULLY after that we have received the knowledge of the truth, there remaineth no more sacrifice for sins,
27 But a certain fearful looking for of judgment and fiery indignation, which shall devour the adversaries.
28 He that despised Moses' law died without mercy under two or three witnesses:
29 Of how much sorer punishment, suppose ye, shall he be thought worthy, who hath TRODDEN UNDER FOOT THE SON OF GOD, and hath COUNTED THE BLOOD OF THE COVENANT, wherewith he was sanctified, AN UNHOLY THING, and hath done despite unto the Spirit of grace?

Verse 26 says, *"For if we sin wilfully after that we have received the knowledge of the truth. . . ."* That sin couldn't just be referring to *any* sin, for if it just referred to *any* sin, then First John 1:9 wouldn't be true. First John 1:9 promises us that if we confess our sins, God is faithful and just to forgive us and to cleanse us of all unrighteousness.

Therefore, Hebrews 10:26 is talking about the sin of rejecting Christ. Paul (who I believe was the author of the Book of Hebrews) was originally writing to Hebrew Christians in this passage. There's a principle in these verses for all Christians, of course. But in New Testament days, the Jewish Christians were tempted to go back into Judaism because of the difficulties of following Christ.

When these Hebrews became Christians, they were ostracized and cut off from their families. They stuck together and helped one another, but they were having it rough, not only financially, but also because of great persecution.

Some of them were tempted to go back to their old life of Judaism, but to do that they would have had to deny that Christ is the Son of God. Hebrews 10:29 says the unpardonable sin is "trodding under foot the Son of God."

In other words, if those Jewish Christians had gone back to Judaism, they would have had to deny that Christ is the Messiah. If they had done that, they would have had to deny that Jesus was born of a virgin. And if they had gone back into Judaism, that

means they would have counted the blood of the covenant wherewith Jesus was sanctified as an unholy thing (Heb. 10:29). If Jesus
isn't the Son of God, and He's not the Messiah, then His blood
would just be like the blood of any other human being — it would
not be holy.

To deny that Christ is the Son of God is the sin Hebrews 10 is
referring to. It's the same as turning away from Him, rejecting
Him, saying, "I don't want *Jesus* anymore." The Bible is saying that
if mature believers willfully and deliberately deny Christ, there
isn't any more sacrifice for their sins.

After all, what made you a new creature to begin with? It was
receiving Jesus Christ as your Savior. It was believing in your
heart that God raised *Jesus* from the dead, and that He is the Son
of God. You obeyed the Bible and believed in your heart and con-
fessed with your mouth Jesus Christ as your Lord and Savior
(Rom. 10:9,10).

Therefore, the sin the Bible is addressing here is denying Christ,
not some other sin a Christian may commit in his lifetime. But one
of the areas where Satan has wreaked great havoc in the Body of
Christ is in this area of the unpardonable sin. Many mental institutions today are filled with people, even believers, who are convinced
by Satan that they have committed the unpardonable sin.

Satan has used this scripture in Hebrews against people who
are not knowledgeable of the whole counsel of God. He has taken
advantage of their ignorance and lied to them and held them in
bondage by telling them that they have sinned "willfully," thereby
committing the unpardonable sin.

Throughout the centuries people have died at the stake because
they wouldn't recant their belief in Jesus. If they had recanted
under great duress, God wouldn't hold that against them. But if
they recanted willingly, of course, that would be different.

Jesus said this woman in the vision also committed the unpardonable sin on the basis of this passage here in Hebrews 10:26-29. As a
mature Christian, understanding fully what she was doing, she willfully trod Jesus Christ underfoot and counted His blood an unholy
thing (v. 29). Therefore, there was no more sacrifice for her sin.

The devil tries to make believers think they've committed the
unpardonable sin. Over the years, I've had people talk to me who
thought they committed this sin unto death.

I've asked them, "Have you trampled underfoot the blood of
Jesus and said that He was *just* a man — not the Son of God? Have

you said Jesus was not virgin-born? Have you said that His blood isn't holy and that it's the same as the blood of any other man? Have you completely rejected Jesus?"

To every one of those questions they've all replied, "No, of course not."

"That verse doesn't apply to you then," I've answered.

People need to understand biblically about the unpardonable sin so the devil can't take advantage of them. Unless a mature Christian who meets all five qualifications in Hebrews 6 willfully says, "Jesus is not the Son of God," or "I don't want *Jesus,*" he has not committed this sin. Baby Christians can't commit that sin by making that statement in a fit of temper or rage or in a fit of passion. In this verse the Bible is referring to a willful, conscious decision.

No matter what Christians have done, or how far away they've wandered from God, even if they have said some things against Jesus in a moment of anger, He won't hold that against them if they repent and confess their sin to Him and turn away from wrongdoing. That's not to condone sin because sin is wrong. But there's a provision for believers when they sin and miss it (1 John 1:9).

That's why if you get out of fellowship with God, you need to get right back in fellowship as fast as you can. You get out on the devil's territory, and it's dangerous because the devil is out to destroy your life (John 10:10).

Actually, the sin of rejecting Jesus can happen in two ways: People can hear the gospel preached and reject Jesus and just keep on rejecting Him. After a while the Holy Spirit won't deal with them anymore about receiving Jesus as their Savior (Gen. 6:3), and those people will spend eternity in hell when they die. The other way people can reject Jesus is if mature believers willfully and deliberately reject Him.

I asked the Lord what would happen to this woman. He said she would spend eternity in the lake of fire and brimstone. In that vision I saw her go down into that place, and I heard her terrible screams.

I knew another person who committed the unpardonable sin. The Holy Spirit dealt with him over a long period of time, but he just kept rejecting the Holy Spirit's dealings. He never would yield to God. I personally talked to him more than once about God. He told me himself that he'd been born again and that God had called him to preach, but he wasn't willing to preach.

Finally, he just went away from the Lord and quit going to

church and got off into sin. I talked to him about the Lord and tried to get him back to God. At the time, he was living in deep sin, doing just about anything you could mention. When I'd talk to him about the Lord, he'd just weep and shake and tremble under conviction. I kept praying for him and talking to him on different occasions over a fifteen-year period, trying to get him back to the Lord.

The last time I talked to this man, he said, "I know everything you're saying is true, all right. But I'm not going to do anything about it." Then he added, "But don't give up on me. Keep on praying for me." So I kept praying for him. I remember one particular night, I was on my knees praying for him in the nighttime, and the Lord spoke to me. He said, "Get up from there!" It was so real, it startled me. So I got up. The Lord said, "Don't pray for him."

"But, Lord," I said, "he told me that he knew You when he was a teenager. He said You called him to preach. That's why I'm praying that he will get back into fellowship with You and return to You like the prodigal son of old." The Lord answered, "No, don't pray for him anymore."

"You're telling me not to pray for him anymore?" I asked. "But he's still here in this life. There's still hope for him."

"No," the Lord said, "he'll never be saved. He will die and go to hell." That came as a shock to me! I said, "Lord, I don't understand that."

Jesus said to me, "Did you ever read in the Old Testament about Ephraim? Don't you know I finally said, 'Leave Ephraim alone. Just don't bother him anymore. Leave him alone.' Why did I say that? Because Ephraim was joined to his idols [Hosea 4:17]. So you leave this man alone."

You see, in a spiritual sense, this man was joined fast to his idols. He had opened wide the door to the devil, and the Lord knew he would never repent. I never did pray for him after that. I just couldn't. Others did, but the Lord told me not to and the man died at an early age. He was about fifty-four years old when he died.

I inquired of his relatives how he died. They said he died cursing God, yet at one time, he was a believer. Isn't that terrible! But that *can* happen when you open a door to the devil and persist in sin and never turn from it and repent.

Was that God's will? Of course not! But, you see, it's dangerous to be in Satan's territory. The devil can mislead people, and it's possible that they can come to the place where they willfully and deliberately don't want anything to do with God.

It's dangerous to listen to the lies of the devil and get out of fellowship with God and get into sin. And it is possible for believers, if they are over in Satan's territory, to just coldly and deliberately not want anything more to do with God.

But you need to realize that there is a vast difference between believers who desire to walk with God, but occasionally stumble and fall, yet don't intend to, and those believers who just willfully and deliberately persist in wrongdoing and intentionally turn away from God and deny Him.

The Last Opportunity

I was holding meetings in west Texas in 1945. One of the board members said to me, "Brother Hagin, I want to ask you a question." He went on to explain that a previous pastor had originally built that church and had pastored it for about thirty years in this town of about 15,000 people. But he had left his wife and had taken up with another woman in that small town. He just lived with her; he never did marry her.

By the time I came to preach at this church, several years had passed since this pastor had run off with this other woman. Every year since that pastor had left the church, a new pastor came to the church but would only stay about a year and leave. The church was trying to live down the bad reputation it had because of that first pastor who had run off with that woman. He still lived in the same town with her, and he ran a gambling hall and did other things that weren't right. He had brought reproach to that church by the way he was living.

Anyway, this board member said to me, "Brother Hagin, about three weeks ago on a Sunday morning, this former pastor suddenly showed up for the Sunday morning service. One of the women in the church gave an utterance in tongues, and this former pastor got up and interpreted it. Could that be right? Could that have been God?"

"Well," I said, "in the first place, have you ever read in the Old Testament that when Saul was backslidden and away from God, he got in with some of the prophets and the Holy Ghost came upon him and he began to prophesy [*see* First Samuel chapter 19]. The Bible says the gifts and calling of God are without repentance [Rom. 11:29]. But that doesn't mean God condoned Saul's sin. So before I can judge whether the interpretation was of God or not, tell me what the message was."

The board member said, "Well, we were all so startled, I don't remember the first part of it, but it ended with, 'This is your *last* call. I'm giving you your *last* opportunity.'"

When this incident occurred, it had been about three years since this former pastor had been in fellowship with God. The board member said to me, "When that former pastor finished the interpretation, he shouted out loud, 'I want everyone to know that as far as Jesus Christ is concerned, to hell with Him!' and he turned and walked out of the building."

The board member said, "When the former pastor interpreted that message by saying, 'This is your last call — your last opportunity,' do you think that was the right interpretation?"

I said, "Yes, that was God. God was talking to this man supernaturally. The man was speaking out of his spirit what the Holy Ghost was saying to him. That interpretation wasn't a message to that church body; God was talking just to *him*. And he got the message. God in His mercy gave him one *last* opportunity to repent and turn from his sin, but the man turned it down. He rightly interpreted what the Holy Ghost was saying to him, and he made his decision to reject Christ, willfully and deliberately."

That's sad, but it can happen. There's a lesson to be learned here. Remember, in this vision, the Lord began His conversation with me by saying, "I'll show you how the devil gets ahold of people, even believers, if they'll let him."

You see, you are on dangerous ground if you begin listening to what the devil is feeding your mind and begin thinking his thoughts and following his suggestions. By thinking wrong thoughts, you can open a door to the devil. If you open the door to the devil, it won't be long before he'll try to control your mind, and you'll become obsessed with his thoughts.

Believers aren't to give any place to the devil in their thought life. The Bible says, *"Neither give place to the devil"* (Eph. 4:27). That means that the devil can't get ahold of believers *unless they let him.* They *can* give him permission, however. But believers don't have to let Satan dominate their thinking because we have authority over him in the Name of Jesus. Satan is not our lord, and we don't have to let him lord it over us even in our thought life.

Christians have a will of their own that God never violates. But Satan *cannot* violate a person's will either. Believers don't need to yield to the devil. God has well equipped and enabled the Body of Christ to be strong in the Lord by thinking God's thoughts after

Him. We don't have to fall prey to the devil and his thoughts because He is not our Lord, Jesus is. We have victory over Satan, but we must not only exercise the authority we have in Christ, we also have to keep the door to our minds closed on the devil by thinking in line with God's Word. That's how we give Satan no access to us and stand strong as members of the triumphant Church.

---

[1] For more information on this subject, *see* Rev. Hagin's study guide, *The Holy Spirit and His Gifts.*

Chapter 6
How To Deal With Evil Spirits

It is dangerous to think the devil's thoughts because his thoughts bring darkness, depression, oppression, and finally error. The woman in the 1952 vision didn't guard her mind, and it caused her to go into error. Because she rejected Jesus, she will spend eternity burning in the lake of fire and brimstone (Rev. 20:15).

I was still kneeling in the kitchen of the parsonage, praying with that pastor for whom I was holding the meeting. As I said, this pastor was this woman's former husband.

When I asked Jesus why He showed me this vision, He said, "I wanted to show you first of all how the devil, demons, or evil spirits get ahold of people, even believers, if they let them. But, secondly, I want you to command the demon that's in this woman to stop harassing, intimidating, and deterring the ministry of my servant _____," and the Lord called the name of that woman's ex-husband, the pastor I was praying with.

This pastor had never told me anything about his former wife. I knew his wife had left him several years before, but I didn't know anything else about the situation until I had this vision praying in his kitchen.

Still in the vision, Jesus told me that although I couldn't deal with the woman myself, for no one, not even God, has authority over the *human spirit* because people have a free will, I did have authority over the evil spirit that was influencing this woman.

Jesus told me that I *could* deal with the evil spirit that was influencing her, because that demon was hindering His servant in the work of the ministry. I found out later that she had been calling her former husband, this pastor, threatening to come to town to make trouble for him.

As a member of the Body of Christ, I had authority over the devil that was hindering and coming against the Lord's servant, this pastor. But that didn't mean this woman would be *delivered* of this evil spirit because she didn't *want* to be delivered. She *wanted* that demon; she didn't want to give it up. Besides, she had already committed the unpardonable sin by denying Christ. But by dealing with the evil spirit that was influencing her, the demon could no longer harass and intimidate God's servant, this pastor.

I asked Jesus, "Lord, how do I deal with the evil spirit in this woman?"

The Lord answered, "You just simply say, 'You foul spirit that is operating and manifesting yourself in the life of _____ (and Jesus called the woman's name), intimidating, harassing, and deterring the ministry of _____, (and Jesus called the pastor's name), I command you to stop in your operations against him. I command you to cease and desist in your maneuvers, in the Name of the Lord Jesus Christ.'"

I said, "Is that all I have to do?"

I thought perhaps I would have to prepare myself and get ready for some big battle or something. Sometimes because of our religious teaching, we think we have to pray for a week before we can exercise our authority over the devil. Or we think maybe we ought to fast several meals before we could attempt to deal with the devil.

But our authority over the devil is in Jesus' Name based on our rights and privileges *in* Christ. Our *authority* over the devil doesn't depend on how long we pray and fast, but we do need to know who we are in Christ. On the other hand, praying and fasting will help make us more sensitive to the leading of the Holy Spirit.

Jesus replied, "That's all you do." "Yes, but, Lord, she's in another state and I'm here," I protested. The Lord replied, "There's no distance in the spirit realm. You can command a devil to stop harassing, intimidating, or deterring someone who is in another state, and he'll have to stop in his operations against the person."

So I dealt with the evil spirit that was working through that woman just as Jesus told me to do. And when I spoke to the demon, he answered me. Jesus had told me I would begin to *see* and *hear* in the realm of the spirit; that was the gift of discerning of spirits in operation. The pastor didn't see or hear anything, but I both saw and heard that spirit as it spoke to me.

The evil spirit said he sure didn't want to stop in his operations against that pastor, but he knew he had to if I told him to. I told him he had to in Jesus' Name. Then still in the spirit realm, I saw the evil spirit run away like a whipped dog. When he did, I started laughing. There is a laugh *in the Spirit*, and it indicates a note of victory.

Then I became tuned back in to the natural realm, and I realized that the pastor was laughing with me. I don't know how long we laughed like that in the Spirit. After it was over, I told him I'd been in the spirit realm — lost in that cloud of glory — but that I

thought I'd heard him laughing too. He said he had been. He told
me he didn't see or hear anything, but he knew I both saw and
heard something.

I asked him what he'd been laughing about. He said he'd gotten
a phone call and a letter that day from his former wife saying she
was going to come to town to make trouble for him and his ministry. When we were praying, the pastor had sensed in his spirit
that the devil who was operating through her had been dealt with.
By faith the pastor could see that devil on the run. I told him I'd
actually seen the spirit that was involved, and that I'd seen it run
away like a whipped dog. That was what we were both laughing
about, so we were both in the Spirit.

Check Up on Spiritual Revelations and Visions

I like to check up both scripturally and naturally on the validity
of spiritual revelations and visions I receive. In other words, I don't
accept revelations and visions just because they occur. I described to
this pastor in detail what I'd seen in the vision. I told him about the
minister (the head of that woman's denomination) going to a certain
hotel where this pastor's ex-wife was staying with another man. I
related to the pastor what his ex-wife had said to the minister.

The pastor exclaimed, "That's exactly what happened! The man
you saw in the vision is the district superintendent of the denomination we belonged to. And that's exactly what he told me that she
said and did."

I had no knowledge of any of that in the natural; there was no
way I could have known that except by the Spirit of the Lord. But I
like to be sure about things I see in the Spirit and check up on
them. I don't just accept everything that happens in the Spirit and
run off with it and accept it or try to build a doctrine on it.

This pastor, this woman's former husband, had since remarried.
I didn't know his first wife had been threatening to cause trouble
for him. Of course the devil in this woman wanted to cause trouble
for him in his church and in the community to deter him from the
work of the ministry. That's what the Lord meant when He said an
evil spirit operating through this woman was harassing and intimidating His servant.

When this pastor had eventually remarried, his denomination
wouldn't have anything more to do with him because he was
divorced. But when the Lord spoke to me in the vision, He called

this pastor *"My* servant." Isn't it strange that the Christians in that denomination wouldn't even call him *brother!*

Harassing the Church

In the vision, Jesus explained to me that a person doesn't have to operate in the gift of discerning of spirits in order to deal with the devil when the devil is harassing, intimidating, or deterring a member of the Body of Christ. We have authority in those situations to command the devil to stop in his maneuvers against a believer.

It doesn't take a gift of the Spirit in those situations in order to take your stand and to exercise your authority over the devil. Jesus also said a believer doesn't need a word of knowledge or to be a minister in order to exercise authority over the devil. *Every* believer has the authority to use the Name of Jesus and to take his stand against the devil (Matt. 18:18; Mark 16:17; Luke 10:19; Phil. 2:9,10).

Jesus explained, "Anytime anyone in the Church or outside the Church is doing anything, saying anything, or acting in any way that embarrasses, hinders, harasses, intimidates, deters, or retards the ministry of the Church, you don't have to have discerning of spirits or a word of knowledge, just *know* it is the devil causing the trouble.

"You are just to command the spirit that's behind the operation against the believer to stop and desist in his maneuvers *in My Name* — in the Name of Jesus. You don't have to deal with the person; deal with the evil spirit behind the operation."

You see, many people — believers and unbelievers alike — unconsciously yield to the devil. Sometimes due to ignorance, people can innocently become a tool of Satan when they *unconsciously* yield to him. But people, even believers, can also *consciously* yield to the devil too.

Although believers have the authority to deal with any *evil spirit* that's influencing a person to harass the Body of Christ, we don't have the authority to deal with the *person* causing the problem. Our authority doesn't extend that far because we don't have authority over the human will, and the person may want the evil spirit. No one can get a person delivered if he wants to keep an evil spirit.

That's why binding the evil spirit behind the operation will not get the person causing the problem *delivered* of evil spirits, for he has free choice and he may want to keep them. But exercising our authority *stops* the evil spirits in their strategy against a believer.

Problems occur in this area when believers try to deal with *people* in the *natural realm*, instead of with *evil spirits* influencing people in the *spiritual realm*. Many times we try to deal with people when we should be dealing with evil spirits, and we get things in a mess.

Now don't misunderstand me. There's a time and a place to deal with people in the natural. But Jesus was talking about those cases where the enemy is working through people to hinder the Church — the Body of Christ. If a person hinders, harasses, or deters the Church, then it is the working of evil spirits through the person.

In dealing in the lives of people to get them *delivered* of a demon, it's a different situation. In most cases, their own will is involved. What do *they* want to do about the situation? Do they want to be delivered? Some people want the situation as it is; they don't want to be free from demons. And in that case, there's nothing you can do about it. When people genuinely want deliverance, you still have to deal with the evil spirit in them by the leading of the Holy Spirit.

On the other side of this issue, we have to realize that not every problem in life is caused by a demon, just as not everything that goes wrong in life is *directly* caused by a demon either. Of course, the devil is ultimately behind all the evil in the world. But because we live in a world where Satan is god (2 Cor. 4:4), problems, tests, and trial will occur.

Jesus said, *"In the world ye shall have tribulation: but be of good cheer; I have overcome the world"* (John 16:33). He also promised us the victory in every situation: *". . . thanks be to God, which giveth us the victory through our Lord Jesus Christ"* (1 Cor. 15:57).

I said there are times when people have to be dealt with in the natural by a person who is in charge, because not everything that happens is caused by an evil spirit. For example, parents need to train and discipline their children in the natural, as well as pray and watch over them spiritually.

But right on the other hand, there is another side to that coin. Many times, good people — even born-again, Spirit-filled people can unconsciously yield to the devil and cause problems in the church. In those instances, you *will* have to deal with the evil spirit that is causing the problems by exercising your authority in Christ.

In most cases, you should deal with an evil spirit privately. However, occasionally a minister may have to deal publicly in his meeting with the devil operating through a person.

But normally in the privacy of your own prayer closet you can just say, "You foul spirit that's operating in the life of So-and-so, hindering and embarrassing this church (or person), I command you to cease and desist in your maneuvers in Jesus' Name."

I was preaching along these lines in a Full Gospel church, and a neighboring pastor in a larger city was having some problems with certain members of his congregation. The pastor where I was preaching gave him my tapes on this subject to listen to.

A couple of years later, the pastor of that neighboring church told me, "There were three families in my church who were causing all kinds of problems. In fact, one of them was my deacon, one was my school superintendent, and one of them was a board member. The deacon was trying to get up a petition to kick me out of the church.

"I had been trying to deal with those three families for a long time in the natural, but I never got anywhere. Nothing I did seemed to work; they still caused all kinds of problems in the church. After I heard your tapes, I realized it was an evil spirit influencing these people, causing all the trouble."

You see, the devil can speak to Christians' minds, and they can repeat what the devil is saying and create division and strife (James 3:14-16). The Bible says that Satan is the accuser of the brethren, and he can influence believers to accuse one another (Rev. 12:10).

The pastor told me that in the privacy of his own study, he simply took authority over the evil spirits causing the trouble in his church and commanded those spirits to stop in their maneuvers against him.

That pastor later told me, "Those people had been causing problems for three years, but they changed almost overnight. They were basically good, Christian people. They just didn't realize they were yielding to the devil and that the devil was using them to come against the church. But once I dealt with the evil spirit causing all the problems, those same people are now my staunchest supporters."

I am convinced the Body of Christ has more authority than we've ever exercised. Instead of rising up and using what is rightfully ours, we are too often prone to drift along, hoping things will get better someday. But we need to remember that the Bible says we wrestle not against flesh and blood (Eph. 6:12). Too much of the time we try to wrestle *with* flesh and blood — with human beings — instead of dealing with the evil spirit causing the problem.

Now don't misunderstand me. As I said, there are times you will have to deal with flesh and blood — you will have to deal with people in the natural. But too much of the time, we're trying to do it *all* in the natural in the energy of the flesh by wrestling with flesh and blood. But thank God for the Name of Jesus, and for the victory He already won for us over the powers of darkness!

The Man in the 1952 Vision

As I said, there were three parts to the 1952 vision. In the first part of the vision, Jesus showed me the Christian woman who became oppressed, obsessed, and finally possessed when she denied Christ.

In the second part of the vision, Jesus taught me how to deal with an evil spirit in a person to *cast it out*. In the second part of the vision, I saw a man. I didn't know him, but I knew he wasn't a believer; he'd never been born again. In the vision Jesus said to me, "I will show you how demons and evil spirits get ahold of a person and how to cast them out of a person."

In the vision I saw an evil spirit come and sit upon this unsaved man's shoulder and whisper in his ear. I don't know what the evil spirit said to the man because Jesus didn't narrate that part. Jesus said to me, "This man began to listen to the devil." The man not only listened to the devil but began meditating on the thoughts of the devil. As he continued to entertain the devil's thoughts, the evil spirit went into the man's mind.

Then in the vision, the man's body became transparent like his body was made out of glass, just as the woman's body had. I could see a black dot in the man's head about as big as a quarter. Jesus explained that this evil spirit had first come from the outside to attack the man's mind through *oppression* in the man's thought life. That is the way the devil begins his operation against a person — through his mind and his thought life.

Jesus said, "Because this man listened to the evil spirit and opened his mind to the demon's suggestions, the evil spirit was able to enter into the man's mind." When the man did that, he became *obsessed* in his mind — in his thinking. He liked dwelling on Satan's thoughts.

Just as Jesus had explained in the case of the Christian woman who had become obsessed and then possessed, Jesus said that this man could do something *himself* about the devil and about thinking those kinds of thoughts, even though he wasn't a believer.

You see, even though this man wasn't a Christian, he still had free choice, and he didn't have to think those kind of thoughts. At any time he could have chosen not to think like that even if he didn't recognized that they were the devil's thoughts. At any time *he* could have changed his thinking; he didn't need anyone to change his thinking for him.

Saved and unsaved people alike can choose to think whatever they want to — good thoughts or evil thoughts — because they have free choice. But the man continued to yield to the devil's thoughts until he became obsessed with those evil thoughts. Then Jesus said to me, "Now he is obsessed with that kind of thinking, and the devil has control of this mind."

You Choose What You Think About

You hear people say all the time, "I just can't help the way I think." But, yes, you can if you want to. The Bible says you can. *You* — not God, and certainly not the devil — are to control your own thoughts.

It makes all the difference in the world what you *think* about. God wants us to keep our thoughts centered on Him and on His Word (Isa. 26:3). But if you want to entertain wrong thoughts, God is not going to stop you; He is not going to override your will. But if you entertain wrong thoughts, you will open a door to the devil in your life.

Don't misunderstand me; God doesn't *condone* wrong thoughts. He's given us instruction in His Word what we are to think about (Phil. 4:8). But if you persist in thinking wrong thoughts, God won't stop you. It's up to *you* what you think about, *not* God. You can think wrong thoughts if you want to, or you can *resist* them and turn away from wrongdoing in your thought life.

Sometimes believers *consciously* or *unconsciously* open the door and invite Satan to come in. Or they may do it *ignorantly* through a lack of knowledge of God's Word, but nonetheless they give Satan consent to come in to their lives through their thought life. A consent of ignorance is still a consent.

How Evil Spirits Let Other Evil Spirits In

In the vision, after the man became obsessed, Jesus narrated, "This evil spirit obsessing this man is one of the rulers of the darkness of this world — one of the higher order of demon spirits. The rulers of the darkness of this world are the ones that get ahold of a person and will eventually possess him, if the person lets him. And there are degrees of possession."

Jesus then explained that when these rulers of the darkness of this world, this higher order of evil spirits, get ahold of an unsaved person, they let other spirits in with them. Jesus said, "I'll show you how this higher order of evil spirits lets in other evil spirits." Then in the vision I saw the evil spirit in the man's mind hold up something that looked like a trapdoor in the top of the man's head.

I watched as that demon that did the possessing let many other evil spirits (they looked like big flies) enter into the man through that trapdoor in the man's head. So many of these big fly-like evil spirits came into the man's mind through that trapdoor, I couldn't count them all. They looked like big flies, but that ruling spirit, the evil spirit that first whispered in the man's ear, looked like a little monkey or an elf.

Jesus talked to me about those evil spirits that looked like flies. He explained that they were of a lower order of evil spirit and primarily obeyed just what they were told. They didn't have much intelligence of their own.

Do we find anything in Scripture about this lower order of evil spirits that look like flies? Yes, we do. Jesus reminded me of the account in Matthew 12:24 when the Pharisees accused Him of casting out devils, not by the finger of God, but by Beelzebub (Matt. 12:24-28). Jesus told me that Beelzebub means "lord of flies" or "lord of the dunghill" (Matt. 12:24-28). In other words, Beelzebub, or Satan, has dominion over and is lord over all demons and evils spirits.

In the vision, Jesus explained that one of the higher class of demons — the rulers of darkness — first approach a person in order to gain access to him and try to get control of him, if the person will allow it. Then once that higher order of demon gains access to the person, the ruler of darkness lets in this lower class of evil spirits too.

Once the ruler of darkness let the other spirits in with it, in the vision, I saw the evil spirit of that higher order go down inside the man into his spirit. Still narrating, Jesus said, "Now the man is *possessed* by that evil spirit."

Jesus explained to me that even in the case of this unsaved man, he was first just *oppressed* by the evil spirit that came to whisper the devil's thoughts to his mind. Then as the man *yielded* to thinking those thoughts, he became *obsessed* with the devil's thoughts. The man kept yielding his thinking to that evil spirit until finally through the man's own *consent* the evil spirit was able to *possess* the man's spirit.

Then Jesus explained to me, "The higher class of demons — a ruler of darkness — got control of the man first, and it is the one that did the possessing. It is always a ruler of darkness that does the possessing. Then that higher order of demon let in all the others with him." All of those evil spirits were in the man, of course, but it was the demon of the higher order that first enticed the man and entered his mind that fully possessed him.

Full Possession

After the Lord showed me how evil spirits gain access to a person, He said to me, "From this night on, when you are in the presence of one who is fully possessed, the evil spirits will recognize you. They will also recognize that you have authority over them."

Jesus was speaking of the authority every believer has in the Name of Jesus. Jesus said, "When a person is fully possessed, the demon in him can use the person's voice. The demon may speak and say, 'I know who you are.' Evil spirits will know you, just as they knew who I was. They will know you just as the demon in the young woman in Philippi knew who Paul and Silas were" (Acts 16:17).

Jesus gave me Mark 5:6,7 and His dealings with the madman of Gadara to substantiate this: *"But when he saw Jesus afar off, he ran and worshipped him, And cried WITH A LOUD VOICE, and said, What have I to do with thee, Jesus, thou Son of the most high God? I adjure thee by God, that thou torment me not."*

The demon that possessed the man knew exactly who Jesus was: *". . . What have I to do with thee, JESUS, THOU SON OF THE MOST HIGH GOD? . . ."* (Mark 5:7). In the natural, the madman himself couldn't have known who Jesus was because he had dwelt in the tombs and hadn't mixed with society.

In the vision Jesus said to me, "Particularly when you are in the presence of those who are *fully* possessed, the evil spirits will recognize you and will speak to you using the person's voice, saying, 'I know who you are.'"

Jesus explained that when a person is fully possessed, the demon's voice speaking through the person can be heard in the natural realm. It doesn't take the gift of discerning of spirits to hear that because the possessing demon uses the person's vocal chords to speak in the natural realm.

Jesus said to me, "If you had been there that day, in the natural realm with your own physical ears you would have heard this man talking to Me. But in reality it was the demon that possessed him doing the speaking — not the man himself."

In other words, when the demon in the madman of Gadara cried out with a loud voice, ". . . *What have I to do with thee, Jesus, thou Son of the most high God? I adjure thee by God, that thou torment me not"* (Mark 5:7), that was heard in the natural realm. The ruler of darkness was speaking through this man, using his voice, and anyone present that day could have heard him say that.

Jesus also said if I had been there that day, I would have heard the possessing demon answer Jesus and say, ". . . *My name is Legion: for we are many . . ."* (Mark 5:9). The possessing demon named Legion was using the man's vocal chords to talk to Jesus.

Jesus said, "But if you had been there, or if any other human being had been present that day, you would *not* have heard all the devils speak up and say to Me, 'Send *us* into the swine, that we may enter into them' [Mark 5:12]. *That* could only be heard in the spiritual realm by the gift of discerning of spirits in manifestation."

You see, when all those demons spoke up and said that to Jesus, they were not talking through the man, using the man's voice. They were speaking in the spirit realm, and Jesus heard them because the gift of discerning of spirits was in manifestation in His life.

Jesus told me that because I had this gift of discerning of spirits, at times I would *see* and *hear* into the realm of spirits when I was in the Spirit. That scares some people, but it shouldn't because ". . . *greater is he that is in you, than he that is in the world"* (1 John 4:4).

Sometimes when I've been ministering in healing lines, for example, I've had evil spirits in people speak to me before I've ever said a word to the person. I heard those evil spirits speak in the spirit realm. People can hear me tell them to leave, but no one else hears the evil spirits talking because they can only be heard in the spirit realm through the gift of discerning of spirits.

For example, sometimes in the healing line evil spirits have said very emphatically to me, "I don't intend to go!" I just say, "You have to go in the Name of Jesus. Leave this person in the Name of Jesus," and the evil spirits always depart and the people are delivered. Many times when I'm in the Spirit, I've seen them depart, although there was no visible manifestation in the person. God's Word works; we have authority over all the power of the devil (Luke 10:19).

Jesus and the Madman of Gadara

Jesus said, "In dealing with evil spirits, you will know the kind of demon you are dealing with by revelation — either through the word of knowledge or discerning of spirits. When I walked up to that madman of Gadara, I discerned what *kind* of a spirit it was that possessed him. It was an unclean spirit: *"For he* [Jesus] *said unto him, Come out of the man, thou UNCLEAN SPIRIT"* (Mark 5:8).

Jesus explained to me, "You see, I was not ministering by some power inherent in Me because I am the Son of God. When I came to this world, I laid aside My mighty power and glory, as the Scriptures say (Phil. 2:6-8). I was ministering under the anointing of the Spirit of God by the gifts of the Spirit, just as any other believer would minister.

"And because I was ministering by the anointing of the Spirit of God, I had to depend upon the Holy Spirit to manifest Himself through Me. In this case, the Holy Spirit manifested Himself through the gift of discerning of spirits. That's the reason I knew it was an unclean spirit that was governing this man."

If you have a revelation of the kind of spirit that is present in a person through a *word of knowledge*, you *know* what kind of evil spirit is present. If you have a revelation of the kind of spirit that is present through the gift of *discerning of spirits*, you *see* or *hear* what kind of evil spirit is present.

Jesus explained to me, "Ordinarily, if there is only one spirit and you command him to come out, he will come out." Then Jesus said something that startled me.

He said, "I had already perceived or discerned that the man had an unclean spirit, but when I commanded the unclean spirit to come out, it didn't come out. So then I asked him what his name was" (Mark 5:8,9).

We can see in Luke's account that Jesus commanded the unclean spirit to come out, but it didn't come out until Jesus found out its name and in this case, its number.

LUKE 8:28-30
28 When he saw Jesus, he cried out, and fell down before him, and with a loud voice said, What have I to do with thee, Jesus, thou Son of God most high? I beseech thee, torment me not.
29 (For he [Jesus] HAD COMMANDED the unclean spirit to come out of the man. For oftentimes it had caught him: and he was kept bound with chains and in fetters; and he brake

**the bands, and was driven of the devil into the wilderness.)
30 And Jesus asked him, saying, WHAT IS THY NAME? And
he said Legion: because many devils were entered into him.**

Jesus explained that the unclean spirit didn't come out of the
man until Jesus asked the evil spirit its name. The unclean spirit
gave its name: "... *My name is Legion: for we are many*" (Mark
5:9). Jesus said in this case, its name and number was the same —
Legion. Legion was its name, but it was also its number. So in dealing with the madman of Gadara, Jesus Himself had to know the
name of the spirit before He could cast it out.

Jesus explained that through discerning of spirits or a word of
knowledge, when I am in the Spirit (or when these gifts are operating through any believer when he is in the Spirit), I would know
what *kind* of spirit possesses a person. But in some cases Jesus
said it would also be necessary to know the *name* of the evil spirit
or sometimes the *number* of spirits involved in order to cast them
out. If an evil spirit didn't come out when I commanded it to come
out, I should ask its name and its number — how many evil spirits
are in the person.

Then still in the vision, Jesus told me to walk up to the unsaved
man I was seeing in the vision. The minute I did, the evil spirit in
the man spoke to me just as Jesus had said it would, saying, "I
know you! I know who you are!"

I said, "Yes, I know you know who I am. And you also know I
have authority over you in the Name of Jesus!"

Then Jesus said to me, "Now tell that evil spirit to be quiet.
Don't let him talk."

Nowhere in Scripture do you find that Jesus ever held a conversation with demons. He always told them, "Hold your peace!"
(Mark 1:25; Luke 4:35). Jesus explained that the only exception to
this is when you command an evil spirit to come out, and it doesn't
come out, then you need to ask the evil spirit his name or the number of evil spirits involved. That is the only case in which Jesus
spoke further to an evil spirit — and it was only to demand its
name (Mark 5:9).

In the vision, I commanded the evil spirit in the man to be quiet
in the Name of Jesus. On the inside of me I knew by revelation of
the Holy Spirit what *kind* of evil spirit was possessing the man and
talking to me. It was a deceiving spirit. So I said, "You foul deceiving spirit, I command you to come out of this man in the Name of

Jesus." Nothing happened; the evil spirit didn't come out.

Then in the vision Jesus emphasized again to me, "When you know the kind of evil spirit it is, and it still doesn't come out, then you need to know its number." So in the vision, I asked the evil spirit possessing the man, "What is your name or number?" Deceiving wasn't the name of the spirit; it was just its *kind*.

The evil spirit in the man answered, "There are nineteen more in here besides me." Once I found out its number, that's all I needed to know. I said, "I command you and all nineteen others to come out of the man in the Name of Jesus." Then in the realm of the spirit, I saw those evil spirits leave the man.

Where Do Evil Spirits Go When Cast Out?

You remember in Mark 5:13, the devils went into the swine and the swine ran off the cliff and perished in the sea. The Bible also says evil spirits ". . . *besought him* [Jesus] *that he would not command them to go out into the deep"* (Luke 8:31).

So I asked Jesus, "Where do evil spirits go when they are cast out of a person?" I'd heard preachers try to cast evil spirits into the abyss or pit (Rev. 20:3). So I asked Jesus if I should cast these spirits into the pit or into hell.

Jesus answered, "No, you can't cast evil spirits into hell or into the abyss. The Bible says that when I would go into the synagogues, those demons would cry out, '. . . *What have we to do with thee, Jesus, thou Son of God? art thou come hither to torment us BEFORE THE TIME?"* (Matt. 8:29).

Jesus said, "You see, their time hasn't come yet. Don't you know that if it were possible to cast evil spirits into the abyss, when I was on the earth, I would have cast all of them in there I could. That would have left that many less for you to put up with."

Why hasn't the time come yet for evil spirits to be cast into the abyss? Because Satan is presently 'the god of this world' until Adam's lease runs out that Satan has been using (2 Cor. 4:4), Satan has a *legal* right — but not a *moral* right — to be here.

I asked Jesus, "What happens to those evil spirits that are cast out of people?"

Jesus said, "Haven't you ever read in My Word, 'When the unclean spirit is gone out of a man, he walks through *dry places* seeking rest'" (Matt. 12:43). Then in the vision, I saw the demon that had possessed the man, walking through dry places.

Jesus continued, "When you cast evil spirits out of people, they walk through the dry places. They are still here on earth seeking rest. And finding none, they try to go back to the 'house' they came out of, if that person will let them back in [Matt. 12:44]. They will stay in that person until they are cast out again or until the person dies."

The person's body or soul becomes the demon's "house." So when the person dies, the demon will leave that "house" and look for someone else to inhabit.

Some years after this vision, I was standing in a hospital room when a man died who had had a serious stomach problem. When he died, something jumped from him to me. (Not all stomach problems are caused by the presence of a demon, but they can be.) That thing hit me in the stomach like I'd been shot with a BB gun, and my stomach began to burn like fire. I said, "No, you don't, devil! You are not getting into me, in Jesus' Name!" And that demon left me immediately.

A Word of Caution

There is something we need to realize about spiritual things. Every revelation or vision must be looked at in the light of God's Word. In other words, just because you've had a vision, don't just accept it and run away with it and begin to build doctrine on it and teach it wherever you go. Compare it with the Word of God and see if it lines up.

If I have a spiritual revelation of any kind, I don't just run out and began acting on it or began teaching it. I stop and think over what I've seen and meditate on it in the light of God's Word before I start implementing what I've learned or teaching it. The Lord told me one time He would rather I be too slow than too fast.

Jesus told me that some people receive a little revelation, and they grab it and run off with it and many times get into error. They usually end up getting things in a mess. It's better to be careful and let the Lord lead and guide you as to how to use spiritual revelations and not run ahead of Him with them.

About two months after this vision, I had the opportunity to implement what I had learned in this vision about dealing with demons. I was holding a meeting at a church in Texas. One of the board members of a church in a nearby city asked me to hold a meeting for them after I closed my meeting. So after I finished my meeting, I drove over to the nearby city and checked into the hotel where the church had made accommodations for me.

In the afternoon, the board member who had talked to me earlier called me on the telephone. He asked, "Brother Hagin, could you help me. You've never met my son, but he is thirty-eight years old and has never been saved. He drinks and takes drugs. He comes to stay with us sometimes, but we can't do anything with him. He has spells and goes wild and starts breaking up the furniture. We've had to call the police to come and put him in jail for our own protection." It seemed the devil had tried to drive this young man insane.

The board member said, "He's here with us now, and he's had one of his spells. He picked up a huge piece of furniture and broke it in two with his bare hands. It's so large, two or three men couldn't have broken it. He picked up a piano and threw it against the wall, just like you'd pick up a book and throw it."

That's supernatural strength! Remember, the Bible says the madman of Gadara broke every chain and fetter (Mark 5:4) because he possessed supernatural strength. The board member asked, "Would you come over and help us?"

I drove to his home. When I got to the house, the man and his wife took me to their son who sat slouched over on a couch with his head in his hands. This couple didn't say one word of introduction as we entered the room. Their son didn't know they had called me or who I was; we had never met before. But the minute I walked into the room, their son immediately looked up at me and said, "I know you! I know who you are! I saw you when you came into town at ten minutes after two o'clock this afternoon!"

He then proceeded to tell me the very street I had come down and told me each turn I had made, calling each street by name. Then he told me the name of the hotel I had checked into. He told me *exactly* the way I came into town, and *exactly* what time I had arrived. No *man* could have known those things.

The demon who possessed that man was using his voice and had revealed these things to him. I answered, "Yes, I know you know me, but in the Name of Jesus, be quiet! In the Name of Jesus, come out of him!"

Just like you'd snap your fingers, the man's countenance and his whole personality completely changed! He brightened up and looked completely normal. There was no other visible manifestation of his deliverance. I didn't see any spirits leave the man, and nothing else happened visibly, but the man was totally delivered.

We make a mistake thinking there always has to be some kind of *manifestation* when someone is delivered of evil spirits. Whether you see the evil spirits leave or not, what's important is that the person is delivered.

The Third Part of the 1952 Vision

There was a third part of the 1952 vision about demons and evil spirits and how to deal with them. In the third part of the vision, Jesus gave me further instruction about how to deal with demons. Here's what happened. As Jesus was talking to me in this vision, all of a sudden a demon ran up between us. It looked a lot like a monkey, but his face was more human looking.

The demon ran up between Jesus and me and began to jump up and down in the air, and as he did, he put out something like a black cloud or a smoke screen. When he did that, it became hard to see Jesus. Then the little imp began to jump up and down and throw his arms and legs out, and in a high-pitched shrill voice, he began to scream, "Yakety yak yak! Yakety yak yak!"

The entire time this was happening, Jesus went right on talking. I could hear Jesus talking, but I couldn't distinguish His words. And then because of that smoke screen, I finally couldn't see Jesus anymore either. This probably lasted just a few seconds, but it seemed like it lasted many minutes.

I thought to myself, *Doesn't Jesus know I can't hear what He's saying! Doesn't He know I'm not getting what He's saying!* And then I thought, *Why doesn't Jesus tell him to stop! Doesn't He know I can't hear Him?*

Finally, in desperation, and without really thinking, I just pointed my finger at that little demon and said, "I command you to cease and desist in Jesus' Name!" When I said those words, that little demon hit the floor, kerflop! The black cloud disappeared, and he just lay on the floor, shaking and trembling like a little whipped pup, crying and whining.

Jesus looked at him and then looked at me, and pointing to the little demon, He said, "If you hadn't done something about that evil spirit, I couldn't have."

I said, "Lord, I know I misunderstood You. You didn't say if I hadn't done something about that demon, You *couldn't* have. You said You *wouldn't* have, didn't You?"

Pointing to the demon as he lay trembling on the floor, Jesus repeated, "No, I said, 'If you hadn't done something about that evil spirit, I *couldn't* have.'"

I shook my head, thinking it was my hearing that was faulty. I said, "Something is wrong with me. I didn't hear right. You didn't say if I hadn't done something about that evil spirit, You *couldn't* have. You said You *wouldn't* have, didn't You?"

He repeated the same words, "No, I said, 'If you hadn't done something about that evil spirit, I *couldn't* have.'"

I said, "Lord, something is wrong. I'm not hearing right," and I repeated my question the third time. I think I know how Jesus must have looked when He got angry and took that rope and drove those money changers out of the Temple (Mark 11:15). It looked to me like His eyes shot little flashes of lightning, and He said, "No! I said I *couldn't* have!"

I said, "I can't accept that. Lord, that's different than anything I've ever preached or heard. Lord, that upends my theology." You see, in religious circles we had always prayed, "God, *You* rebuke the devil" or "Jesus, *You* rebuke the devil."

The Lord answered, "Sometimes your theology needs upending."

I said, "I've never heard anything like that in my life. Lord, I won't accept any vision, or any divine visitation, I don't care if I am seeing You and hearing You talk to me as plain and as real as any man in the natural — I won't accept that unless You can prove what You're saying to me by the holy written Word of God. The Bible says, 'By the mouth of two or three witnesses, let every word be established' [Matt. 18:16]. I won't believe what You are telling me unless You can give me three witnesses from the New Testament."

You see, we live under the New Covenant or the New Testament. I'm not so concerned about the Old Covenant. Now don't misunderstand me. I believe it, of course, and I understand its value. But I'm not trying to get back under the Old Covenant and live under its rules and regulations because it was written for spiritually dead people; they weren't born again. Under the New Covenant, we are made new creatures and our human spirits are recreated.

Jesus smiled so sweetly at me and said, "I'll go you one better. I'll give you four."

Jesus said to me, "To pray that I, the Lord Jesus Christ, or that God the Father would do anything about the devil is to waste your time."

I said, "Dear God, I've wasted a lot of time!" A lot of folks today are wasting their time!

Then Jesus said, "God the Father and I have done all that We are ever going to do about the devil until the time when the angel of God will come down from Heaven and bind the devil with a chain and put him in the bottomless pit for a thousand years [Rev. 20:1-3]. Until that time, Heaven is not going to do anything else about the devil."

You see, God sent Jesus, and Jesus already did something about the devil: ". . . *For this purpose the Son of God was manifested, that he might DESTROY THE WORKS OF THE DEVIL*" (1 John 3:8). Jesus defeated the devil in His death, burial, and resurrection (Col. 2:15). Now the believer is expected to exercise his rightful authority over the devil.

Jesus said, "In every Epistle that's written to the Church — to believers — if the writer of the Epistle said anything about the devil, he always told believers that *they* were to do something about the devil. I'm going to give you four references to prove that believers themselves have authority over the devil."

Believers, Not God, Must Exercise Authority Over the Devil

Jesus began with Matthew 28:18 to show me that believers are the ones on the earth who have authority over the devil.

MATTHEW 28:18
18 And Jesus came and spake unto them, saying, ALL POWER is given unto me IN HEAVEN and IN EARTH.

Jesus said, "When I arose from the dead, I immediately said to My disciples, 'All power is given to Me both in Heaven and in earth'" (Matt. 28:18).

"Now this Greek word translated 'power' is also translated *authority* elsewhere in the New Testament. So you could read this verse, 'All *authority* is given unto Me both in Heaven and in earth.'

"Now," Jesus said to me, "if you stop reading at the end of verse 18, you'd say to Me, 'Why, Lord Jesus, *You* do have authority on earth against devils and demons. You *can* do something on the earth about the devil because this verse says You have authority on the earth.' But I immediately took My authority on the earth and delegated it to believers — to the Church. I immediately said, '*Go YE.* . . .'"

MATTHEW 28:19,20
19 GO YE therefore, and teach all nations, baptizing them in the name of the Father, and of the Son, and of the Holy Ghost:

20 Teaching them to observe all things whatsoever I have commanded you. . . .

MARK 16:15,17
15 And he [Jesus] said unto them, GO YE into all the world, and preach the gospel to every creature. . . .
17 And these signs shall follow them that believe; In my name shall they CAST OUT DEVILS. . . .

Jesus said to me, "The first sign that is to follow believers is that in My Name they shall cast out devils. Believers couldn't cast out devils if they didn't have authority over them. I gave the Church that authority. In fact, a better way to say that would be, 'In My Name believers shall exercise authority over devils.'"

So many times Christians ask the question, "Why does God permit the devil to do such terrible things on the earth? Why doesn't God do something about the devil?"

There are many things that happen in life that we wonder about. But, really, God is waiting for *us* to exercise our authority and do something about the devil. His Word stands behind the authority He's given us.

But so many times we just bow down and let the devil run over us, waiting for God to do something about the devil, when *we* just need to take our stand against him with the Word and put him on the run. *We* need to do something about the adverse circumstances in our own lives by taking authority over Satan and standing our ground against him with the Word, claiming what belongs to us.

Then Jesus gave me James 4:7 as the second scriptural witness that believers have the authority on the earth over the devil.

JAMES 4:7
7 Submit yourselves therefore to God. RESIST THE DEVIL, and he will FLEE from you.

James was writing to the Church — to believers — when he told them to resist the devil. Jesus said to me, "James didn't say, 'Get your pastor to resist the devil for you.' Or 'Get fellow Christians to resist the devil for you.' He said *you* are to resist the devil. You couldn't resist the devil if you didn't have authority over him."

I saw this truth. James didn't say, "Go get Jesus to rebuke the devil." Or "Go get God to resist the devil for you." He said, "*You* resist the devil and he will flee from *you*" (James 4:7). *You* is the understood subject of the sentence.

I looked up the word "flee" in the dictionary later and saw that one definition of "flee" is *to run away from as in terror.* Demons and evil spirits are not afraid of us, but they are afraid of Jesus, whom we represent. Therefore, because we are in Christ, they will flee from us when we take our authority over them in Jesus' Name.

Some have said, "I'll just write in a request and have a preacher pray for me. I'll write to that Hagin fellow. He's got faith. Maybe if he prays, the devil will leave me alone." No, each believer has to take authority over the devil for himself. We don't need to get someone else to do something about the devil for us.

Satan can't take any authority in your life unless you give him authority. Of course, if you don't exercise your authority over him or take a stand against him in the tests and trials he brings against you, then nothing will be done about the situation, because *you* are the one in authority on the earth through Jesus' Name.

Then Jesus gave me First Peter 5:8 as the third scriptural witness that believers have authority over the devil.

1 PETER 5:8,9
8   Be sober, be vigilant; because your adversary the devil, AS a roaring lion, walketh about, seeking whom he may devour:
9   WHOM RESIST STEDFAST IN THE FAITH. . . .

The Bible says, "your *adversary* the devil," so we know we do have an enemy. The word "adversary" means *an enemy* or *an opponent.* It means *one who is arrayed against us.*

But remember this adversary is a defeated foe; therefore, he can only walk about *as* a roaring lion. The Bible doesn't say he *is* a roaring lion. That isn't to say your adversary isn't real; he is very real. But he has been defeated by Jesus Christ.

Why is Satan walking about as a roaring lion? Because he is "seeking whom he may devour." He isn't trying to devour sinners; they already belong to him. He is seeking to devour Christians, and he will devour them if they let him.

What are you going to do about the devil? Are you going to stick your head in the sand like an ostrich and hope he'll go away? Are you going to let him devour you? No! A thousand times no! Stand your ground with the sword of the Spirit and the Name of Jesus in the victory Jesus won over him and put him to flight!

When Jesus appeared to me in this 1952 vision, it was the heyday of the healing revival, and some people in that day had gotten off in this area of the devil and evil spirits just as they have today. Because of this error, Jesus had to bring correction in the area of demonology in order to get the Body of Christ back on track and in the middle of the road again.

Our problem has been that we want someone else to take care of the devil for us. Notice that Peter wrote his epistle to Christians; he didn't write it to sinners. In other words, he was telling Christians to resist the devil. He wouldn't tell them to resist the devil if it was impossible for them to do it.

After Jesus pointed out these scriptures proving that believers have authority over the devil, He said to me, "If Peter had been like some believers today, he would have said, 'Word has come to us that God is using our beloved brother Paul in an unusual way. Paul is laying hands on cloths and handkerchiefs, and diseases and evil spirits are departing from people. Therefore, I suggest you write to Paul and get one of those handkerchiefs.' But Peter didn't tell believers that. Peter told believers, '*You* do something about the devil *yourself.*'"

Look again at First Peter 5:9: "*Whom* [YOU] *resist stedfast in the faith. . . .*" "You" is the understood subject of that sentence. "*You* resist the devil and he will flee from *you.*" "*You* resist the devil steadfast in *your* faith in God's Word." That comes right back to the fact that *you* are the only one who can resist the devil in your own life. You resist the devil by your faith in what God says in His Word.

Jesus said to me, "That's the reason if you hadn't done something about that devil, I *couldn't* have." I saw it then! As a member of the Body of Christ, *I* had the authority over that devil that jumped up between Jesus and me. And if I hadn't exercised my authority over that evil spirit, nothing would have been done about him.

That's why you need to put the devil on the run with the Word of God. However, if your mind hasn't been renewed with the Word, you are in trouble because you probably wouldn't know how to take your rightful position in Christ so you can take your stand against the enemy. And because of your lack of knowledge, you'd let the enemy defeat you because you wouldn't know who you are in Christ and the authority you really possess.

Jesus also gave me Ephesians 4:27 as the fourth scriptural witness that proves believers are the ones who have authority over the devil.

EPHESIANS 4:27
27 Neither give place to the devil.

Paul was writing to Christians, saying, "Don't give the devil any place in *you.*" If the Bible says not to give the devil any place, it stands to reason that you *can* give the devil place in your life. On the other hand, if you can keep from giving him a place in you, then you must have authority over him.

Actually, the devil can't take any place in you unless you give it to him by permission or ignorance or just by failing to exercise the authority that already belongs to you.

How are you to keep the devil from taking a place in you? You'll have to submit to God first. Only then will you be in a position to resist the devil. *Then* when you resist the devil, he *will* flee (James 4:7).

When Jesus gave me these scriptures, I saw how we had been missing it. The Church has tried to get *God* to rebuke the devil for us. Or we've tried to get *Jesus* to deal with the devil in our lives. We've tried to get *someone else* to exercise *our* authority over the devil for us, and it won't work because Jesus delegated that authority to each one of us.

Then Jesus said to me, "These are the four scriptural witnesses I told you I would give you instead of just two or three. I am the first, James is the second, Peter is the third, and Paul is the fourth.

"These scriptures establish the fact that the believer has authority on earth, for I have delegated My authority over the devil to the Body of Christ. *If believers don't do anything about the devil, then nothing will be done about him in their lives.*"

God has already done all He is ever going to do about the devil in our lives because God sent Jesus to dethrone Satan! So if we allow Satan to ride roughshod over us, it's because *we* have not taken our stand against him with the Word.

Other Scriptural 'Witnesses'

ROMANS 6:14
14 For sin shall not have dominion over you: for ye are not under the law, but under grace.

Paul writing to believers said, ". . . *sin shall not have dominion over you* . . ." (Rom. 6:14). Another translation says, "For sin shall not lord it over you."

If anything has dominion over you, that means it lords it over you. The Bible is saying that sin is not to lord it over you. Sin and

Satan are synonymous terms. It wouldn't be an injustice to read
that verse like this: "For *Satan* shall not have dominion over you."

Why shouldn't Satan have dominion over you? Because if you're
born again, you're not under the law of sin and death; you're under
grace (Rom. 6:14; 8:2). And Satan is not your lord, Jesus is (Col.
1:13). Therefore, sin and Satan can't dominate you, unless you
allow it.

John also wrote a letter to believers. He addressed this same
subject.

> **1 JOHN 4:1-4**
> **1   Beloved, BELIEVE NOT EVERY SPIRIT, but TRY THE
> SPIRITS WHETHER THEY ARE OF GOD: because many
> false prophets are gone out into the world.**
> **2   Hereby know ye the Spirit of God: Every spirit that con-
> fesseth that Jesus Christ is come in the flesh is of God:**
> **3   And every spirit that confesseth not that Jesus Christ is
> come in the flesh is not of God: and this is that spirit of
> antichrist, whereof ye have heard that it should come; and
> even now already is it in the world.**
> **4   Ye are of God, little children, and HAVE OVERCOME
> THEM: because greater is he that is in you, than he that is
> in the world.**

Verse 1 says, *"Beloved, believe not every spirit. . . ."* That verse
surely fits us today. Many folks today are believing every spirit and
every spiritual experience, vision, and manifestation. But, no, we
are to examine spiritual experiences in the light of God's Word and
*". . . every spirit that confesseth not that Jesus Christ is come in the
flesh is not of God . . ."* (1 John 4:3).

Don't just believe every spirit. John says, *". . . try the spirits
whether they are of God: because many false prophets are gone out
into the world"* (v. 1).

Notice that the Bible talks about false prophets in connection
with evil spirits. That's because prophets operate in the spirit
realm and they should be motivated by the Holy Spirit, but too
many times they are motivated by wrong spirits because they don't
discern the difference.

Verse 4 says, *"Ye are of God, little children. . . ."* That refers to
our position in Christ and our rightstanding with God. It also
refers to our authority over the devil because as children of God we
are seated with Christ in heavenly places (Eph. 1:20).

Then what does the rest of that scripture say? *"Ye are of God, little children, and have overcome THEM . . ."* (1 John 4:4). Who is "them" referring to? What have believers overcome? The word "them" is referring to the evil spirits that John mentioned in the previous verses. In other words, when Jesus overcame Satan, because we are *in* Christ, Jesus' triumph over Satan is our triumph! In Christ we are to enforce Satan's defeat in our lives by standing against the devil with God's Word.

The Bible doesn't say, "You are going to overcome evil spirits and demons in the sweet by and by." It said, "You *have* overcome them because *'. . . greater is he that is in you, than he that is in the world'"* (v.4).

The Bible says, *". . . Christ in you, the hope of glory"* (Col. 1:27). Jesus spoiled and put to naught principalities and powers and made a show of them openly by triumphing over them in the Cross (Col. 2:15). Therefore, because Jesus overcame the devil and every evil spirit, and you are in Christ, you have overcome them too. That's a past-tense fact!

When Jesus overcame Satan and his host of evil spirits and demons, God marked that down as though every believer did it because we are *in* Christ. Jesus was our Substitute. He defeated Satan for us, not for Himself.

Therefore, if you're born again, you have the Greater One — the Victor over Satan — living on the inside of you.

John G. Lake once said that he got so mad about these fellows who are always running around talking about demons all the time and magnifying the devil, that he almost wanted to cuss. They magnified the devil by always talking about him and what he's doing in their lives and on the earth and how great his power is.

Lake said some people talk like the devil is a great big fellow — a huge giant — and God is a little bitty fellow, maybe two feet tall. People who talk like that say, "You'd better watch out for the devil." These people are so devil-conscious, they very seldom talk about Jesus. But the more you magnify the devil, the greater he is going to become in your life.

Some believers seem to have more respect for the devil and his ability and believe in him more than they do in God!

Take your place in Christ. Stand your ground on God's Word. Be careful about keeping company with people who are always talking about the devil and who don't magnify the Word of God. And don't pick up on every spiritual "fad" that's going on. Stay with the Word. Preach *the Word*, not what the devil is doing. And stay in the middle of the road doctrinally and avoid extremes, including in this area of demons.

You don't have to go looking for the devil, but if he shows up, kick him out. You have authority over him in Jesus. Put him on the run with the Word. The devil knows that when you find out who you are in Christ and begin to take your rightful position of authority over him, he won't be able to keep you under his thumb anymore.

Chapter 7
The Wisdom of God

God has provided a glorious inheritance for every believer. That inheritance includes dominion over all the works of darkness, including sin, sickness, disease, and spiritual death.

But in order for us to take advantage of our authority in Jesus so we can successfully stand against the devil's strategies in every circumstance, the eyes of our spiritual understanding need to be enlightened.

The believer's inheritance in Christ is the wisdom of God, and it was hidden throughout previous ages until it was revealed through Jesus Christ. Grasping that truth and walking in the reality of God's inheritance for us as saints is the key to taking our place as the triumphant Church, reigning as kings in *this* life.

The riches of our inheritance are revealed more fully in the Book of Ephesians than in any other book of the Bible. In Ephesians chapter 1 and 3 are Spirit-inspired prayers, which apply to believers everywhere because they were given by the Holy Spirit to the Body of Christ.

EPHESIANS 1:16-23
16 [I] Cease not to give thanks for you, making mention of you in my prayers,
17 That the God of our Lord Jesus Christ, the Father of glory, MAY GIVE UNTO YOU THE SPIRIT OF WISDOM AND REVELATION IN THE KNOWLEDGE OF HIM [and of being *in* Him]:
18 The EYES OF YOUR UNDERSTANDING BEING ENLIGHTENED; that ye may know what is the hope of his calling, and what [are] **the riches of the glory of his inheritance in the saints,**
19 And what is the exceeding greatness of his power to usward who believe, according to the working of his mighty power,
20 Which he wrought in Christ, when he raised him from the dead, and set him at his own right hand in the heavenly places,
21 FAR ABOVE ALL PRINCIPALITY, and POWER, and MIGHT, and DOMINION, and EVERY NAME THAT IS NAMED, not only in this world, but also in that which is to come:

22 And HATH PUT ALL THINGS UNDER HIS FEET, and
gave him to be the head over all things to the church,
23 Which is his body, the fulness of him that filleth all in all.

EPHESIANS 3:14-21
14 For this cause I BOW MY KNEES UNTO THE FATHER
OF OUR LORD JESUS CHRIST,
15 Of whom the whole family in heaven and earth is named,
16 That he would grant you, according to the riches of his
glory, TO BE STRENGTHENED WITH MIGHT BY HIS
SPIRIT IN THE INNER MAN;
17 That Christ may dwell in your hearts by faith; that ye,
being rooted and grounded in love,
18 MAY BE ABLE TO COMPREHEND WITH ALL SAINTS
WHAT IS THE BREADTH, and LENGTH, and DEPTH, and
HEIGHT;
19 And to know the love of Christ, which passeth knowledge, that YE MIGHT BE FILLED WITH ALL THE FUL-
NESS OF GOD.
20 Now unto him that is able to do EXCEEDING ABUN-
DANTLY ABOVE ALL that we ask or think, ACCORDING
TO THE POWER THAT WORKETH IN US,
21 Unto him be glory in the church by Christ Jesus
throughout all ages, world without end. Amen.

If you are a believer, you can pray these prayers for yourself by
putting "I," "me," and "my" where Paul says "you" and "your."

In these prayers, the Holy Spirit wants to reveal to believers
"the spirit of *wisdom* and *revelation* in the *knowledge* of Jesus"
(Eph. 1:17). What is the wisdom and knowledge God wants to
reveal to the believer about Jesus Christ?

The Holy Spirit wants the eyes of our understanding opened to
understand Jesus' complete victory over Satan in the triumph of the
Cross. He wants us to understand what Jesus' seating on High
really means to the believer. The wisdom and knowledge the Holy
Spirit wants to reveal to us is the believer's joint-seating with Christ
as a benefit of our redemption. Joint-seating with Christ is a position of authority and triumph over Satan. God wants us to see what
we have as rights and privileges by being in Christ.

Revelations in Line With the Word

In the last church I pastored in 1949, I did a lot of extra praying
and seeking God. Every opportunity I'd have, I prayed these prayers
in Ephesians and Philippians over and over for myself. Scripture is

given by the Holy Spirit, so it never loses its inspiration and power.

The Holy Spirit, writing through Paul, wants you as a believer to pray for the eyes of your understanding to be enlightened. The word "enlightened" means *illuminated* or *flooded with light.* Another translation says to pray that the eyes of your *heart* will be flooded with light.

After praying these prayers for a number of months, one day I was praying at the altar and the Lord spoke to me and said, "I am going to take you on to revelations and visions." That came as a result of praying these prayers thousands of times for myself. Revelation from the Word of God began to come to me and kept on coming. I am talking about revelations in line with the Word.

Finally, I said to my wife, "What in the world have I been preaching!" I had been in the ministry fourteen years, but in six months of praying these prayers for myself, I received so much revelation from the Word of God that it seemed like I was a brand-new person.

That's what Ephesians 1 is talking about — insight into the knowledge of *Jesus* and understanding of the knowledge of His Word.

It was in the winter of '47 and '48 that understanding in line with God's Word by the Holy Spirit began to come to me. Then in the '50s the visions started coming. From 1950 through 1959, the Lord Jesus Himself appeared to me eight different times. Three out of the eight times He talked to me for an hour and a half and brought me further revelation concerning the Word of God.

One revelation the Spirit of God brought to me was the believer's authority in Christ over Satan. In fact, in the 1952 vision when Jesus talked to me for an hour and a half, I received understanding concerning demons and evil spirits. This understanding came after praying these prayers for the eyes of my understanding to be enlightened. Jesus Christ, the Head of the Church, gave me biblical truths in that vision so believers could be enlightened about Satan's wiles and strategies and not get off into error.

Believers have been ignorant of Satan's devices, so he has been able to take advantage of them. But the Spirit of God wants believers to get the wisdom and revelation of the knowledge of Jesus and His Word so the eyes of their understanding will be enlightened to know their authority *in Christ.*

God wants believers to know they are no longer subject to Satan because they have been delivered from his dominion and authority (Col. 1:13). God wants the Body of Christ to know that we aren't a defeated Church — we are a *triumphant* Church. We are to reign in life through Jesus Christ because we have a position of authority over the devil. When the eyes of our understanding are enlightened, we can stand in our place of authority as the triumphant Church upon the earth.

Jesus' Authority

When Jesus began His public ministry, He came into contact immediately with demonic forces and evil spirits. Demons and evil spirits had wrought evil unhindered down through the ages. Satan and his hosts had reigned as kings in the spirit realm and held men in the bondage of spiritual death. No one had authority to dethrone Satan and his hosts or to rule over them or to even challenge their authority or rulership upon the earth.

For example, in the Old Testament, we don't see people casting evil spirits out of anyone or taking authority over the devil because under the Old Covenant no one had any authority over the devil or evil spirits. But when Jesus came on the scene in His earth walk, it was different. Evil spirits *and* man instantly recognized Jesus' authority as He walked upon this earth.

> **MARK 1:21-24**
> **21 And they** [Jesus and His disciples] **went into Capernaum; and straightway on the sabbath day he entered into the synagogue, and taught.**
> **22 And they were astonished at his doctrine** [teaching]**: FOR HE TAUGHT THEM AS ONE THAT HAD AUTHORITY, and not as the scribes.**
> **23 And there was in their synagogue a man with an UNCLEAN SPIRIT; and he cried out,**
> **24 Saying, Let us alone; what have we to do with thee, thou Jesus of Nazareth? art thou come to destroy us? I KNOW THEE WHO THOU ART, the Holy One of God.**

Throughout the New Testament, we see that demons and evil spirits instantly recognized and knew Jesus. Here in Mark, the unclean spirit in this man not only knew who Jesus was, but he also recognized Jesus' *authority*.

Even the scribes, Pharisees, and the people in the synagogue recognized Jesus' authority. They marvelled and were astonished because Jesus taught with *authority*, not as the scribes taught. Both men and demons recognized *Jesus*' authority and bowed before it.

Demons feared Jesus because He proved Himself to be the Mas-

ter over the devil. Even in the first recorded encounter Jesus had
with the devil, Jesus proved Himself to be triumphant over Satan.

Jesus' Defeat of Satan

The first recorded encounter Jesus had with the devil occurred
after Jesus was baptized by John in the Jordan River. Right after
Jesus was baptized, the Scripture says, *"Then was Jesus led up OF
THE* [Holy] *SPIRIT into the wilderness to be tempted of the devil"*
(Matt. 4:1). Many times people have the idea that the Holy Spirit
only leads us into good, easy places, where the going is never hard.
But that's not always true. As we grow and mature in Christ, we
find out that sometimes it's in the hard places where we grow the
most in God.

Jesus was led by the Spirit of God into the wilderness to be
tempted by the devil. But, thank God, even in His temptation,
Jesus proved Himself to be Master over the devil. Jesus overcame
Satan in this encounter with the *Word of God.* Three times Jesus
overcame Satan with the words, "It is written" (Matt. 4:4,7,10;
Luke 4:4,8,12). Jesus didn't do "battle" with Satan; He simply stood
His ground and overcame Satan with *the Word* alone.

In Jesus' earth walk, from the day of His temptation when He
was *led* by the Spirit in the wilderness to be tempted of the devil,
until the day Jesus willingly *surrendered* Himself to the will of God
on the Cross — He defeated Satan in every encounter.

Jesus' complete and total victory over Satan is clearly shown
throughout the Word of God.

HEBREWS 2:14
**14 Forasmuch then as the children are partakers of flesh
and blood, he [Jesus] also himself likewise took part of the
same; that through death he might DESTROY HIM THAT
HAD THE POWER OF DEATH [spiritual death], that is, THE
DEVIL.**

HEBREWS 2:14 *(American Standard Version)*
**14 Since then the children are SHARERS in flesh and
blood, he also himself in like manner partook of the same;
that through death HE MIGHT BRING TO NOUGHT HIM
THAT HAD THE POWER OF DEATH, that is, the devil.**

The *King James Version* of the Bible says that Jesus "destroyed"
Satan who had the power of death — spiritual death or separation

from God. That doesn't mean Jesus destroyed Satan in the sense that Satan ceased to exist. The meaning is a little clearer in the *American Standard Version*. It says Jesus put Satan "to nought." In other words, Jesus conquered Satan and stripped him of his power and authority.

When Hebrews 2:14 says Jesus destroyed Satan who had the power of *death*, the Bible is not talking about physical death. Physical death will eventually be put underfoot (1 Cor. 15:54), but until it is, people still die physically.

There are three kinds of death referred to in the Bible. First, *spiritual death* (John 5:24; Eph. 2:1) or separation from God. Second, the Bible talks about *physical death* (Phil. 1:20,21). Third, the Bible refers to the *second death* which is eternal separation from God and being eternally cast into the lake which burns with fire and brimstone (Rev. 20:13-15).

Hebrews 2:14 is talking about *spiritual death*. It's saying that Jesus destroyed the authority of Satan who had power over *spiritual death* or *eternal separation* from God. Those who accept Jesus Christ as their Lord and Savior never have to fear "the lord of death" and being eternally separated from God.

Looking at Hebrews 2:14 in other translations sheds more light on Jesus' triumph over Satan. For example, *Moffatt's* translation says, ". . . by dying HE MIGHT CRUSH HIM WHO WIELDS THE POWER OF DEATH . . . the devil. . . ."

Conybeare's translation says that Jesus destroyed the authority of the "lord of death" and allowed us to be *partakers* of Jesus' victory over him. The *American Standard Version* says we are *sharers* in Jesus' victory over the devil.

We are not only *partakers*, but we are *sharers* in Jesus' victory over Satan. That means we are sharers in the resurrection power of God. And now God is asking us to share with Him in giving the world the message of Jesus' victory so those in bondage to Satan can be delivered from his captivity.

Another passage in the Book of Revelation not only shows us Jesus' complete defeat of Satan, the lord of death, but it shows us that Jesus took the keys of death and hell from the devil. *Death* and *hell* are no longer under Satan's jurisdiction.

REVELATION 1:17,18 *(American Standard Version)*
17 And when I saw him, I fell at his feet as one dead. And he laid his right hand upon me, saying, Fear not; I am the first and the last,

18 And the Living One; and I was dead, and behold, I am alive for evermore, and I HAVE THE KEYS OF DEATH [spiritual death] **and of HADES** [Hell].

When Jesus conquered Satan in His death, burial, and resurrection, He stripped from Satan all his authority over spiritual death. Jesus now has ". . . *the keys of hell and of* [spiritual] *death"* (Rev. 1:18).

In other words, everyone who accepts Jesus Christ as his Lord and Savior is redeemed from the dominion of Satan who had the power of spiritual death. Believers are redeemed from spiritual death itself and aren't separated from God when they die. They will forever be with God (2 Cor. 5:6,8).

We can also see the victory of Jesus over Satan in Colossians 2:15.

COLOSSIANS 2:15
15 And having spoiled principalities and powers, he made a shew of them openly, TRIUMPHING OVER THEM in it [the Cross].

The phrase "having spoiled principalities and power" is a little blind to us. Of course, the principalities and powers that Jesus "spoiled" refer to satanic beings. Let's look at some other translations of Colossians 2:15 to get a better understanding of what Jesus did when He spoiled these principalities and powers.

COLOSSIANS 2:15 *(Conybeare)*
15 . . . He [Jesus] **DISARMED the Principalities and the Powers** [which fought against Him]. . . .

COLOSSIANS 2:15 *(Phillips)*
15 . . . he [Jesus] **EXPOSED THEM, SHATTERED, EMPTY and DEFEATED, in his final glorious triumphant act!**

Colossians 2:15 tells us that Satan and his evil hosts were spoiled, disarmed, stripped of their power, exposed, shattered, emptied and defeated by our Lord Jesus Christ. And Jesus made an open example of their complete defeat. This verse also shows us Satan's *eternal defeat.*

When we understand how the word "spoiled" was used in biblical times, it gives us a clearer picture of Jesus' complete victory over the powers of darkness when He was raised from the dead. In Bible days, when one king fought against another king and defeated him in battle, it was said that the defeated king was "spoiled." The victor would parade the captured king and other important prisoners through the town as a trophy of triumph. The victors would make a show of the enemy's defeat, openly displaying their complete downfall publicly before everyone.

The Bible says Jesus did that to Satan. Jesus "spoiled" Satan, displaying His triumph and Satan's defeat before three worlds: Heaven, earth, and hell (Phil. 2:9,10). He disarmed and stripped Satan of his authority and took the keys of death and hell from him (Rev. 1:18), thereby stripping from Satan his authority over spiritual death — eternal separation from God.

Another translation of Colossians 2:15 reads, "Having put to nought principalities and powers, He made a show of them openly triumphing over them in the Cross."

To "put to nought" means to *reduce to nothing*! Jesus reduced principalities and powers to nothing. He completely stripped them of their authority. First John 3:8 says, ". . . *For this purpose the Son of God was manifested, that he might DESTROY* [put to nought and reduce to nothing] *the works of the devil*." The reason Jesus came to this earth was to put to nought the works of the devil and reduce him to nothing!

Dethroned Powers

The Body of Christ needs the eyes of their understanding enlightened to understand Jesus' complete defeat of Satan. This is *the wisdom of God* that God wants each believer to understand.

> **1 CORINTHIANS 2:6,7**
> **6 Howbeit we speak WISDOM among them that are PER-FECT** [mature]: **yet not the wisdom of this world, nor of THE PRINCES OF THIS WORLD, that come to nought:**
> **7 But we speak THE WISDOM OF GOD. . . .**

Don't let the word "perfect" in verse 6 throw you. Another word for "perfect" is *full grown* or *mature*. No one is perfect in the flesh, but God does expect us to mature and grow up spiritually.

> **1 CORINTHIANS 2:6,7** *(Moffatt)*
> **6 We do discuss 'wisdom' with those who are MATURE; only it is not the wisdom of this world or of the DETHRONED POWERS who rule this world,**
> **7 It is the mysterious WISDOM OF GOD that we discuss, that hidden wisdom which God decreed from all eternity for our glory.**

Verse 6 tells us that Satan has been *dethroned*. The wisdom of the mature or full-grown Christian whose understanding has been enlightened by the Holy Spirit is that Satan has already been dethroned and the believer has victory over him in Christ. Let that sink in!

Satan and all of his demon forces are *dethroned*. "Dethroned" is defined as *to remove from a throne or place of prominence: deposed.* The word "deposed" means *to remove from office, position, or authority, especially high office.*

Satan has been dethroned by Jesus Christ at the Cross of Calvary and in His resurrection. Satan has been removed from his *throne*, his place of *prominence*, his place of *authority* — and from his *high office*. Jesus already did that for every believer.

Satan has no authority over the believer, unless the believer gives him access or authority through lack of knowledge of God's Word, disobedience, or failure to exercise his rights in Christ.

The fact that Satan has been dethroned and stripped of his authority is the wisdom the Holy Spirit is trying to get across to the Body of Christ — the triumphant Church — in these Spirit-inspired prayers in the Book of Ephesians.

The wisdom of God is that believers only need to stand in Jesus' victory over the devil because they are *in* Christ. Jesus' victory over the devil is their victory. That's why believers don't need to make war on an enemy that is already defeated.

The *wisdom of God — Bible* wisdom — is that Satan is a defeated foe. But that's *not* the wisdom of the world. Satan, the god of this world, doesn't want people to know that.

The wisdom of the god of this world is that believers still have to struggle and war against the hosts of darkness in an effort to try to defeat and overcome them.

Satan wants believers to spend their time trying to fight a "war" that has already been fought and won by Jesus because the devil knows that is a waste of their time.

Of course Satan still wields power over unsaved people in the world because they don't know he's been dethroned. Satan's "wisdom" is that *he* still rules and reigns in the affairs of men.

Satan has even blinded the minds of some Christians so *they* believe that too. That's why believers need to get the eyes of their understanding enlightened — to see the truth and power of the finished work of the Cross.

The Seating and Reigning of Christ

After Jesus was raised from the dead, the Bible says God *highly* exalted Him to a position of honor at the right hand of God the Father and gave Him a Name which is above every name.

PHILIPPIANS 2:9-11
9 Wherefore GOD also HATH HIGHLY EXALTED HIM [Jesus], and given him a name which is ABOVE every name:
10 That at the name of Jesus every knee should bow, of THINGS [beings] IN Heaven, and THINGS [beings] IN EARTH, and THINGS [beings] UNDER THE EARTH;
11 And that EVERY TONGUE should confess that Jesus Christ is Lord, to the glory of God the Father.

EPHESIANS 1:19-22
19 And what is the exceeding greatness of his power. . . .
20 Which he wrought in Christ, when he raised him from the dead, and SET HIM AT HIS OWN RIGHT HAND IN THE HEAVENLY PLACES,
21 FAR ABOVE ALL PRINCIPALITY, and POWER, and MIGHT, and DOMINION, and EVERY NAME THAT IS NAMED, not only in this world, but also in that which is to come.
22 And hath put all things under his feet, and gave him to be THE HEAD OVER ALL THINGS to the church.

God not only gave Jesus a Name which is above *every* name, but at the Name of Jesus every being in all three worlds — Heaven, earth, and hell — must bow and confess Jesus' Lordship and dominion. God also seated Jesus in the highest position in the universe, at His own right hand, and made Him head over all things (v.22).

These verses don't say, "God raised Jesus from the dead and set Him *above* all principality, power, might, and dominion." They say that God set Jesus "*far above*" all principality, power, might, dominion, and every name that is named.

Your Position in Christ

How does Jesus' seating in the highest position in the universe affect you, the believer? What is your position because you're in Christ?

EPHESIANS 2:1,2,4-6
1 And you hath he quickened [made alive], who were dead [spiritually dead] in trespasses and sins;
2 Wherein in time past ye walked according to the course

**of this world, according to the prince of the power of the air
[the dethroned powers], the spirit that now worketh in the
children of disobedience: ...
4 But God, who is rich in mercy, for his great love wherewith he loved us,
5 Even when we were dead in sins, HATH QUICKENED
US TOGETHER WITH CHRIST, (by grace ye are saved;)
6 And HATH RAISED US UP TOGETHER, and MADE US
SIT TOGETHER IN HEAVENLY PLACES IN CHRIST
JESUS.**

According to Ephesians 2:6, believers are seated with Christ in
heavenly places. Joint-seating with Christ is *"far above"* all principalities and powers of darkness. Evil spirits can't influence the
believer who has joint-seating with Christ *far above* all principality
and power!

Our seating and reigning with Christ in heavenly places is a
position of authority, honor, and triumph — not failure, depression,
and defeat.

As a believer, your seating with Christ is part of your inheritance *now*. This is where you are *already* seated because when
Jesus was seated in triumph, you were seated with Him.

The word "hath" in verse 6 is past tense: God has already raised
you up together and made you sit in heavenly places in Christ Jesus
in a position of honor and triumph. You rule and reign with Christ
in this life *now* — if you'll just exercise your rightful authority.

Therefore, your position in Christ *far above* principalities and
powers has already been accomplished. But you need to exercise
the authority that belongs to you in that position of reigning with
Christ over principalities and powers before it will profit you.

Our *position* as believers is one of joint-seating with Christ in
heavenly places. That may not always be our *circumstance*, but
that is our *position*.

If you want to rise above your *circumstances,* take advantage of
your *position* in Christ.

Look at this passage in *Weymouth's* translation.

EPHESIANS 2:4-6 *(Weymouth)*
**4 But God, being rich in mercy, because of the intense
love which He bestowed on us,
5 Caused us, dead though we were through our offences,
TO LIVE WITH CHRIST—it is by grace that you have been
saved—
6 RAISED US WITH HIM from the dead, and**

ENTHRONED US WITH HIM IN THE HEAVENLY REALMS as being IN CHRIST JESUS.

God enthroned us with Jesus in the heavenly realms. Does that sound like a Church that's defeated and is still having to do battle to gain mastery over Satan? No, God designed the Church of the Lord Jesus Christ to be triumphant because we are *sharers* and *partakers* of Christ's victory over Satan.

Because the believer is in Christ, when Christ sat down, the believer sat down with Him *far above* principalities and powers. The Church, the Body of Christ, is *in Christ*. The body is connected to the head. Jesus is the Head of His Body — the Church.

If Jesus the Head triumphed over the devil, is the Body of Christ to be any less triumphant since we are *in* Christ? Of course not! It is our *legal right* to enjoy joint-seating with Christ in heavenly places in a position of authority and triumph *far above* all principalities and powers. If you will take advantage of your joint-seating with Christ, you will begin to triumph in life!

Believers don't have to *try* to be seated far above principalities and powers with Christ. They don't have to *pray through* to be seated with Christ in heavenly places. They don't have to *struggle through* to attain that position, or *fight through* demons to be seated in a place of victory with Christ.

The believer's position and seating in Christ is a *fact*. It has already happened. That position was attained *for us* through our Lord Jesus Christ. Now all we have to do is enjoy the rights and privileges that already belong to us as joint-heirs with Christ.

In these Spirit-anointed prayers, the Holy Spirit is endeavoring to get across to the Body of Christ that their joint-seating with Christ far above the realms of darkness is their legal inheritance.

But believers won't be able to take advantage of what rightfully belongs to them in their inheritance in Christ unless the eyes of their understanding are enlightened to see what they really possess in this life. We can't possess what we don't know belongs to us.

When believers get the revelation of their position in Christ, what a difference it will make in their lives. They will no longer be the defeated Church. They will take their place as *the triumphant Church*, which was God's design from the foundation of the world.

The unredeemed thinking of so many believers is that they are helpless against the devil and are always subject to defeat and failure: "The devil is after me all the time." "The devil is going to get me!" "We don't have much in this life, but when we all get to Heaven, what a glorious future awaits us."

Yes, believers have a glorious *future* to look forward to because they will forever be with the Lord. But the Holy Spirit wants believers to know the glorious *present* they possess right now because of their position in Christ! Believers need to take advantage of what belongs to them in Christ.

Because of our position in Christ, God is the strength of our life. The psalmist asks the question, "Of whom shall I be afraid?" (Ps. 27:1). We don't have to be afraid of anything, including Satan, demons, or evil spirits because of Jesus' victory at the Cross.

ROMANS 8:37-39
37 Nay, in all these things WE ARE MORE THAN CON-QUERORS THROUGH HIM THAT LOVED US.
38 For I am persuaded, that neither death, nor life, nor ANGELS, nor PRINCIPALITIES, nor POWERS, nor things present, nor things to come,
39 Nor height, nor depth, NOR ANY OTHER CREATURE [Satan or evil spirits]**, shall be able to separate us from the love of God, which is in Christ Jesus our Lord.**

The Body of Christ — the triumphant Church — is more than a conqueror over all the power of the enemy because we're *in* Christ (Luke 10:19; Rom. 8:37). Perhaps believers have sung too much the song, "Oh, Lord, just keep me near the Cross."

No, you don't want to stay at the Cross. You want to come on up to the throne and sit in your rightful position as a joint-heir with Christ in heavenly places (Eph. 2:6; Gal. 4:7; Rom. 8:17). You want to take your place of authority *far above* principalities and powers so you can rule and reign in life with Christ.

Come *by* the way of the Cross, but don't stay there. Come on to Pentecost and get filled with the Holy Spirit. But don't stop there either. Come on to the throne where you are seated *in* Christ and take your authority in Christ. It's a position of authority, not because of who you are, but because of who *He* is.

Is the Body of Christ seated in heavenly places far above principalities and dominions in the power of their *own* strength? No! We are seated in heavenly places in the power of *God's* might (Eph. 1:20-22; 6:10).

Look at Ephesians 1:22 in the *American Standard Version.* I want you to see a truth in this verse.

EPHESIANS 1:22 *(American Standard Version)*
22 And he put ALL THINGS IN SUBJECTION UNDER HIS
[Jesus'] **FEET, and gave him to be head over all things to the**
church.

This scripture is saying that *all* things — whether it's Satan, principalities, powers, thrones, or dominions — they are all under subjection to the Lord Jesus Christ. And because we are in Christ, evil spirits are subject to us in Jesus' Name.

How many things did God put under Jesus' feet? *All* things! That includes Satan, demons, evil spirits, sin, sickness, poverty, and disease. We are Christ's body on the earth, so that means all things have been put under our feet too.

Is God *going* to put *all things* under Jesus' feet and therefore under our feet? No, that's *future* tense. God *"hath"* put all things under his feet" (1 Cor. 15:27; Eph. 1:22). That's *past* tense. Satan is already under Jesus' feet, so he's under our feet, too, because we're in Christ.

If Satan is under our feet that means he has no authority over us — we have authority *over* him. Is that something the believer has to try to attain to? No, it's an accomplished fact because of the believer's joint-seating with Christ.

If believers really understood what that means, Satan would never be able to lord it over them again. And if this truth ever dawns on the Church, they will take their rightful place in Christ as the triumphant Church, reigning as kings in life.

You see, our joint-seating and ruling with Christ is the climax of the redemptive work of Christ. After the resurrection, Jesus was exalted to the highest seat in the universe. He was given *all* dominion, *all* authority, and *all* power. Not only that, but all dominion, authority, and power was put beneath Jesus' feet, which means it's under our feet since we're the Body of Christ.

That's why Satan can't rule over *you* unless you allow him to through ignorance of your rights and privileges in Christ or you open the door to him. Too many times, believers just open the door and invite Satan to come in.

Another scripture shows us the authority we have because Satan is under our feet.

LUKE 10:19
19 Behold, I give unto you power [authority] **TO TREAD ON**
SERPENTS and SCORPIONS, and over ALL THE POWER
OF THE ENEMY: and nothing shall by any means hurt you.

In Luke 10:19, Jesus used the terms "scorpions" and "serpents" figuratively as a type of the enemy's power. He was talking about Satan and all his host of demons and evil spirits. We know this because Jesus said, "I give you power or authority over all the power of the *enemy*."

Jesus was saying that no power of the enemy — no principality, power, ruler of darkness, nor spiritual wickedness in high places — can hurt us as we take our stand of authority in Christ. We can *tread* upon Satan and his hosts because he's under our feet.

Looking at Luke 10:19, there are two different Greek words translated as "power." The first word for "power" is *exousia* or *authority*. The second word for "power" is *dunamis* which means *strength* or *ability*.

Actually a better translation of this verse would be "I give you *authority* over all the power of the enemy." Translated as "power," people think, "That means *I* have power." Then they realize, "But I don't *feel* any power."

You don't have any *power* in *yourself*, but you do have *authority* in *Christ*. That's different. In themselves believers don't have any *power* over the devil, but they do have *authority* over the devil.

Our authority in Christ is like a policeman's authority when he stands out in the street to direct traffic. He doesn't have any *power* or *personal strength* to hold back those cars; he doesn't have that kind of *ability*. But he does have that kind of *authority*, and people recognize that authority and honor it.

So Jesus was actually saying in Luke 10:19, "I give you authority to tread upon devils, demons, evil spirits and over all the power of the enemy. And because of the authority in My Name, none of the power of the enemy can harm you."

God Himself is the force and power behind your authority in Christ. The believer who is fully conscious of the divine power behind him and of his authority in Christ can face the enemy without fear or hesitancy.

The Wisdom of Being in Christ

Now go back and read First Corinthians 2:6, and you will understand the wisdom of God more clearly.

1 CORINTHIANS 2:6,7 *(Moffatt)*
6   We do discuss 'wisdom' WITH THOSE WHO ARE MATURE; only it is NOT the wisdom of this world or of the

**DETHRONED POWERS who rule this world,
7 It is the mysterious WISDOM OF GOD that we discuss,
that hidden wisdom which God decreed from all eternity
for our glory.**

What is the wisdom of God that those who are spiritually mature
in the Word will see and understand? It is knowledge of the inheritance that God has already prepared for them in Christ; it is the wisdom of knowing who they are *in* Christ. The wisdom of God is that
believers only need to stand against demons in the finished work of
the Cross — in the victory that Jesus Christ already won *for* them.

If believers would begin to stand in their position of authority in
Christ against a foe that has already been *defeated* and *dethroned*,
it would solve so many of their problems.

Many well-meaning believers have fallen into the error of thinking *they* have to do something to *overcome* the devil. They seem to
think that somehow they have to "fight" the devil and conquer him.

According to First Corinthians 2:6, one reason believers have
fallen into this error is that they aren't mature in the Word: "We
speak the wisdom of God to those who are *mature.*"

People who are wrestling against the devil in their own
strength, always trying to defeat a "dethroned power," are not yet
mature or *full grown* in the Word. I didn't say that — the Bible said
that: ". . . *we speak wisdom among them THAT ARE PERFECT*
[mature or full grown]: *yet not the wisdom of this world. . . . But we
speak THE WISDOM OF GOD . . .*" (1 Cor. 2:6,7).

The wisdom of God is the wisdom of His Word. Your mind will
have to be renewed to the wisdom of God — the wisdom of *God's
Word* — to see what Jesus has already wrought for you in your
redemption. That's what will make you mature in your knowledge
of being in Christ.

When believers have the eyes of their understanding enlightened, they will understand exactly how complete the plan of
redemption really is. Those who are still waging war on the devil
haven't had the eyes of their understanding enlightened to see the
wisdom of God. But when you are mature in the Word and have the
wisdom of God — *Bible* wisdom — you know Satan and his hosts
are already conquered, defeated, dethroned, and deprived of their
power and that *you* are the triumphant one in Christ.

But you will have to stand your ground with the Word of God
against Satan because his wiles are deceptive, and he will try to

blind your eyes to make you think he has power and authority over *you*. He will always try to get you out of the realm of faith in God's Word by making you doubt the Word, doubt God, and doubt what God has told you. That's why the fight against him is in the arena of faith — faith in God and faith in God's Word — not in trying to defeat an enemy who is already defeated.

One reason many believers are having so much trouble with the devil is that they are always trying to do something *themselves* about the devil, instead of *acting on* what the Word says *Jesus* already did about the devil. That means they aren't doers of the Word. They say, "Let's declare war on the devil!" and they try to carry out some kind of combat against him.

But when you understand that Satan is dethroned, you know war has already been declared on the devil, and the victory has been won by the Lord Jesus Christ. Jesus Christ arose the Victor! So just take your position of joint-seating with Christ in His victory over the devil.

If Satan and his cohorts have been dethroned, then why are the hosts of darkness ruling over so many *believers*? Either believers don't *know* their authority in Christ, or they aren't *exercising* their authority in Christ.

Satan will keep on ruling people in the world who aren't saved, of course, because they don't know any better. But if believers will preach the gospel to unsaved folks, they'll get saved and come out from under Satan's dominion.

The Church is to preach the good news to every creature and tell them that they don't have to be dominated by the devil anymore. That's how we are to "wage war" on the devil! When people get ahold of the good news in Christ and are born again, Satan won't be able to rule over them anymore. That is how believers are to put Satan's kingdom to nought and reduce it to nothing.

The Authority in the Name of Jesus

The key to our glorious inheritance and our authority over the powers of darkness is the Name of Jesus. Believers have authority over the devil in the Name of Jesus, not in themselves. But I think even Full Gospel folks have almost thought the Name of Jesus is just to be used like a magic charm one wears to ward off evil forces or something. Believers haven't really understood what they possess in their inheritance because of that Name.

All the power and authority Jesus has is invested in His Name. Believers have been authorized to use His Name (John 14:13,14).

We know we've been authorized to use the Name of Jesus in prayer because Jesus said, *". . . Whatsoever ye shall ask the Father IN MY NAME, He will give it you"* (John 16:23).

Praying according to the Word of God is one way believers take their place of authority in Christ on the earth.

But Jesus also said to the believer, *". . . In my name shall they* [believers] *cast out devils . . ."* (Mark 16:17). Therefore, we have authority over the devil in the Name of Jesus.

PHILIPPIANS 2:9,10
9 Wherefore God also hath highly exalted him, and GIVEN HIM A NAME which IS ABOVE EVERY NAME:
10 That at THE NAME OF JESUS every knee should bow, of things [beings] **in heaven, and things** [beings] **in EARTH, and things** [beings] **UNDER THE EARTH.**

The Name of Jesus has authority in three realms: Heaven, earth, and hell. The devil recognizes the authority of Jesus' Name; he knows he has to bow to that Name. And the devil also recognizes the authority *you* have *in* Christ because of that Name. But *you* must recognize your authority and exercise it and take a stand against the devil in Jesus' Name.

Blessed With All Spiritual Blessings in Christ

This authority over the devil is the true possession of every child of God. It belongs to every one of us and it is one of the spiritual blessings of our inheritance as saints in Christ.

EPHESIANS 1:3
3 Blessed be the God and Father of our Lord Jesus Christ, who hath blessed us with ALL SPIRITUAL BLESSINGS in heavenly places in Christ.

In Jesus' redemption, everything Jesus wrought — everything He bought and secured in His victory over Satan — He did for the Body of Christ — you. Jesus' triumph and victory belongs to every single believer.

Because we are blessed with *all* spiritual blessings, that would certainly include triumph and authority over Satan, otherwise it wouldn't be *all* spiritual blessings.

The *American Standard Version* says, "Blessed be the God and Father of our Lord Jesus Christ, who hath blessed us with *every* spiritual blessing in the heavenly places in Christ." That includes your victory in Christ over Satan and all his evil hosts.

In other words, in Christ, *every single* spiritual blessing belongs to you *now.* You don't have to work or struggle or fight demons to attain to *all* spiritual blessings; they are already yours as you appropriate them by faith in the Word and exercise what rightfully belongs to you. But all spiritual blessings are only ours because we are *in Him.*

You hear some people say, "But So-and-so seems to get more blessings than I do." We look at certain people and think they are *especially* blessed of God. But you won't find that in Scripture anywhere; God has no favorites.

People who enjoy the blessings of God, including their rightful authority over the devil, just know how to take advantage of what belongs to them to a greater degree than those who don't appropriate the blessings of God. If you don't know about your inheritance and authority in Christ, you will not be able to partake of what is rightfully yours.

Every one of us in the Body of Christ is blessed with *all* or *every* spiritual blessing in Christ, so no one has a corner on the authority we possess over the devil in Jesus' Name. The least member in the Body of Christ can be fearless in the face of demons, devils, and evil spirits because of who he is in Christ. No one is blessed with any more spiritual blessings than anyone else in the Body of Christ.

It's to be regretted that every member of the Body of Christ doesn't take advantage of what belongs to him, because his authority over the devil belongs to him whether he knows about it or not. But a person can't take advantage of something he doesn't *know* about or *exercise.*

Only The Truth Acted Upon Sets You Free

The eyes of your understanding need to be enlightened so you can *know* and *exercise* your authority in Christ before it will benefit you. In other words, you can *know* what is yours, but not *act* upon it. You can *know* what the Word says, but not be a *doer* of the Word.

Any blessing, right, privilege, or authority can belong to you, but if you don't know about it, you won't act on it. Or if you don't act on what you *know* and *exercise* and *appropriate* what has been given to you, it won't benefit you. It won't become a reality to you even though it's your legal possession.

That's why you need to know what belongs to you in Christ. But just knowledge of what belongs to you isn't enough. *It's knowledge acted upon that brings results.*

The devil doesn't want the people of God to find out the authority that actually belongs to them in Christ. This is one way Satan tries to defeat the child of God. He knows when the child of God finds out his legal, lawful authority in Christ, he will enjoy victory over him.

That's why Satan tries to obscure this knowledge and blind people's eyes and understanding and keep this vital knowledge from them. But when the child of God knows the truth and acts on that knowledge, he can no longer be dominated by the devil.

JOHN 8:32
32 And ye shall know the truth [the Word]**, and THE TRUTH** [the Word] **SHALL MAKE YOU FREE.**

You have to *know* the truth before the truth can make you free. That's what this verse is saying. Then once you know the truth of God's Word about who you are in Christ, it's *acting* on the truth you know that makes you free.

That's so important, I'm going to say it a little differently so you can grasp the meaning:

You must *know* the Word before the Word can make you free.
Then you have to *act on* the Word you *know*.
The Word you *know* that you *act on* makes you *free*.

When you act on the Word you know, you will enjoy victory over satanic forces in every circumstance of life.

2 CORINTHIANS 2:14
14 Now thanks be unto God, which ALWAYS CAUSETH US TO TRIUMPH in Christ, and maketh manifest the savour of his knowledge by us in every place.

God promised us the victory in every circumstance of life, so tests and trials don't have to overcome you. The Bible didn't say, "Thanks be to God, who causes you to triumph once in a while over Satan and circumstances." Because Jesus triumphed over all of those satanic forces — His triumph is your triumph because you are in Him.

2 CORINTHIANS 2:14 *(Conybeare)*
14 But thanks be to God who leads me on from place to place in the train of His triumph, TO CELEBRATE HIS VIC-TORY OVER THE ENEMIES OF CHRIST [demons].

In the face of these facts, what should our attitude be toward the devil and his works? One of cowering in fear at the devil? No! We are more than conquerors through Him who loved us (Rom. 8:37).

As the Body of Christ, we are taking Jesus' place on the earth. Jesus is the Head and we are His Body. We are acting for Jesus on this earth in the affairs of life. Jesus is the Destroyer of the adversary's authority, and we are to enforce that defeat on this earth.

Satan Shall Not Have Dominion Over Believers

We are talking about the riches of our inheritance in Christ. The Bible says we have been translated out of the kingdom of darkness into the Kingdom of God's dear Son (Col. 1:13). Therefore, our inheritance includes the fact that the works of darkness have no legal authority or dominion over us.

Paul wrote to the believers at Rome, saying, *"For sin shall not have dominion over you: for ye are not under the law, but under grace"* (Rom. 6:14). In a sense, sin and Satan are synonymous terms. Therefore, we could read this verse, *"Satan shall not have dominion over you."*

Another translation reads, "Sin shall not lord it over you." You could read it: "Satan shall not lord it over you."

Why can't Satan lord it over believers? Because he's not our lord, and he's been put under our feet! Jesus is our Lord and the Head of the Church, not Satan.

Jesus is the only One who is to have dominion over us! He is the One who rules us, not only corporately as the Body of Christ, but individually as well.

For example, if symptoms of distress and deficiency of any kind from the enemy try to attack my body or mind, I just say, "Oh, no you don't, Satan. You can't put that on me. Jesus has dominion over me. Jesus is My Healer and My Deliverer. He is not the destroyer.

"Jesus is the Life-Giver, and He is my Lord. Satan, you are not my lord, and you can't triumph over me. I refuse to accept or permit anything that belongs to you. You can't bring me depression, oppression, sickness, or disease. I refuse to permit it in Jesus' Name."

When I take my stand against Satan in Jesus' Name using my rightful authority, the enemy can't bring me any of his evil works. When I am a doer of the Word, Satan *can't,* he *doesn't,* and he *won't* be able to defeat me because Jesus' Lordship over me is declared in the Word, and I stand upon my rights and privileges in Christ. Jesus' dominion over me is real, and I submit only to Him as my Lord.

That is acting on the truth, and it will make you free.

The Shadow of the Valley of Death

Once we understand that we have been delivered out of Satan's control and we are no longer under the dominion of Satan or spiritual death, we can understand more clearly what Psalm 23 is saying to us.

PSALM 23:1,4-6
1   The Lord is my shepherd; I shall not want. . . .
4   Yea, though I walk through THE VALLEY OF THE SHADOW OF DEATH, I will fear no evil: for thou art with me; thy rod and thy staff they comfort me.
5   THOU PREPAREST A TABLE BEFORE ME IN THE PRESENCE OF MINE ENEMIES: thou anointest my head with oil; my cup runneth over.
6   Surely GOODNESS and MERCY shall follow me all the days of my life: and I will dwell in the house of the Lord for ever.

There is a truth in Psalm 23 that the Body of Christ has failed to receive and appropriate for their lives. You understand, of course, that many of the psalms are prophetic or Messianic. But we are living in Psalm 23 right *now.*

Psalm 23 says, *"Yea, though I walk through the valley of the shadow of death, I will fear no evil . . ."* (v. 4). This Psalm is quoted all the time at funerals, but actually this is referring to Satan's domain here on earth, and it is referring to spiritual death, not physical death.

You and I are walking through *the valley of the shadow of death* in this life because Satan is the god of this world. Spiritual death and its effects are on every side. Sin, sickness, disease, poverty, and everything else that Satan brings surround us in this life.

But Jesus declared that we are *in* the world, but not *of* the world (John 17:16,18). That correlates with a valuable truth we find in Psalm 23:5: *"Thou preparest a table before me in the presence of mine enemies. . . ."*

Who are our enemies? The devil himself is certainly our enemy; the Bible calls him our adversary (1 Peter 5:8). Evil spirits, demons, sickness, disease, and poverty are all our enemies. Anything that would bind or hinder us is our enemy.

The Table of Provision

In Psalm 23 God is telling us that right in the midst of Satan's domain where the devil is ruling over those in darkness as the god of this world and where the effects of spiritual death are all around us — God prepares a table for us in the very presence of those enemies!

Yes, demons, devils, and evil spirits are here and we sometimes feel their presence and their effect. But even so, God prepares a table for us right in the midst of them!

Why does God prepare a table for us in the presence of our enemies? Why don't we just *get rid* of our enemies? We can't. As I've said, they have a right to be here, and they are going to stay here until Adam's lease on this earth runs out. That's why it is so important for believers to stand in their victory and partake of the table of the Lord's provision, because those evil spirits will be here to try to hinder us, tempt us, and keep us from receiving God's best in life.

But right in the presence of our enemies — demons and evil spirits — God has prepared a table of abundant provision — the riches of the glory of His inheritance in the saints — for every believer in the Body of Christ!

The reason many Christians are defeated in life is that even though they are seated with Christ in heavenly places at the table of the Lord's provision, they aren't *appropriating* what belongs to them at that table. All the *riches* of being *in* Christ are included at the table of the Lord's provision.

Many believers are not even looking at the provisions God has made for them in the Word. Instead of looking at their rights and privileges in Christ, including their authority over the devil, they are looking at the enemy. Their focus in life is on the devil and his works, not on Jesus and His finished work of redemption.

They are always talking about devils, demons, and demonic activity instead of the riches of God's abundant grace and the "all spiritual blessings" that belong to them in Christ. They're not standing in the finished work of the Cross as the triumphant Church, reigning in life through Jesus Christ.

No, just forget about looking at the enemy. Don't keep your eyes focused on him. Yes, demons and evil spirit are here; we don't deny their presence. But, thank God, *God* has prepared a table of *abundant* provision before us in the midst of them all.

The table the Lord has prepared for us is a table of *abundant riches of provision.* For example, on that table of provision is the new birth, the baptism of the Holy Spirit, authority over the devil and evil spirits, and healing. On that table of provision is *anything* we would need to put us over in life.

On that table of provision is victory and deliverance from anything that would try to bind or hinder us or keep us from being successful in life. On that table is blessing and benefit, triumph and victory — not failure and defeat. On the table of provision is anything else we need from the time we are born again until we step off into eternity.

"Well, why don't I have God's blessing then?" you ask. Well, the table is prepared for you, but you may be ignorant of the blessings that are rightfully yours on the table — *the riches of your inheritance in Christ.* Or maybe you don't even know the table of provision is right there in front of you because the eyes of your understanding have not been enlightened to see God's abundant and rich provisions for you.

Maybe you don't know you're seated at a table of triumph — not at a table of defeat — so you're letting Satan walk all over you. Or you may know the provisions — all spiritual blessings — are on the table, but you're not appropriating them into your own life. You're not exercising your authority over the devil by faith in the power of God's Word.

Just reach out and take what is yours on that table. Your Heavenly Father has prepared it all for *you.* Use the Name of Jesus because you have authority in that Name.

We need to focus on God and what He has provided, instead of on the devil and what he's doing. We need to focus on the riches of our inheritance in Christ and the rights and privileges that legally belong to us as a result of being *in* Him. Appropriate for yourself the riches of being *in* Him. Focus on your heavenly position in Christ where we are seated *far above* all powers and principalities and all the evil works of the enemy.

It is true that we *were* the defeated, conquered ones before we accepted Jesus Christ as our Savior. Before we knew Jesus, we *were* ruled over by Satan. We didn't know Satan and all his demons were *defeated* and *dethroned* by the King of kings and the Lord of lords.

Reigning in Life

Because of Jesus' victory over Satan at the Cross, instead of being defeated, conquered, and ruled over, now in Christ we *reign* as kings in *this* life here in *this* world. Because we are *in* Christ, Satan is under our feet. Before we served as slaves to Satan and spiritual death, but now we *reign* in life through Jesus Christ. This is part of the riches of our inheritance in Christ.

ROMANS 5:17
17 For if by one man's offence death reigned by one; much more they which receive abundance of grace and of the gift of righteousness shall REIGN IN LIFE BY ONE, JESUS CHRIST.

Does this sound like a Church that is being ruled over and dominated by demons and evil spirits? No! When does the Bible say we will reign over Satan and his evil schemes against us? In the sweet by and by? When we all get to Heaven? No, believers reign as kings in the realm of life now. We who are born again have become new creatures in Christ Jesus, and we are now the victorious ones, not the defeated ones. We are the triumphant church, not the defeated Church.

We reign as kings in life through Jesus Christ *now*. This is part of the wisdom the Holy Spirit is trying to get over to the Body of Christ in these Spirit-inspired prayers in the Book of Ephesians. In times past, we served as slaves of Satan, but now we walk in the newness of life (Rom. 6:4). Now because of our joint-seating with Christ in heavenly places, we reign as kings through the Lord Jesus Christ.

This is the message the Holy Ghost through Paul is endeavoring to get across to the Body of Christ. God wants the eyes of our understanding enlightened so we can understand that *we reign with Christ* in this life.

God wants us to know we have victory over Satan in every contest and circumstance, even as Jesus had victory over Satan when He was on the earth. We don't have to struggle to be victorious; we just need to stand our ground with the Word against a defeated foe according to what we already possess in Christ.

It doesn't take all day to stand against evil spirits if you know your authority in Christ. Just speak the Word to them in the Name of Jesus, and they have to go. *You* don't have to fight with them because they've been defeated and dethroned. By standing on the Word against them, you are standing in Jesus' victory.

I'll be honest with you. I don't know whether it's my righteous indignation that gets stirred up or whether I just get plain mad, but something rises up within me when I hear preachers teaching people to fear the devil: "You'd better be careful! The devil might hear you." Or "You'd better be careful. The devil might try to lay sickness and disease on you."

I have authority over myself and my house. If the devil ever comes knocking at my door with sickness, poverty, lack, or oppression, I tell him, "Don't come to *my* house. You'll have to go peddle that junk somewhere else because I won't receive it!"

But I *don't* have authority over the devil in *your* life. Ultimately you'll have to learn to stand against the devil for yourself. Of course, if you are a baby Christian, I can make my faith work for you. But in the final analysis, God will expect you to take authority over the devil for yourself.

If you've already accepted sickness or disease (or anything else the devil tries to bring your way), then you've got a mess on your hands, and you'll have to do something about it. But, thank God, something *can* be done in the Name of Jesus.

If you give someone else permission, they can pray for you in faith, but, really, *you* need to do something about taking authority over the devil for yourself. That's one way you grow in who you are in Christ. Take authority over Satan, sickness, disease, or whatever the enemy is trying to get you to receive. Stand against it for yourself in the Name of Jesus. Believers make a mistake by accepting what the devil brings to them.

You will be defeated if you don't recognize who is *in* you and the authority you have in Christ. By failing to recognize that the Greater One dwells *in* you, you will allow the devil to take advantage of you.

It's one thing for Satan to dominate unsaved people who are in the kingdom of darkness; they're under his authority. But Satan and his cohorts are dominating too many Christians who don't *know* their authority or don't *exercise* their authority.

That's why the believer needs to come to prayer understanding that all those spiritual forces have been defeated by Jesus. When the believer prays, he needs to pray from a position of victory because he is seated with Christ in heavenly places, looking down on a defeated foe.

When you come to prayer, pray from a seated position in Christ far above principalities and powers where you have joint-seating with Christ. Jesus' victory is *your* victory. Because of what Jesus did, you are free from Satan's dominion.

Too often Christians just hang on and try to do the best they can, not realizing what their inheritance in Christ really entitles them to. Instead of taking their rightful place in Christ as victors, they magnify the devil, and that gives him access in their lives.

You can dwell on the negative side of things and you will become what you dwell on. What you are *thinking* about and *dwelling* on is what you are *believing*. What you are *believing* is what you are *talking* about. And eventually what you are *believing* and *talking* about is what you will *become*.

This applies in this area of demons and demonic activity too. If you think the devil's thoughts, you will become depressed, oppressed, and you can go into error. Or you can think on the Word, and your thinking can become enlightened, illuminated, and flooded with light.

You can go around preaching how powerful the devil is, or you can get on the positive side where the eyes of your understanding have been enlightened to see the wisdom of God. Then you will be on the *scriptural* side and the *victory* side where you belong as a believer because of your triumph *in* Christ.

Because I know Jesus defeated the devil, *that*'s what I *think* on and *talk* about. And the Greater One puts me over in life and causes me to succeed because I'm giving place to *God* and the power of His Word, not to the devil.

Christians are defeated because they believe "greater is he that is in the world than He that is in me." They have it backwards in their thinking. Then they go to confessing that.

Many are defeated in life because they have a negative confession; they're always talking on the negative side of things, and that opens a door to the devil in their life.

They're always telling what they're *not* and what they *don't* have and about their weaknesses, failures, and lack. Invariably they go down to the level of their confession.

If you believe and confess that the devil's power is greater than God's power, Satan will defeat you. But if you stand your ground in your blood-bought rights in Christ and confess that, you will rise to the level of your confession and inheritance.

What a change would take place in your life if you stood your ground on the Word of God against every attack of the enemy in every test or trial! What a change would take place if you maintained a positive confession in Christ so you give no ground to the devil in your life!

Then you would rise to the level of your confession — you would take your rightful place in Christ and you would be able to possess what Christ has already wrought for you. You would take your rightful place as the triumphant Church of the Lord Jesus Christ over all the power of the devil.

The Triumphant Church — Not the Militant or Defeated Church

There are some people today who are talking about the militant Church. Among them there are those who say that the Church of the Lord Jesus Christ needs to fight devils in order to be successful.

But I'd rather talk about the triumphant Church because that's scriptural. Jesus' triumph over Satan is every believer's triumph. And every believer can enjoy that triumph and victory if he will walk in the light of His inheritance in Christ.

Those who continually talk about the militant Church are those who are always trying to fight the devil: "We're waging war on the devil. It's going to be tough! We are in for a battle!"

People who talk like that all the time need the eyes of their understanding enlightened to see that the battle has already been won by Jesus Christ. Now they just need to *stand* in that victory.

When the eyes of your understanding have been enlightened to see your rightful position in Christ — *that it is a position of victory* — then when you do encounter the forces of the devil, you'll know what to do about them. Because of your authority over evil spirits in Christ, you will stand against them with the Word of God and put them in their place.

The Body of Christ is triumphant. Thank God we can triumph over sin, sickness, disease, poverty, and bad habits because of our inheritance in Christ. And we can triumph over devils, evil spirits, and anything else the enemy would try to bind us with because Jesus already defeated them for us.

There was no reason for Jesus to enter into the tremendous contest for our redemption except for *us* — in order to redeem us out of the hands of the enemy. Thank God, He did it to redeem a Church — a Body of believers — who would partake of their inheritance in Christ and rule and reign in triumph and victory over the devil in the affairs of life. What Jesus did, He did for us, and Jesus' defeat over Satan belongs to us.

What is ours in Christ requires nothing but the taking or appropriating by faith. We don't have to struggle to believe for something that already belongs to us. But we do need to know it's ours or we won't take our rightful position in Christ and take advantage of what is already ours.

Wherever God's plan of redemption is unveiled, people are saved, and they can become masters over their circumstances and over demon forces, instead of allowing the devil to dominate them.

The Body of Christ never needs to yield in cowardice to the forces of darkness or submit to satanic domination. No, we must arise boldly in the Name of Jesus and take our place in our inheritance as sons and daughters of the Most High God as the triumphant Church!

Chapter 8
Spiritual Warfare: Are You Wrestling or Resting?

Spiritual warfare is a subject some Christians are overemphasizing today in a way that is not in line with the Word of God. Actually, some of what is being taught in the Body of Christ in this area of spiritual warfare and demonology is scripturally in error. That's why it would benefit us to study the Word to see how to deal *scripturally* with Satan and his strategies.

Many believers become fearful if you talk about the devil, demons, and evil spirits and their activities. Many people seem to think it would be better not to ever mention the devil or evil spirits. But if you don't teach believers scripturally from the Word of God how to deal with the devil, the enemy will just run rampant and hold high carnival in their lives because they won't know their scriptural authority.

> **2 CORINTHIANS 2:11**
> 11 Lest Satan should get an advantage of us: for we are not ignorant of his devices.

We need to know our enemy. The Bible says we are *not* to be ignorant of Satan's devices. Satan has not changed the least bit in the world. The devil is the same old devil he has always been, and he uses the same tactics he has always used. He is the same devil Paul had to deal with when he penned these words that we aren't to be ignorant of his devices. And one of Satan's devices is to get people off into the extreme, even in the area of spiritual warfare, so they become unfruitful in the Kingdom of God.

It seems on any Bible subject, it is most difficult for the Body of Christ to stay in the middle of the road. Many believers either get in the ditch on one side of the road or on the other side of the road. In either ditch, they become ineffective because extremes and excesses never produce any fruit to the glory to God.

Actually, the greatest enemy that has robbed the Church, even in this area of demonology and spiritual warfare, is *wrong thinking* and *wrong believing*. That's what initially opens a door to the devil.

And actually, some people are even thinking wrong and believing wrong about the subject of spiritual warfare, and it is going to get the Body of Christ off track unless we get back on the Word of God.

Wrong thinking and wrong believing eventually lead to wrong actions. For example, one error wrong thinking and wrong believing has produced in some believers is that they are trying to fight the devil and pull down strongholds over cities and nations. We need to look at that practice in the light of God's Word to see if it's scriptural. We need to know what the Word of God says on any subject and *think* and *believe* and *act* in line with God's Word. Then we will get Bible results.

There is legitimate spiritual warfare, of course. Spiritual warfare is a *Bible* subject and one that we should be interested in because every one of us must take our stand in spiritual warfare at one time or another in our Christian life.

After all, there is a truth to the fact that there is an adversary arrayed against us and that we are in the army of the Lord. However, people often take those truths and run off with them into extremes and error. Their thinking seems to be, "Well, an army fights the enemy to defeat him, so let's fight the devil so we can defeat him."

But Jesus already "fought" the devil and won. That's why Jesus said to us, *"Occupy, till I come"* (Luke 19:13). We're to take our stand on the Word against a defeated foe. Therefore, we are in the army of the Lord, all right, but it's the *occupying* army. The occupying army is not in battle. The occupying army is just *enforcing* the victory that's already been won by our Commander in Chief, the Lord Jesus Christ. That's why believers shouldn't magnify the *battle*; they should magnify the *triumph*!

'War' and 'Warfare' in the Epistles

Some people emphasize spiritual warfare to the point that you would think it is the only subject taught in the Bible. But you'll find that real spiritual warfare is entirely different from what many people think it is. For example, as you study the New Testament, particularly the epistles, it is amazing how seldom the words "war" and "warfare" are mentioned.

It is also amazing to note that when the words "war" or "warfare" *are* used in the epistles, never once are the words "devil" or "Satan" used in connection with them. Let's look at the words "war" and "warfare" as they are used in the epistles, which were written to us, the Body of Christ.

For instance, in First Corinthians 9:7, Paul asks the question, *"Who goeth a WARFARE any time at his own charges? who planteth a vineyard, and eateth not of the fruit thereof? or who feedeth a flock, and eateth not of the milk of the flock?"* Paul isn't referring to combating the devil. He's simply making the point that ministers should be adequately paid.

Second Corinthians 10:3-5 is another place in the epistles where the words "war" and "warfare" are used.

> **2 CORINTHIANS 10:3-5**
> **3   For though we walk in the flesh, we do not WAR after the flesh:**
> **4   (For the weapons of our WARFARE are not carnal, but mighty through God to the pulling down of STRONG HOLDS;)**
> **5   Casting down IMAGINATIONS, and every high thing that exalteth itself against the knowledge of God, and bringing into captivity every THOUGHT to the obedience of Christ.**

If you take these verses out of their context you can make them say anything you want them to say. Second Corinthians 10:3-5 has been widely used to apply to battling demons over cities and countries. But it's clear by the context that Paul is talking about something different.

Paul isn't referring to battling demonic forces over geographical areas. He is admonishing believers to take control of their own *thoughts* and *imaginations* so they can prevent the devil's lies from getting a stronghold in their *minds*.

You see, the devil can't get into a believer unless the door is open. An uncontrolled mind and wrong thinking have as much to do with opening the door to the devil as wrong believing and wrong talking do. Believers need to know those are the major battlefields in life.

The Bible says, *". . . God is not mocked: for whatsoever a man soweth, that shall he also reap"* (Gal. 6:7). There's a certain truth in using this verse to tell sinners they will reap the consequences of what they sow in sin. But actually, Paul was writing to *believers* when he said that.

Believers are going to reap what they sow — whether it's good or bad. Believers are sowing *words* and *acts* and *deeds* every day from which they will eventually reap a harvest — good or bad — and demonic activity is not necessarily even involved.

Most important of all are the words you sow, because the Bible says there is *life* and *death* in the power of the tongue (Prov. 18:21). And wrong *thinking*, wrong *believing*, and wrong *speaking* are ways believers knowingly or unknowingly open a door to the devil in their lives. That's how believers allow the devil to build strongholds in their minds and lives.

Therefore, reading Second Corinthians 10:3-5 in its entire context, it is telling believers that the truth of God's Word is a spiritual force mighty enough to overcome the lies and deception Satan tries to bring against our minds to bring us into bondage.

What else do the epistles say about "war" and "warfare?"

> **1 TIMOTHY 1:18,19**
> **18 This charge I commit unto thee, son Timothy, according to the prophecies which went before on thee, that thou by them mightest WAR a good WARFARE;**
> **19 HOLDING FAITH, and A GOOD CONSCIENCE; which some having put away concerning faith have made shipwreck.**

How did Paul tell Timothy to war a good warfare? *By holding faith and a good conscience.* In other words, Paul is simply telling Timothy, "Stay in the fight of faith. Fulfill the call of God on your life. That is how you are going to war a good warfare in this life."

The devil isn't even mentioned in these scriptures. The statement is simply a challenge to Timothy as a young minister to fulfill his ministry and not be deterred by any opposition he would face. Paul gives another admonition to Timothy in Second Timothy chapter 2 about warring.

> **2 TIMOTHY 2:3,4**
> **3 Thou therefore endure hardness, as a good soldier of Jesus Christ.**
> **4 No man that WARRETH entangleth himself with the affairs of this life; that he may please him who hath chosen him to be a soldier.**

When we read the entire context of this passage, we find it has nothing to do with the devil. Paul is simply saying, "Stay committed to the call of God on your life, regardless of the cost." Paul is telling believers that there's a price to pay to be good soldiers of Jesus Christ; it takes discipline and dedication.

Paul is giving Timothy an illustration to remind and encourage him to keep himself free from the cares of this world and from any hindrances that would distract him from serving God and ministering effectively.

Then in James 4:1,2 we see the terms "war" and "wars" used in reference to fights, controversies, and strife which occurred because of believers' uncontrolled *flesh* problems.

> **JAMES 4:1,2**
> 1 From whence come WARS and FIGHTINGS among you? come they not hence, even of your LUSTS that WAR in your MEMBERS [body or flesh]?
> 2 Ye lust, and have not: ye kill, and desire to have, and cannot obtain: ye fight and WAR, yet ye have not, because ye ask not.

The word "war" here is used to describe the results of unrestrained fleshly activities, and it has nothing to do with the devil. According to James, spiritual warfare has to do mostly with fighting the lusts of the flesh that come to destroy our spiritual development and hinder our growth in Christ.

We need to crucify our flesh today just as Christians did back then (Gal. 5:24). When we don't crucify the flesh and "keep our bodies under" (1 Cor. 9:27), we can count on having trouble in life, and it's not even necessarily demonically inspired.

Finally, Peter refers to warfare in First Peter 2:11 when he says, *"Dearly beloved, I beseech you as strangers and pilgrims, abstain from fleshly lusts, which WAR against the soul."* Again there is absolutely no reference whatsoever to the devil. Just as James did, Peter uses the word "war" to vividly describe the battle between the lusts of the flesh and the soul — the mind, will, and emotions.

Paul also referred to the unregenerate flesh warring against the mind in Romans chapter 7.

> **ROMANS 7:23**
> 23 But I see another law in my members [body or flesh], WARRING against the law of my MIND, and bringing me into captivity to the law of sin which is in my members [body].

We have looked at scriptures in the epistles where the words "war" and "warfare" are used. The devil isn't mentioned one single time in any of these scriptures. Yet to hear some people talk, you would think spiritual warfare is the only subject in the Bible!

Doctrinally speaking, some people have made a mountain out of a molehill. I suppose that's because some Christians want to blame everything on the devil. But in the epistles, the words "war" and "warfare" primarily have to do with putting the flesh under and controlling one's thought life. He can only do that by the Word of God and with the help of the Spirit of God.

Many believers are trying to get victory in life some other way. But what they need to realize is that *genuine spiritual warfare has to do mostly with the mind and the flesh and fighting the good fight of faith* (1 Tim. 6:12). Those who wage a good warfare keep their mind renewed and their flesh in check and know how to stand in faith on the promises in God's Word.

Keeping the body under subjection and controlling our thought life is not widely taught in the Body of Christ, so many believers allow the lusts of their flesh to run rampant and uncontrolled. Many Christians who have fallen into sin blame it on the devil, but they never would have sinned if they had taken charge of their own mind and flesh. They may claim that Satan caused them to sin, but the truth is that Satan found an open door through which he could get into their lives. They were either thinking wrong thoughts or they weren't crucifying their flesh.

One of the greatest failures of the Charismatic Movement is that there has been so little teaching on sanctification and separation from the contaminating lusts of the world (2 Cor. 6:17; 2 Peter 1:4). Much of what believers blame on the devil is the result of their own lack of sanctification and separation from the world. We separate ourselves from the world by obeying the Bible's instructions in Romans 12:1 and 2. If believers will obey those scriptures, the majority of spiritual warfare they will ever encounter in life will already be settled.

I am not denying the existence of the devil or that he is our adversary. But when a believer learns by the Word of God to control his own thoughts and to gain mastery over his own flesh, he will have no difficulty in enjoying great victory over the devil who was defeated, stripped of his power, brought to nought, and reduced to nothing nearly 2,000 years ago by the Lord Jesus Christ.

I am telling you what the Word says on the subject of spiritual warfare. Rather than always trying to stand *against* something, why don't we just stand *for* something — the truth of the Word of God and Jesus' victory over Satan at the Cross of Calvary. As we stand for the truth and get the Word on the inside of us, situations in our lives will begin to be corrected. We need to stay on the offensive, preaching the Word, not on the defensive constantly trying to battle a defeated foe as if we have to "defeat" him again and regain the victory Christ already won for us.

Do Christians Wrestle With Demons?

So we can see that the epistles use the words "war" and "warfare" to describe the conflict between the flesh and the mind and between the flesh and the recreated spirit. Then what does the Bible have to say about "wrestling"? Does the New Testament teach that believers need to wrestle with demons?

> EPHESIANS 6:10-17
> 10 Finally, my brethren, BE STRONG IN THE LORD, AND IN THE POWER OF HIS MIGHT.
> 11 Put on the whole armor of God, that ye may be able to STAND against the wiles of the devil.
> 12 For we WRESTLE not against flesh and blood, but against principalities, against powers, against the rulers of the darkness of this world, against spiritual wickedness [wicked spirits] in high places.
> 13 Wherefore take unto you the whole armor of God, that ye may be able to WITHSTAND in the evil day, and having done all, TO STAND.
> 14 STAND therefore, having your loins girt about with truth, and having on the breastplate of righteousness;
> 15 And your feet shod with the preparation of the gospel of peace;
> 16 Above all, taking the shield of faith, wherewith ye shall be able to quench all the fiery darts of the wicked.
> 17 And take the helmet of salvation, and the sword of the Spirit, which is the word of God.

Wrestling denotes strenuous effort, doesn't it? According to these scriptures, we do "wrestle" against the devil; we do have the devil to deal with in life. But read that verse of Scripture in context with the whole counsel of God's Word — that Jesus defeated Satan for us and redeemed us from Satan's dominion.

Well, does the scriptural word for "wrestling" mean *war*? No, certainly not. There is a vast difference between *wrestling* and *warring*. If you've ever seen a wrestling match, you know there is a vast difference between wrestling and fighting a war.

One of the meanings of the word "wrestle" in *W. E. Vine's Expos-*

itory Dictionary of Biblical Words is *to sway.* If we will let him, the enemy will come against us and try to sway us and get us out of faith and into doubt and unbelief about the Word so he can defeat us. But if we stand our ground in faith, he *cannot* sway us from the Word. Therefore, the "wrestling" we do is not fighting the devil, but it is a "fight" sometimes to hold fast to our *faith* in God's Word.

You see, the term "wrestling" in Ephesians 6:12 is used figuratively, just as the word "run" is used figuratively in Hebrews 12:1: *". . . let us RUN with patience the race that is set before us."* The Bible doesn't use the word "wrestle" to tell believers to get into heavy spiritual combat to wrestle against the devil in prayer.

No, the Bible is trying to show believers that our opposition in this life comes from the spiritual realm and that we are not to fight against flesh and blood, but we are to take our stand on the Word of God and enforce our victory against a defeated foe.

We can accept the victory Jesus Christ already wrought for us and enforce Satan's defeat in every situation or we can lose the faith fight. God doesn't want us to lose, but by failing to believe the Word of God — who we are in Christ and what we already possess in Christ — and by failing to exercise our authority in Christ against the devil, we can allow Satan to gain the upper hand in any situation.

So if you don't read the entire context of this passage in Ephesians chapter 6, but only focus on verse 12, you can become confused and defeated because you'll think, *I'm in for it! I've got to wrestle against all those principalities, powers, and forces of darkness in order to try to defeat them.*

But anytime we overemphasize one part of a scripture and take it out of context, it's too easy to make it mean something it isn't saying. And if we overemphasize one verse to the exclusion of other scriptures, we don't really have the whole counsel of God on the subject. What we need to do is get our thinking straightened out and begin believing in line with the *whole* counsel of God's Word.

For example, just reading verse 12, you can see how people could become overwhelmed, thinking *they* have to wrestle and *overcome* evil spirits. But that's how people become devil-conscious. And instead of *resting* in the finished work of the Cross, they try to *wrestle* a foe who they forget is defeated! That gives the devil access to hold high carnival in their minds, bodies, and lives because they aren't believing what the Word says Jesus already did for them.

By overemphasizing just that one verse alone rather than the whole counsel of God, people place the emphasis not on what Christ has *already* done for believers, but rather on what the Christian must *yet* do in order to get victory over the devil. That is unscriptural because every believer *already* participates in Jesus' victory over Satan.

We must constantly keep in mind the whole counsel of God. Although Ephesians 6:12 says we do wrestle against principalities and powers, the Bible says in other verses that we are in a battle against a foe that has already been defeated! So read Ephesians 6:12, but instead of "camping" there and trying to build a doctrine on that *one* verse alone always doing *warfare* against the devil — look at the whole counsel of God on this subject.

For example, read Ephesians 6:12, "We wrestle against principalities and power," and read that scripture with Colossians 2:15: "... *having SPOILED principalities and powers, he* [Jesus] *made a shew of them openly, TRIUMPHING OVER THEM in it* [the Cross]."

And then look at Luke 10:19: "*Behold, I give unto you* [the Body of Christ] *power to tread on serpents and scorpions* [the devil and his evil forces], *and over all the power of the enemy: and NOTHING SHALL BY ANY MEANS HURT YOU.*"

Yes, we are in a battle all right, but it's against principalities and powers that Jesus already defeated in his death, burial, and resurrection! Notice also in Luke 10:20 that Jesus admonished the disciples not to rejoice in their authority over the devil but to rejoice in their relationship with God and in the fact that their names are written in the Book of Life. So our focus is *not* to be on a battle with a defeated enemy, but it is to be on a relationship with a mighty and loving God.

Some people are advocating that the Body of Christ is to fight devils. But why would we have to fight an enemy that has been dethroned from his place of authority!

Yet some folks are coming to church dressed in army fatigues, and instead of worshipping *God*, they spend all of their time yelling, screaming, and trying to do "battle" against the devil in prayer. They use scriptures such as Second Timothy 2:3,4 to justify these practices: "... *endure hardness as a GOOD SOLDIER of Jesus Christ. No man that WARRETH entangleth himself with the affairs of this life. . . .*"

Actually, in both Second Timothy 2:3,4 and in Ephesians 6:12, Paul is speaking symbolically. He is using the words "soldier," "warreth," and "wrestling" figuratively. Paul was using an illustra-

tion from the Roman army of the day so people could relate to what
he was saying. Paul used concepts that the people of the day could
understand. We can see this when we read this passage in the *context* in which it was written.

2 TIMOTHY 2:3-6
**3   Thou therefore endure hardness, as a GOOD SOLDIER
of Jesus Christ.**
**4   No man that WARRETH entangleth himself with the
affairs of this life; that he may please him who hath chosen
him to be a SOLDIER.**
**5   And if a man also STRIVE FOR MASTERIES, yet is he
not crowned, except he strive lawfully.**
**6   The HUSBANDMAN that laboureth must be first par-
taker of the fruits.**

In these verses, Paul uses military, athletic, and agricultural
terms to illustrate various aspects of the ministry. He uses the
word "soldier" in verses 3 and 4 to depict the hardiness, discipline,
and dedication it sometimes takes to fulfill the call of God. The
expression, "striving for masteries" in verse 5 refers to winning
first place in an athletic event. And the word "husbandman" refers
to a farmer reaping a crop.

So based on these scriptures taken out of context, if we're supposed to be a "militant" Church so we can fight the devil — then
based on Second Timothy 2:3-6, we should also be an "athletic"
Church and all come to church in sweatsuits, or we should be an
"agricultural" Church and come dressed like farmers!

Do you see how ridiculous this is? We were never meant to
establish outward *practices* based on verses used as *illustrations*.
These verses were only meant to illustrate different aspects of the
Christian life and ministry.

Some folks — good, well-meaning Christian people — are coming
to church or going to prayer meetings to make war on the devil in
prayer. We aren't supposed to "make war" on the devil. We are to
stand our ground of victory in Christ enforcing the truth of God's
Word, because Satan was thoroughly whipped at the Cross of Calvary.

Also, constantly doing battle and warring against the devil
couldn't be scriptural because it negates Jesus' victory over Satan
at Calvary. Because of Jesus' victory over Satan, now believers only
need to take their place of authority in the finished work of the
Cross and appropriate by faith what Jesus did for them.

Wrestling in the Spiritual Realm

The Church of the Lord Jesus Christ just needs to learn to stay balanced. Overemphasizing just one scripture to the exclusion of others or exalting something other than God's Word, including unbiblical practices, can get believers off on doctrinal tangents. A person can take any Bible subject and overemphasize it and make the Bible say something it really doesn't say.

That's what some Christians have done with this issue of "wrestling" the devil. They have resorted to using fleshly tactics such as yelling and screaming at the devil to try to "defeat" him. But the wrestling the believer does against the forces of evil is *not* done in the natural realm with fleshly tactics. It's done in the spiritual realm by faith in the Word.

Some believers are even taking the scripture about wicked spirits in heavenly places (Eph. 6:12) out of context and advocating that we have to get up higher *physically* in order to do battle with the wicked spirits in the heavenlies in prayer! What they really need to do is get down where the *real* battle is — in the mind and flesh!

What these people are doing is trying to *physically* attain to the place where God has already seated us *positionally* in the heavenlies in Jesus Christ (Eph. 2:6). We are already *far above* principalities and powers in our position in Christ.

Not only that, but the Bible says, ". . . *Whatsoever ye shall bind ON EARTH shall be bound in heaven . . .*" (Matt. 18:18), and ". . . *if two of you shall agree ON EARTH as touching any thing that they shall ask, it shall be done for them of my Father which is in heaven*" (Matt. 18:19). The Bible says we are to do these things on *earth*; it never mentions that we have to get up into the spiritual atmosphere to try to deal with the devil! All that Jesus and the disciples accomplished, they accomplished *on the earth*, not up in heavenlies above the earth.

Paul and Silas Prayed the Power of God Down

If you want to know if a spiritual practice is scriptural, look in the Word and see if you find Jesus or His disciples doing it. For example, what did the disciples do when they were faced with great satanic opposition?

Certainly Paul and Silas were experiencing warfare with the enemy when they were beaten and cast into prison (Acts 16:18,22,23). There's no doubt about that. The devil was the one stirring up those people against them. It wasn't God who caused Paul and Silas to be cast into prison; it was the *devil* operating behind the situation. The devil was opposing the Church and the gospel message in warfare by working through men.

Well, did Paul and Silas find a way to get up into the earth's atmosphere so they could fight the devil? Did they war and wrestle and yell at the devil and fight demons in tongues?

No, when Paul and Silas were cast into prison, their feet were put in stocks, and they were in a stationary position, deep in the innermost prison (Acts 16:23-26). Well, then how could they get up in the heavenlies to contend with the powers of darkness that were opposing them? They didn't need to! They praised *God* until the power of the Holy Spirit came down!

Right here on earth, at midnight, Paul and Silas prayed and sang praises to *God*, and God heard and delivered them (Acts 16:25). You see, *praying* and *singing praises* is a type of scriptural "wrestling" in the *spiritual* realm because you have to stay in faith to do it! And because God responds to faith (Heb. 11:6), He reached down and shook that old jail and delivered Paul and Silas.

We don't need to get up into the heavenlies to deal with evil spirits! We ought to be interested in tapping into the power of God that's already available to us as believers right here on earth! Yes, the word "wrestling" shows us that there is a *spiritual* conflict between the believer and the devil. But the wrestling is done in the arena of faith — in the spiritual realm — not in the natural realm. It is a fight based on standing firmly on the promises in God's Word and on the finished work of our redemption.

Scriptural 'Wrestling' — The Fight of Faith

Once believers understand their authority in Christ and begin to appropriate the finished work of the Cross, they will understand exactly what kind of "wrestling" it is that believers are to engage in.

Believers don't have to *overpower* and *overcome* the devil or wrestle him in their own strength. We only "wrestle" demonic forces by our faith in God's Word from a *position of victory* seated with Christ because we have authority over demons in Christ. That's why the only wrestling we engage in is the faith fight. If we are in any other fight, we are in the wrong fight: *"Fight the good fight of faith . . ."* (1 Tim. 6:12).

You see, sometimes you have to "wrestle" to stay in faith,

because as long as the devil can keep you in the *sense realm* where he is god, and you look at the circumstances, he'll whip you every time. But as long as you stay in the *faith realm* depending on God's Word to put you over, you'll whip him every time.

The faith fight — trusting God's Word to work for you — is the only fight the Bible says believers are to fight. The Bible says, *"Let us labour therefore to enter into that rest, lest any man fall after the same example of unbelief"* (Heb. 4:11). We labor to come into God's rest of faith: *"For we which have BELIEVED do enter into rest . . ."* (Heb. 4:3). Some believers are laboring and laboring, trying to defeat the enemy. They just need to enter into the rest of faith because they believe the Word.

If you are a believer, you are *in* Christ and you have authority over satanic forces *now*. You don't have to labor to attain authority over Satan because Jesus provided that in your redemption by defeating those principalities and powers for you. So you are not coming to prayer with the idea that *you* have to whip principalities and powers. Jesus did that *for you* on the Cross.

Yes, these principalities and powers try to come against our lives. But these same principalities and powers that folks in the Old Testament had such a struggle with — Jesus defeated them under the New Covenant and put them to nought. This is the wisdom of God, not the wisdom of the dethroned powers of this world who try to blind our eyes to our victorious position in Christ (1 Cor. 2:6; Col. 2:15).

So when you come to prayer, always pray from the understanding that the same principalities and powers the Bible says we wrestle against in Ephesians 6:12 were thoroughly *defeated*, *dethroned*, and *stripped of their authority* in your life by Jesus Christ (Col. 2:15).

How are we going to help other people deal with the devil? By teaching them what the *Word* says. Tell them who they are in Christ and what their blood-bought covenant rights and privileges are in their redemption. Tell them about their authority over the devil and how to use their authority in Christ to deal scripturally with the powers of darkness.

Be Strong in the Lord

The Bible says in Ephesians 6:10 that the believer is to ". . . *be strong in the Lord, and in the power of his might."* You hear folks say, "Well, I'm *trying* to be strong." But the Bible doesn't say a thing in the world about being strong in yourself. Paul said,

". . . when I am weak, then am I strong" (2 Cor. 12:10).

Many times in the circumstances we face in life, we can feel weak, empty, and helpless in ourselves. But, thank God, we can lean on the promises of God. We can go to the Rock, and stand fast on His Word. Paul said, *". . . we were pressed out of measure, above strength, insomuch that we despaired even of life: but we had the sentence of death in ourselves, that WE SHOULD NOT TRUST IN OURSELVES, BUT IN GOD which raiseth the dead"* (2 Cor. 1:8,9).

Trusting in God is trusting in His Word. This is where many believers are missing it; they're trying to be strong in their own strength and don't realize all the strength they need is found in the Word.

The reason you need to be strong in the Lord and in the power of His might is so that you can stand your ground against the wiles of the devil *"in the evil day"* (Eph.4:13). The evil day is when Satan will come to test, try, and tempt you, and you will have to be strong in the Lord and in the power of His might so you can take your stand of faith against him.

One way you become strong in the Lord is by *putting on the whole armor of God* (Eph. 6:11-18). You put on the full armor of God for two reasons:

1. You wear the armor of God for protection in your prayer life. Once you have the armor on, you are ready to pray — you are dressed for prayer. The object of putting on the armor is so you can enter into prayer.
2. You wear the armor to help you stand in life against the wiles, tests, and trials of the devil.

The Armor of God

If we need the armor of God to make us strong in the Lord, then we need to take a closer look at it. Notice the Bible says first, *"PUT ON the whole armor of God . . ."* (Eph. 6:11). In *Strong's Exhaustive Concordance of the Bible*, the word for "put" is *enduo*. It has the sense of *sinking into a garment*; *to invest with clothing*; *to array or clothe*; *to endue, have*, or *put on something*.

So to be strong in the Lord you need *to put on* or *sink into* the armor of God as your protection against the wiles of the devil. Then in verse 13, the Bible says, *". . . TAKE UNTO YOU the whole armour of God. . . ."* According to *Strong's Exhaustive Concordance of the Bible*, the word "take" means *to take up*. In other words, once you've got the armor of God on, then you've got to do something with it — use it!

Paul used an example of the armor of a Roman soldier here to give us a picture of what the armor of God is like. The *helmet of salvation* is the knowledge of your position in God because of your salvation and redemption in Christ.

The helmet of salvation is directly related to the prayers Paul prayed for the Church in Ephesians 1:17-22: *"That the God of our Lord Jesus Christ . . . may give unto you the spirit of wisdom and revelation IN THE KNOWLEDGE of HIM. . . ."*

The helmet of salvation includes having your mind renewed to know and understand your rights and privileges in Christ and who you are in Christ. The helmet of salvation protects your mind — Satan's chief battleground.

The *girdle of truth* represents a clear understanding of God's Word. Like a soldier's belt, it holds the rest of the armor in place. Your loins must be girded with the truth of God's Word because you aren't going to get anywhere in prayer unless God's Word abides *in* you (John 15:7). A successful prayer life must be based on the promises in God's Word.

Then you must have on the *breastplate of righteousness*. That refers to your rightstanding with God. When you accept Jesus, you become the righteousness of God in Christ (2 Cor. 5:21). You wouldn't be any match against the devil if you didn't have rightstanding with God. But because of your redemption in Christ, you do have rightstanding with God, and you are seated as a joint-heir with Christ: *"And if children, then heirs; heirs of God, and joint heirs with Christ"* (Rom. 8:17).

Your feet must be *shod with the preparation of the gospel of peace*. To be effective in prayer, you must walk in the light of God's Word (1 John 1:7). As the psalmist of old said, *"The entrance of THY WORDS giveth light . . ."* (Ps. 119:130). It's hard to walk when the path before you is dark. But with the light of God's Word, you never have to walk in darkness under Satan's dominion.

As soon as the light of God's Word comes, faith is there. Feeding and meditating on God's Word brings *light* and *faith* because *". . . faith cometh by hearing, and hearing by the word of God"* (Rom. 10:17). And faith in God's Word is your major defense against Satan's onslaughts against your mind and your life.

Then you must take up the *shield of faith*. Notice verse 16 says, *"ABOVE ALL, taking the shield of faith. . . ."* Why does the Bible say, "above *all*"? Read the rest of that verse: *"ABOVE ALL, taking the shield of faith . . . WHEREWITH ye may be able to quench all the FIERY DARTS of the wicked.*" Above everything else take the shield of faith because that's what you use to quench the enemy's fiery darts that he'll try to assail against you.

The shield of faith has to be used in your everyday life and also in your prayer life. While you're praying, the devil will send every kind of fiery dart to your mind to get your attention diverted to keep you from staying in faith. You will have to quench every one of his fiery darts with the shield of faith in God's Word.

Then you also need to use the shield of faith in your everyday life against the devil because you need to stay in faith on a daily basis, not just while you're praying. You need to think faith thoughts and speak faith words continually so you don't give the devil a place in you. If you stay in the arena of faith in the promises of God, you will be able to stand against Satan and put him on the run.

The Sword of the Spirit

What about *the sword of the Spirit*? Did you ever stop to think about it? Every part of the armor is protective or defensive, except one, and that is the sword of the Spirit. The sword of the Spirit — the Word of God — is the only part of the armor you fight Satan with.

You don't fight Satan with the helmet; it protects you. You don't fight Satan with the shield of faith or the girdle of truth; they protect you. You don't fight Satan with your breastplate of righteousness or shoes of peace; they protect you. But you do fight Satan with the Word of God — the sword of the Spirit. It is the only *offensive* weapon the Bible mentions.

What is the scriptural way to deal with these forces of darkness? It's with the sword of the Spirit. How did Jesus deal with the devil in His earthly ministry?

For one thing, Jesus never went looking for the devil to do spiritual combat with him. Yes, the Bible says that Jesus was tempted by the devil (Luke 4:1,2). But when Satan tempted Jesus to oppose Him from bringing redemption to mankind, Jesus did not groan against the devil for three hours or try to pull down Satan's strongholds. He was protected by truth and righteousness, so He simply *stood* His ground and used the sword of the Spirit, the Word of God.

In every temptation, Jesus said, *"It is written"* (Matt. 4:4,7,10; Luke 4:4,8,12). Jesus Himself quoted the Word of God, using the Word against the devil as a sword. In that sense, Jesus was "fighting" or "wrestling" with the devil. But the only weapon Jesus used against the devil was faith in *the Word of God*. He didn't fight Satan any other way. And the devil left, defeated. If Jesus wrestled with the devil using the Word, then that's how we should deal with the devil too.

In this encounter with the devil, Jesus showed us how to wield the sword of the Spirit as an offensive weapon against Satan. Jesus is our example, even in spiritual combat with the devil.

Think about it. If we didn't know how to use the sword of the Spirit, we could have all the other pieces of armor in place, and we would still be at a disadvantage. But, thank God, we can just stand in faith on the Word, using the sword of the Spirit against Satan by jabbing him in every encounter, speaking the Word, saying, "It is written!"

Why does the Bible call the Word of God "the sword of the Spirit"? The word "Spirit" and "anointing" are often used synonymously in the Bible. The Bible says the yoke shall be destroyed because of the anointing (Isa. 10:27). God's Word is anointed. So we could say *the sword of the anointing* — the Word of God — breaks the yoke of Satan's bondage.

Go after any yoke that binds you with the sword of the Spirit — the sword of the anointing! Free yourself from those things Satan tries to bind you with and walk in the liberty Jesus already purchased for you by using the sword of the anointing — God's holy written Word!

The Power in the Blood of Jesus

What else does it mean to ". . . *be strong in the Lord, and in the power of his might*" (Eph. 6:10)? We can't be strong in the Lord without appropriating the saving power of His blood.

COLOSSIANS 1:13,14
13 Who hath DELIVERED US FROM THE POWER OF DARKNESS, and hath translated us into the kingdom of his dear Son:
14 In whom we have redemption THROUGH HIS BLOOD, even the forgiveness [remission] **of sins.**

Every benefit and blessing we possess in our redemption, including complete and total victory over Satan, is based on Jesus and His triumph over Satan at the Cross. We have victory over Satan because of Jesus' shed blood. The oldtimers in Pentecost understood a truth about the blood of Jesus. They would plead the blood against the devil. That's scriptural.

When you plead the blood against the devil, you are really

pleading your covenant rights of protection against the enemy (Isa. 54:17; Luke 10:19; Phil. 2:9,10; Col. 1:13).

REVELATION 12:11
11 And they overcame him [Satan] **by the BLOOD OF THE LAMB, and by the word of their testimony....**

A missionary told an interesting testimony once about the power in the blood of Jesus for protection. This woman was left alone in a mission station in a foreign field, and a peculiar kind of scorpion was common in that area. Its sting was deadly; no one had ever survived who was stung by it.

This missionary was down in the village one day, and one of these deadly scorpions stung her. It scared her at first because she was alone in the missionary station; all the other missionaries were gone. She related, "At first, I panicked. Then I just said, 'I plead the blood of the Lord Jesus Christ against this scorpion sting.'"

The natives in that area all watched her, expecting her to fall down dead. But she never did swell up or show any sign of sickness whatsoever. Those natives watched her as she went on about her business. In fact, the whole village followed her around because they were sure she was going to die.

That missionary never did experience any ill effects. She just pled the blood of the Lord Jesus Christ and stood on her covenant rights of protection, and she never experienced any harm (Isa. 54:17; Mark 16:18; Luke 10:19). As a result of that miracle, most of those natives were saved.

Yes, we have to deal with Satan and those things that try to come against us to hurt and destroy us. But there is victory in Jesus and in His blood. Let's not magnify the devil and his work and what he's doing in our lives. Let's magnify the victory we have in our blood covenant in Christ over all the works of the devil.

The Believer's 'Battle' Stance — To Stand

Once you have the armor on, you are ready to take your position of "battle" against the devil. However, because of Jesus' victory over Satan and the believer's position in that triumph, the Bible only gives us one position of "warfare" against the devil: "Having done all, STAND" (Eph. 6:13).

Notice how many times the word "stand" is used in Ephesians 6:11-14. The word "attack" is *never* used. The Holy Spirit is telling the believer his position in the good fight of faith against the enemy is a stand of faith and a stand of resting on the promises of God. He is *to stand* against the devil with the Word.

1. *"Put on the whole armour of God, that ye may be able TO STAND against the wiles of the devil"* (Eph. 6:11).
2. *". . . take unto you the whole armour of God, that ye may be able to WITHSTAND in the evil day . . ."* (Eph. 6:13).
3. *". . . and having done all, TO STAND"* (Eph. 6:13).
4. *"STAND therefore, having your loins girt about with truth . . . the breastplate of righteousness: . . . your feet shod with . . . the gospel of peace; above all, taking the shield of faith, wherewith ye shall be able to quench all the fiery darts of the wicked"* (Eph. 6:14-16).

The position the believer takes is not one of wrestling as if *he* had to defeat the devil, for the battle has already been fought and won on Calvary. But sometimes there is strenuous effort or "wrestling" in *standing* against the enemy based on your faith in God's Word. But that's the only position of "battle" the Bible mentions — to *stand* and to *withstand* the devil with the full armor of God, using the anointed sword of the Spirit against him.

The Bible says believers are to stand against the enemy wearing the armor of God so they can successfully withstand the devil in the evil day of testing, trial, and temptation (v. 13). Whether we like it or not, the Holy Ghost is telling the Body of Christ that the evil day is coming when the enemy is going to come against each one of us. But Jesus said, *". . . In the world ye shall have TRIBULA-TION: but be of good cheer; I have OVERCOME the world"* and that includes the god of this world, Satan (John 16:33; 1 Cor. 4:4).

What are you going to do when Satan comes against you? Are you going to get all the saints to pray for you? That will only help temporarily. Have you ever noticed that no believer can stand against the tests and temptations of the devil just because the saints pray for him? Sooner or later, each of us has to stand our ground on the Word against the wiles of the devil for ourself. And if we don't do it, it won't be done.

Stand Fast in Faith

Once you have your armor on, the only position the Bible tells you to take against Satan is *to stand* against him — that means to enforce his defeat with the Word of God. Paul said, "Stand, stand, withstand, and stand." He never said "attack, attack, counterattack, and attack."

The purpose of putting on the armor is so that we can stand against the wiles or the craftiness and deceit of the devil. The Bible does not say we are to put on the Bible so we can attack the devil, but rather so we can stand successfully against his attack.

When I say "stand," I am using this word in reference to our enemy Satan. This is not to be confused to mean that we are not to *go* into all the world and preach the gospel (Matt. 28:19; Mark 16:15). In reference to the *world* we are to go, but in reference to the *enemy* we are to stand.

Therefore, in true spriitual warfare, we do not go looking for the devil. But when he shows up, we deal with him. Ephesians 6 doesn't instruct us to fight against the devil, but to put on the whole armor so we can stand against the attacks which Satan launches against us. We take the sword of the Spirit and fight the good fight of faith by enforcing Satan's defeat and our triumph over him.

The Bible also tells us exactly *how* to stand strong against the enemy. We do it by the Word and by our steadfast, unwavering faith in the Word.

> **1 CORINTHIANS 16:13**
> **13 Watch ye, STAND FAST in the FAITH, quit [act] you like men, be strong.**

> **2 CORINTHIANS 1:24**
> **24 . . . for by FAITH ye STAND.**

The word "stand" in this verse means *to be stationary* and *to persevere*. The word "fast" means *firmly fixed; stable; unyielding*. Your position against the devil is to stand firmly fixed, stable, and unyielding on the promises of God's Word for your life. You are to be firmly fixed in your perseverance of faith in God's Word.

Stand Fast in Grace

Since Satan is a defeated foe, now it is up to us to take our *stand* against him in the *faith* and also the *grace* the Lord Jesus Christ has provided for us: *"Let us therefore come boldly unto the throne of grace, that we may obtain mercy, and FIND GRACE TO HELP in time of need"* (Heb. 4:16).

ROMANS 5:1,2
1   Therefore being justified by faith, we have peace with
God through our Lord Jesus Christ:
2   By whom also we have access by faith into this GRACE
wherein WE STAND. . . .

Why would the Holy Spirit through Paul tell the Body of Christ
to stand fast in faith and in the grace of God? Because everything
in the world, including our adversary Satan, will try to pull us out
of faith and try to get us to walk by sight and by our own strength.

The Bible says, *"There are . . . so many kinds of voices in the*
world, and none of them is without signification" (1 Cor. 14:10).
And if you listen to all the voices round about you — even some
well-meaning friends, preachers, and theologians — you could be
pulled back from walking by faith and be tempted to walk by sight
and by circumstances. But, thank God, we're firmly fixed, standing
on God's Word and in God's grace. And that is God's provision for
protection against the onslaughts the enemy would try to assail
against us.

It's only your faith in God and His Word that will enable you to
stand successfully against the devil. First Corinthians 16:13 says,
"Watch ye, stand fast in the faith, quit [act] *you like men. . . ."* In
other words, "Don't be a baby in faith and just give up when Satan
comes against you. *Stand* against him with the Word." We were all
spiritual babies when we were first born again, but babies grow up.
We're not supposed to stay babies in our dealings with the devil.
We are to put *him* on the run.

Satan will tempt you to doubt God and His Word, and he will
use adverse circumstances and tests and trials to do it. But in the
face of every adversity, you'll have to learn to stand your ground
firmly fixed on God's Word. You'll have to learn to be spiritually
mature by becoming strong in faith and in the grace of the Lord
Jesus Christ so you can successfully *stand* against the enemy's lies
and deceptions (Rom. 5:2).

Stand Fast in One Spirit

PHILIPPIANS 1:27
27   Only let your conversation [your manner of life and con-
duct] be as it becometh the gospel of Christ: that whether I
come and see you, or else be absent, I may hear of your
affairs, that YE STAND FAST IN ONE SPIRIT, with one
mind striving together for the faith of the gospel.

Standing in faith and *standing in God's grace* are mighty fortresses against the devil. But the Bible also says we are *to stand fast in one spirit.* Strife and discord always open a door to the devil (James 3:16). When you stand strong in unity and forbid Satan to bring strife and division, you prevent him from gaining any ground in you.

Believers will probably never see every little thing just exactly alike because we are all at various stages of spiritual growth and development. But just because we disagree on minor issues doesn't mean we can't be in one spirit and one accord. Believers stand strong against the enemy by being in one spirit and by not allowing division and strife. Even in the face of differences, believers must learn to stand fast in one spirit if they are going to maintain a strong defense against the devil.

If you are standing fast in one spirit you can disagree without being disagreeable. Walking in love closes the door to the devil. When you get over into the Spirit and you walk in love, many issues you thought were so important don't seem to be so important any more. We shouldn't let little issues divide us. Be one — stand fast in one spirit.

Stand Fast in the Lord

PHILIPPIANS 4:1
1 Therefore, my brethren dearly beloved and longed for, my joy and crown, so STAND FAST IN THE LORD, my dearly beloved.

What else does the believer do to take his *stand* against Satan? The Bible says we are to stand fast in the Lord. What does that mean? The answer is found in Ephesians 6:10.

EPHESIANS 6:10
10 Finally, my brethren, be STRONG IN THE LORD, and [be strong] **IN THE POWER OF HIS MIGHT.**

Taking our stand against Satan includes taking our rightful position in Christ. Did you notice in Ephesians 6:10 that the Bible says we are to be strong in two areas:

1. Be strong IN THE LORD, *and*
2. Be strong IN THE POWER OF HIS MIGHT.

To be strong in the Lord, you'll have to be strong in His Word. But what is the power of God's might? The power of God's might is the Holy Ghost. Go through the New Testament and notice how many times "power" is mentioned in connection with the Holy Spirit. Some of these verses are listed below (*See* also Acts 10:38; Rom. 15:13,19; 1 Thess. 1:5).

> **LUKE 4:14**
> **14 And Jesus returned in the POWER of the SPIRIT into Galilee....**

> **LUKE 24:49**
> **49 And, behold, I send the PROMISE [the Holy Spirit] of my Father upon you: but tarry ye in the city of Jerusalem, until ye be endued with POWER from on high.**

> **ACTS 1:8** *Amplified*
> **8   But you shall receive POWER — ABILITY, EFFICIENCY and MIGHT — when the HOLY SPIRIT has come upon you....**

> **1 CORINTHIANS 2:4**
> **4   And my speech and my preaching was not with enticing words of man's wisdom, but in demonstration of THE SPIRIT and of POWER.**

You won't be able to be strong in the power of God's might without being filled with the Holy Spirit and without praying. Part of taking a victorious stand against the devil is to be filled to overflowing with the Holy Spirit. You won't be able to stand strong against the devil as an empty vessel.

Fervent Prayer

Look at James 5:16 in connection with the power of the Holy Spirit. One way the believer continues to be filled with the Holy Spirit so he can stand in the power of God's might is by effectual fervent prayer.

> **JAMES 5:16**
> **16 . . . The effectual FERVENT PRAYER of a righteous man AVAILETH MUCH.**

The *King James Version* says the fervent prayer of a righteous man avails much. But just *how* much does fervent prayer avail? What are the possibilities of the power that is made available by fervent prayer?

The Amplified Bible gives us more light about how much the prayers of a righteous man avail: ". . . The earnest (heartfelt, continued) prayer of a righteous man MAKES TREMENDOUS POWER AVAILABLE — DYNAMIC IN ITS WORKING" (James 5:16 *Amp.*).

Tremendous, dynamic *power* is made available in effectual *fervent* prayer. Now read Ephesians 6:10 and 18 again.

EPHESIANS 6:10,18
10 . . . be strong in the Lord, AND in the POWER of HIS MIGHT [making tremendous power available by the Holy Spirit]. . . .
18 PRAYING always with all prayer and supplication in the Spirit. . . .

The power of God is always available, but prayer brings that power into manifestation. Earnest, fervent praying makes tremendous power available. Praying not only makes tremendous power available — but the power in fervent prayer is *dynamic* in its action. Earnest, fervent prayer is one way the believer gets filled to overflowing with the Holy Spirit — the power of God — to stand strong against the enemy.

Once you have put on the full armor of God and you are strong in the Lord and in the power of His might, then you are ready to pray. With the armor on you are ready to make tremendous power available by the help of the Holy Spirit. When you wear the whole armor of God and you are strong in the Holy Spirit, *then* the Bible says you are in a position to pray *effectually*.

How does prayer relate to spiritual warfare? Because the battle in true spiritual warfare is first in the believer's own mind and flesh. But then it is in prayer and in faith. And many times the victory is won by standing your ground on the Word in the arena of prayer. Many times the reason we're not ready for the battles we encounter in the *natural* realm in life is that we haven't entered into the prayer arena and the fight of faith as we should have in the *spiritual* realm.

Or to say it another way, we're not "prayed up" and full of the Holy Ghost. When you're not prayed up, it's easy to be defeated when Satan comes along to test you.

In Ephesians 6:10-17 Paul took some time in talking about the armor of God to get us ready for verse 18: *"PRAYING always with all prayer and supplication in the Spirit. . . ."* Once you have the armor on, only then are you ready to pray with heartfelt, continued prayer (Eph. 6:18; James 5:16). "Praying *always*" denotes the fact of not giving up in prayer, but continuing to pray.

The prayer mentioned here is not some special type of prayer or some special spiritual activity the believer engages in to try to dethrone Satan or pull down strongholds over communities, cities, states, or nations.

Paul is talking about a lifestyle of communion and fellowship with God so we can resist the wiles and deceptions of the enemy that try to discourage and defeat us. By maintaining a lifestyle of fellowshipping in God's Presence, we'll be able to pray effectively with all prayer and supplication in the Spirit.

The Bible doesn't tell the believer to aggressively attack the devil or the devil's kingdom in prayer. No, the believer is to fervently reach out in prayer for other saints and for ministers who are reaching the lost: "*PRAYING ALWAYS . . . FOR ALL SAINTS*" (Eph. 6:18).

Another translation of this verse says, "Praying with all *manner* or all *kinds* of prayer and supplication in the Spirit." So just wrestling against the devil all the time in prayer couldn't be scriptural because it's not praying with all manner or all kinds of prayer.

'Warring' Tongues

If you follow the leading of the Holy Spirit, He will lead you to pray with all *manner* of prayer, not just one kind of prayer, because He will lead you in line with what the Word says.

That's why those in the Body of Christ today who overemphasize the "warfare" aspect of prayer couldn't be praying with "all manner of prayer and supplication in the Spirit." They claim there is an unction of the Holy Spirit in prayer, a tongue that only the devil knows, that is used to combat the devil and to do warfare against Satan in the Spirit.

But there is no scripture to support that we are to pray against the devil or to combat the devil in tongues. Not one single time is tongues mentioned in the Bible in connection with the devil. Even if the Holy Spirit did give you an unction in prayer to deal with the devil, that is only as the Holy Spirit leads, and you can't teach that to others (1 Cor. 12:11).

In other words, you can't announce to people, "Let's everyone war against the devil in tongues." If there is an unction that should come by the Holy Spirit in prayer, it's as the *Holy Spirit* leads, not as man leads or directs, and it will be in line with the Word of God.

Also, another reason this doctrine of "warring tongues," or trying to defeat the devil in prayer, is not scripturally balanced is that it focuses prayer, not on fellowshipping with God the Father, but on "battling" the devil and wicked spirits in heavenly places. So Satan, *not* God, becomes the focus of our spiritual attention and activities.

The whole idea behind "warring tongues" is that these tongues are a way to "plow through" the demon spirits that infest the heavenlies above the earth. It's true that evil spirits are up there in the heavenlies. But people who are teaching others to pray in warring tongues are trying to use fleshly weapons to try to do a spiritual job.

The teaching of warring tongues ignores the biblical emphasis of tongues and the finished work of the Cross of Calvary. The Apostle Paul wrote that when the Christian speaks in tongues he is speaking mysteries unto *God* (1 Cor. 14:2),and he is magnifying God (Acts 10:46). The Bible also says the believer is edifying himself when he prays in tongues (1 Cor. 14:4; Jude 20). And God sometimes speaks to man through the spiritual gift of diversity of tongues (1 Cor. 12:28). These are the biblical uses of the gift of tongues.

Ignoring the biblical use of tongues, this teaching on "warring tongues" strives to make speaking in tongues something that is done *against* the devil instead of *unto* God. And it takes the believer's focus away from God to focus on the devil.

Thank God for praying with other tongues. But don't waste your time praying in tongues trying to defeat an already defeated foe. Instead yield to the Holy Ghost, and let Him use you as you pray in tongues to be a blessing to humanity. That is the most effective way to gain ground for God and do great damage to the devil's kingdom of darkness.

You see, *in principle* nowhere in the Bible are we taught to pray against the devil in tongues. And *in practice* nowhere in the Bible do we find believers doing it.

In every instance when believers pray, they are praying to a faithful and loving Heavenly Father who hears and answers prayer. Jesus Himself tells us who we are to pray to: ". . . *Whatsoever ye shall ASK THE FATHER in MY NAME, he will give it you*" (John 16:23). This extreme "warring" teaching, however, ignores this biblical emphasis and makes speaking in tongues something that is done *against the devil* instead of *unto God.*

Instead of leading saints into deeper spirituality, this teaching and its extreme practice actually leads believers into fleshly extremes and excesses because it focuses mainly on *experiences* in prayer. This extreme teaching leads believers into error because the emphasis is not on what Christ has already *accomplished* for the believer in His redemption, but on what the believer has *yet* to do to achieve victory over the devil.

You see, instead of emphasizing the triumph of Jesus over Satan, the finished work of the Cross, the triumphant position of the believer in Christ, and the authority that is resident in each believer, this warfare teaching portrays believers as being oppressed and defeated and still under the lordship of Satan, trying to "war" his way free to a place of victory.

The emphasis is not on what *Christ* has already done, but rather it is on what the believer must still do *himself* in order to get victory over the devil. So the believer is instructed to "groan" and to "war" in tongues in order to obtain victory.

Study for yourself the New Testament instruction on dealing with the devil (Eph. 4:27; James 4:7; 1 Peter 5:9). Only when believers submit themselves to God and give the devil no place in them will they be able to resist the devil and take their stand on the Word of God against him. *Then* the devil *will* flee. Only when believers have done their part can they deal effectively with the devil and stand successfully against him with the Word of God.

Actually, the error in this extreme spiritual warfare teaching is one of *focus* and *position.* True biblical authority over the devil is exercised from a seated and victorious position in Christ *far above* all principalities and power in which the believer recognizes that the enemy is defeated and stripped of his authority.

That doesn't mean we are to overreact to error by neglecting and ignoring what is genuine and scriptural. For instance, the Church cannot afford to back away from valid intercession and true spiritual warfare, which come as a result of the promptings of the Holy Spirit. The Body of Christ should and must press into the genuine and biblical operations of the Spirit of God and be fervent in prayer as the Scriptures teach. There is a genuine prayer and supplication that the Church must stir itself up to participate in.

Yes, there are spiritual battles to be fought and won in prayer. But the fight in prayer is a faith fight. Spiritual battles in prayer are fought and won from a seated position in Christ far above principalities and powers where the believer recognizes that the enemy is under his feet (Eph. 1:3,22) and therefore *looks down* on a defeated foe.

Much damage has been done to the Body of Christ by a lack of solid biblical teaching in this area. The Word of God tells us that the Word is to dwell in us ". . . *richly in ALL WISDOM . . .*" (Col. 3:16).

It is the wisdom of God's Word dwelling in the believer richly that brings maturity in dealing biblically with the devil. A lack of scriptural teaching and sound wisdom in God's Word has resulted in foolish practices occurring in the Body of Christ that are hurtful to people. They are harmful because they're extreme and cause people to get in the ditch on one side of the road into fanaticism, excess, and error.

Also, the Body of Christ needs to be careful about ministers who teach certain practices that are not demonstrated in the Word of God. Just because some ministers teach and demonstrate certain practices in their services, that doesn't mean what they are doing is right or scripturally sound.

Ministers need to be careful what they feed the flock of God. Paul told Timothy, *"Preach the word . . ."* (2 Tim. 4:2). People need to be taught what the Word has to say about the enemy so they aren't ignorant of Satan's devices. But stay with *the Word*, not opinion or experiences. Experiences can be helpful, but only if they're in line with the Word. Ministers should be careful to lay a foundation with the Word of God first.

TITUS 2:1
**1   But speak thou the things which become SOUND DOC-
TRINE.**

People need to be careful that what they teach about spiritual warfare is doctrinally sound. Some people teach that they have further revelation about warfare that's out beyond the Word of God.

There are no revelations outside of the Word. Any revelation you have that comes from *the Spirit of God* is in line with the Word of God. People get off into the devil's territory when they leave the Word. They say they are following the Spirit, but you can't follow the Holy Spirit apart from the Word. *Put the Word first and the Spirit second.*

When people endeavor to follow what they call the "spirit," but they leave the Word, they open themselves up to deception. For example, a certain minister had a marvelous ministry for years that was based on the Word of God. But some years later, a pastor friend of mine attended several of this man's meetings. My pastor friend said there were a few things that were doctrinally off, but they weren't crucial to the truth of the gospel. But then this pastor said, "I went back another night, and the minister told some 'revelations' he'd had."

The pastor had known this minister for thirty years, and the man had been in the ministry many years. But it doesn't matter how long you've been in the ministry, or how doctrinally correct you've been in the past, if you leave the Word, you throw yourself wide open for satanic deception.

This pastor friend of mine told me, "I went up to him after the service and said, 'I've been going along with you on some things you've said because they weren't all that important. But tonight you said some things, and you're just going to have to give me chapter and verse for it.'"

Remember the Bible said, ". . . *In the mouth of two or three witnesses shall every word be established*" (2 Cor. 13:1). If people would only heed this scripture, it would keep them from building doctrinal aircastles and going into deception on the basis of one scripture taken out of context.

This minister replied, "Oh, you won't find what I'm preaching in *that thing*," referring to the Bible. "I'm way out beyond *that!*"

If a person is out beyond the Word of God, he's out too far for me. Don't leave the Word and try to follow the Holy Spirit. It won't work. You'll be out in a realm where Satan can deceive you. There is a reason Paul told Timothy to preach *the Word* (2 Tim. 4:2). Putting the Word first will always keep you scripturally balanced so you don't open yourself up doctrinally to Satan's deceptions.

I've told people for more than fifty years, "Examine what people say by the Word, and if it doesn't line up with the Word, don't accept it, whether it's me teaching or someone else." It's what the Word says that counts. Put the Word first. I'm against extremes in any area, because extremes and teachings that go beyond the Word do damage to the Body of Christ.

We need to realize that as in all spiritual subjects, there's just a fine line between true spirituality and excess and fanaticism. So let's just be open to the Word of God and to the Spirit of God, and let Him lead and teach us. Stay down the middle of the road doctrinally; let's not get into a ditch on either side of the road.

No matter who teaches on any Bible subject, you need to study the Bible yourself to determine whether what is being taught is right. Don't accept what someone teaches just because he claims to be an "expert." You can't accept what anyone says on any biblical subject unless the person backs it up with the Word of God.

In the study of demonology and spiritual warfare, as with all Bible subjects, be careful to "rightly divide" what the Bible says on the subject (2 Tim. 2:15). That way you won't be ignorant of Satan's devices, but instead you'll stand fast in faith and stop his strategies in every circumstance. As you obey the Word instead of people's opinions or experiences and you engage in true biblical warfare, you'll overcome the enemy's attacks every time!

Chapter 9
Pulling Down Strongholds

Evil spirits like to remain in the locality where they have established strongholds. The Bible gives us an example of this in Mark chapter 5 when Jesus delivered the madman of Gadara. The evil spirits that inhabited the man didn't want Jesus to send them *out of the country*.

> **MARK 5:9-13**
> 9 And he [Jesus] asked him, What is thy name? And he answered, saying, My name is Legion: for we are many.
> 10 And he BESOUGHT HIM MUCH that he would NOT send them away OUT OF THE COUNTRY.
> 11 Now there was there nigh unto the mountains a great herd of swine feeding.
> 12 And all the devils besought him, saying, Send us into the swine, that we may enter into them.
> 13 And forthwith Jesus gave them leave....

Those evil spirits didn't want to leave that locality, so they asked to go into a herd of swine. Jesus gave them permission (v. 13).

Strongholds in Certain Regions

We can glean from this passage of Scripture that demons do like to gang up in certain parts of the world or in certain countries. For example, in my travels it's easy for me to discern what kinds of spirits are in a given locality.

I can drive through a city and know what spirits predominate there, not because of any spiritual gifts operating in my life, but just by spiritual perception.

Every Christian should have enough spiritual perception about them to discern what spirits predominate in a given locality. Sometimes there are predominately immoral or occult spirits, or spirits promoting foreign religions. Small towns, not just large cities, can have spiritual strongholds or spirits ruling over them too.

The evil spirits that dominate a city will try to get into the local churches if there are people in the church who will yield to them and let them in.

Spirits in the Church

My wife and I were visiting in a certain town once, and the pastor in that town wanted me to preach in his church. I was in the field ministry at the time teaching the Word. He kept asking me to hold a meeting in his church.

Finally, I told him I wasn't going to do it. I explained I didn't want to preach in that town unless God definitely told me to. You see, in that city the people prided themselves on being conservative; actually, they were so conservative in the area of giving that they were stingy. The same spirits that predominate in a city will get into the church if believers let them.

I told the pastor that the town was full of reserved, conservative people, motivated and influenced by stingy devils and demons. I told him those demons had gotten into his church and that the people wouldn't support me if I went there. His eyes got big and his mouth fell open. He asked, "Has anyone been talking to you?" I replied, "No one but the Lord."

I told that pastor, "The people in your church don't treat ministers of the gospel right! That's why I won't come." Unless God tells you to, there's no use going to a group like that anyway. They can't receive God's best because they mistreat God's servants; they are being motivated and influenced by evil spirits.

A "stingy" church is not scriptural. The Bible says, ". . . *Thou shalt not muzzle the ox that treadeth out the corn. And, The labourer is worthy of his reward*" (1 Tim. 5:18). Paul was quoting the Old Testament (Deut. 25:4), but he was talking about those in the ministry (1 Cor. 9:7-14).

When church members yield to evil spirits like that it gives the devil a right of way in the church. It grieves the Spirit of God, and He will be hindered from manifesting Himself the way He wants to. We need to realize that as Christians we don't have to listen to the devil. And we don't have to yield to him either! We don't have to allow the god of this world to dominate our thinking or our actions.

Pulling Down Strongholds

So whatever kind of spirits dominate in a city, those same spirits will try to get into the church if people in the church yield to them and let them in. We can see this, for example, in Paul's Epistles to the Corinthians.

Corinth at that time was one of the most immoral cities of the East. The immoral spirit that had control of the city got into the church because someone in the church let it in through wrongdoing. There was a man in the church who was cohabiting with his father's wife. Paul had to deal with these moral issues in his Epistles to the Corinthian church.

1 CORINTHIANS 5:3-5
3   For I verily, as absent in body, but present in spirit, have judged already, as though I were present, concerning him that hath so done this deed,
4   In the name of our Lord Jesus Christ, when ye are gathered together, and my spirit, with the power of our Lord Jesus Christ,
5   To deliver such an one unto Satan for the destruction of the flesh, that the spirit may be saved in the day of the Lord Jesus.

Notice in this passage that Paul only dealt with the man and his sin; he didn't deal with a "ruling spirit" in the church *or* in the city. It's true that evil spirits which predominate in a city will try to get into the church unless believers and the church as a whole learn to stand against them. However, in our day there has been an extreme teaching in this area.

Some people today are getting into a ditch with some of the things they are doing in the name of spiritual warfare. Spiritual warfare is biblical. But some marvelous and dear Christians have gotten into excess by some extreme practices that are *not* biblical.

Although a lot of these extremes are listed under what they call "pulling down strongholds," they do not line up with what we read in the New Testament. Some of these dear, misguided people believe they are actually pulling down entire strongholds over cities and nations through such excess in prayer as "warring" tongues.

Actually, we have no direct scriptural support for pulling down demonic strongholds over entire cities and nations, especially in the sense of warring tongues and yelling at the devil. We need to go back to what the Word of God says.

What does the Word of God say specifically about pulling down strongholds? And according to the Bible, what is a "stronghold"?

2 CORINTHIANS 10:4,5
4   (For the weapons of our warfare are not carnal, but mighty through God to the pulling down of STRONG

HOLDS:)
**5 Casting down IMAGINATIONS, and every high thing
that exalteth itself against the knowledge of God, and
bringing into captivity every THOUGHT to the obedience of
Christ.**

In these verses, Paul defines what a stronghold is. Because
some have failed to keep this in mind, they have taken one verse
and gone to the extreme with it. For example, some have taken the
phrase "the weapons of our warfare are mighty for the pulling
down of strongholds" in verse 4 out of its setting and tried to use it
to present a complete doctrine by itself. By taking verse 4 out of the
context of the next verse, they begin to make it say something that
it really isn't saying.

But reading verse 4 by itself as a complete doctrine can leave
the wrong impression. You would be missing what Paul is really
talking about here unless you read verse 4 about strongholds in the
context in which it was written.

Actually, in this passage Paul is talking about a believer taking
charge of his mind — his own *thinking.* He is talking about *mental*
bondages — thoughts, reasonings, and arguments — which are
contrary to God and His Word.

Paul is primarily talking about casting down *reasonings, imaginations,* and *thoughts* — *not* casting down demonic strongholds
over cities and nations.

The meaning comes through more clearly in *The Amplified Bible.*

2 CORINTHIANS 10:4,5 *(Amplified)*
**4 For the weapons of our warfare are not physical
(weapons of flesh and blood), but they are mighty before
God for the overthrow and destruction of strongholds.**
**5 [Inasmuch as we] refute ARGUMENTS and THEORIES
and REASONINGS and every PROUD and LOFTY THING
that sets itself up against the (true) knowledge of God; and
we lead every THOUGHT and PURPOSE away captive into
the obedience of Christ, the Messiah, the Anointed One.**

The biggest battle you will ever "fight" is in this area of the
thought life and the mind. It all starts right there. Fighting the
battle of the mind so you can stay in faith is the way to victory in
every area of life.

Well, what are you going to do about *that* battle? In order to
successfully fight that battle, you're going to have to renew your

mind with the Word and cast down reasonings, imaginations, and vain thoughts that are contrary to the Word, because Satan will try to bombard your mind.

The devil's strategy is to sidetrack believers from fighting the true spiritual battle, which is taking every thought captive to the obedience of God's Word.

Satan knows that believers who stay in faith in the Word are dangerous to him because they can fulfill God's will in the earth for their lives.

That's why Satan likes it when believers get off into error and excess trying to fight demonic strongholds over cities and nations. He knows those strongholds can't be once and for all pulled down before the time — before Adam's lease on this earth runs out.

So the devil is laughing the whole time believers are hollering at him in the flesh trying to pull him down over cities. Believers who fight the devil on those terms are actually defeating themselves by having to continually rely on their own fleshly efforts.

They are either trying to pray down the victory that is already theirs, or they are trying to pray down ruling spirits that cannot be pulled down before the time.

Let's look at this passage in Second Corinthians in some other translations, so we can understand better what the Bible is talking about by the word "stronghold."

2 CORINTHIANS 10:4,5 *(Moffatt)*
4   The WEAPONS OF MY WARFARE are not weapons of the flesh, but divinely strong to demolish FORTRESSES —
5   I demolish THEORIES and any RAMPART thrown up to resist the knowledge of God, I take every project prisoner to make it obey Christ.

2 CORINTHIANS 10:5 *(TCNT)*
5   We are engaged in confuting ARGUMENTS and pulling down every BARRIER raised against the knowledge of God. . . .

2 CORINTHIANS 10:5 *(Phillips)*
5   Our battle is to bring down every DECEPTIVE FANTASY and every imposing defense THAT MEN ERECT against the true knowledge of God. . . .

2 CORINTHIANS 10:5 *(Knox)*
5   Yes, we can pull down the CONCEITS OF MEN, every BARRIER OF PRIDE which sets itself up against the true

knowledge of God.

You can readily see that this passage is talking about taking thoughts, imaginations, arguments, theories, reasonings, deceptive fantasies, conceits of men, and barriers of pride and bringing *them* into subjection to the true knowledge of God — the *Word of God.*

This is not telling me to take captive the thoughts in your mind and pull them down. I can take authority and control of my *own* thoughts, but I can't take authority over *your* thoughts.

You see, because the mind is the greatest area of "battle" for the attacks of Satan, the devil's strategy is to erect strongholds in our thinking that "exalt themselves against the true knowledge of God."

That is one reason believers need the full armor of God with the helmet of salvation and the shield of faith — so they can protect themselves from Satan's attacks on their minds. And the Bible teaches that we are to repent of wrong thoughts and conform to the image of Christ in our thinking (Rom. 8:29; Phil. 2:5). That is one of our greatest defenses against Satan.

There is an overemphasis today on some aspects of spiritual warfare, that is based in part on a misapplication of this scripture here in Second Corinthians 10:4 and 5 about "pulling down strongholds," and on the scripture in Ephesians 6:12 about "wrestling." But both of these passages of Scripture must be taken in the contexts in which they were written, not lifted out of context to build extreme doctrines of spiritual warfare.

I believe in spiritual warfare, of course, and in spiritual militancy in the sense of being aggressive and fervent in the Word and in the Holy Ghost. Be aggressive to preach the Word. Be aggressive and fervent to preach the new birth, the baptism of the Holy Ghost, healing, and the believer's rights and privileges in Christ. Be aggressive to preach faith and prayer and to preach against devils and demons.

But in our day there is an extreme emphasis being placed on the subject of spiritual warfare and spiritual militancy to the exclusion of other Bible truths which can get the Church off into a ditch.

Yes, we should be fervent in the Word, fervent in prayer, and fervent in evangelism. "Militancy" meaning *fervency* is fine. But when people teach others to focus all their spiritual activity on the person of the devil — that is both dangerous and unscriptural.

Where this is the most obvious is in the practice of trying to dethrone Satan over cities. Militancy is taken out of bounds when we get the idea that we have to accomplish something which Jesus has already accomplished for us. Why would believers want to dethrone Satan or principalities and powers?

The truth is that Jesus has already defeated Satan for us (Col. 2:15). As the Church, we triumph in that victory — the victory Christ has already won for us at the Cross. Our job now is to make manifest the savor of that victory through the knowledge of God's Word (2 Cor. 2:15). We continue to triumph in that victory in our daily lives as we walk in God's Word.

We don't have to win the battle over Satan. Jesus has already won the victory for us. We must simply walk in the light of God's Word concerning that victory, and Jesus' victory over the devil will become manifest in our daily lives.

The fact that Satan and his hosts are still here should not disturb us. They will continue to be here until Adam's lease runs out. While they are here, we can continue to enforce the reality of their defeat by the Word. Colossians 2:15 says that Jesus *"having spoiled principalities and powers, he* [Jesus] *made a shew of them openly, triumphing over them in it* [the cross]*."* We are to be triumphant in Jesus' victory.

The fact that Satan rules over the lives of others through strongholds of deception does not mean we have to re-enter into battle with him as Jesus did. We can use the Name of Jesus in prayer to bind and break his hold over people and then we can simply enforce Satan's defeat through the preaching of the Word. The light of God's Word will dispel the darkness of Satan's deceptions in people's lives.

We don't have to war in the flesh by trying to defeat Satan through excesses such as warring tongues and yelling at the devil. The business of trying to do battle with evil spirits in the heavenlies is an effort of the flesh to try to defeat an already defeated foe.

However, in some Christian circles today, dethroning Satan over cities and nations through spiritual warfare and violent intercession is seen as an absolute prerequisite before any revival or effective evangelism can take place. *But you can't find that in the Bible.*

Study the Gospels and the Book of Acts for yourself to see what Jesus and His disciples did to bring revival. One thing you'll notice is that Jesus and His disciples didn't pull down demonic powers ruling over entire cities or countries. Jesus and His disciples only dealt with demons in connection with *individual* people.

But I find it very interesting that in reading the Book of Acts, the disciples don't make any reference to the type of warfare and militancy that is being taught in some places in the Church today.

It's also interesting that we don't find this kind of warfare *practiced* in the Book of Acts either. No, the Book of Acts shows us a Church that is conscious of the Presence of God and focused on teaching people the Word of God for themselves so they can be successful in every area of life — not one that is all consumed with fighting the devil.

Study the accounts given in the Book of Acts about what was *taught* to the people and what was *practiced* by the disciples. You will find it is contrary to much of the emphasis taught and practiced in some circles in the Body of Christ today. The Book of Acts emphasizes the teaching of sound doctrine and preaching the gospel to bring people into the Kingdom of God, not fighting devils and bringing down strongholds.

We don't have scripture for pulling down strongholds over cities and nations, but we do have scriptural grounds for binding the operations and strategies of principalities and powers in their attacks against us (Matt. 18:18; Luke 10:19; Phil. 2:9,10).

We do that with the Word of God and the Name of Jesus. We take our stand against the enemy with the Word of God, just as Jesus did (Matt. 4:4-10).

Let's look at the ministry of Jesus to see what He did since Jesus and His disciples certainly turned the world of that day upside down.

Well, how did they do it? If they did it by doing direct battle with the devil then we have scriptural grounds to do the same thing. But if they didn't, then we shouldn't be doing it either.

Believers should follow the *doctrine* we see *practiced* in the New Testament.

Did Jesus Try To War Against Devils In His Earthly Ministry?

Looking at the ministry of Jesus, what *did* Jesus do to change towns and cities? Did He have to pull down strongholds through militant prayer as He went from city to city? Did He find it necessary to "discern" the ruling spirit in every city and then do war against it?

And did Jesus and His disciples teach others to identify the ruling spirit over cities in order to pull down strongholds? No, we don't find scripture where they did.

Study the Gospels for yourself. You will find that the focus of

Jesus' ministry was that He just traveled from place to place teaching and preaching the gospel — *the Word* (Matt. 4:23; 9:35; Luke 13:22). He put the Word first, and the Word set people free from Satan's dominion.

LUKE 4:18,19
18 The Spirit of the Lord is upon me, because he hath anointed me TO PREACH THE GOSPEL to the poor; he hath sent me to heal the brokenhearted,TO PREACH DELIVERANCE to the captives, and recovering of sight to the blind, to set at liberty them that are bruised,
19 TO PREACH the acceptable year of the Lord.

Jesus was sent to *teach* and *preach* the gospel, not to focus on tearing down strongholds over cities and nations. It was the preaching and teaching of the gospel that brought strongholds down in people's lives!

If it were possible to tear them down over cities, Jesus would have taught the people to do that, but He didn't. The Bible says Jesus set the captives free from Satan's bondage by teaching the people what the Word says and to walk in the light of the Word (John 8:32).

We need to do what Jesus did. Preach deliverance by preaching the Word. Notice Luke 4:18 doesn't say Jesus *prayed* deliverance. It says He *preached* deliverance.

In other words, He told people what *the Word* said: *"If the Son* [the Word made flesh] *therefore shall make you free, ye shall be free indeed"* (John 8:36). People were delivered as the Word set them free.

In the scripture that we do have, Jesus prayed His prayers to the Father (Mat. 11:25; Luke 23:34 John 11:41,17:1).

Did the Early Church Try To War Against the Devil Over Cities?

Read the Book of Acts for yourself and see if there is specific scripture stating that the disciples made it a point to fight ruling demonic princes over cities, regions, or countries.

Actually, when the Early Church came together and spoke in tongues, the Bible says they were declaring the wonderful works of God: *". . . we do hear them SPEAK IN OUR TONGUES THE WONDERFUL WORKS OF GOD"* (Acts 2:11). They weren't fighting the devil in tongues. They weren't pulling down strongholds over Jerusalem. They were extolling *God*. God was the focus of their praying.

Let's look at biblical examples of how believers prayed when they faced great opposition from the devil. Did they fight and war against devils when Satan came against them? No, they didn't.

For example, in Acts 16:25, Paul and Silas overcame the opposition of the enemy by praying and praising God. Peter and John also faced an attack (Acts 4:3,5-7). It came through men. They were commanded not to preach and teach anymore in the Name of Jesus (Acts 4:18).

When Peter and John were finally let go, they went to their own company and prayed to God. According to the Book of Acts, these believers didn't battle in tongues against principalities and powers in the heavenlies. They didn't "wage war" against the devil or try to pull down religious devils over the city. What did they do?

ACTS 4:24
24 And when they heard that, THEY LIFTED UP THEIR VOICE TO GOD with one accord, and said, LORD, THOU ART GOD, which hast made heaven, and earth, and the sea, and all that in them is.

They didn't magnify the problem or the devil. They extolled and magnified God. I'm not saying that their praise and worship didn't indirectly affect the spiritual opposition of the devil. I'm saying it was not their primary concern.

It's sad, but some believers spend most of their time praying against the devil and talking about him. Listening to them, you would think that Jesus was "poor ole Jesus," who didn't accomplish anything when He died and rose from the dead and spoiled principalities and powers and put them to nought (Col. 2:14,15). There's nothing that will sap the praise to God out of your prayers like focusing all your attention on the devil.

In Acts chapter 4 when the Early Church was facing great opposition from the devil, these believers lifted their voices to God *in faith*. They stayed in faith; they didn't try to fight the devil in prayer. They talked about how big God is, and then they brought God's *Word* to Him in prayer (Acts 4:25-28).

Actually, from verses 25 through 28, the believers talked about how big God is and about the great things He had done. Then they talked about what the Word of God said about their situation.

ACTS 4:25-28
25 Who by the mouth of thy servant David hast said, Why

did the heathen rage, and the people imagine vain things? 26 The kings of the earth stood up, and the rulers were gathered together against the Lord, and against his Christ. 27 For of a truth against thy holy child Jesus, whom thou hast anointed, both Herod, and Pontius Pilate, with the Gentiles, and the people of Israel, were gathered together, 28 For to do whatsoever thy hand and thy counsel determined before to be done.

Then finally in verse 29 they talked about the problem. But notice that this entire prayer lasts from verse 25 through 30, but they only talked about the problem in one verse (v. 29).

ACTS 4:29,30
29 And now, Lord, BEHOLD THEIR THREATENINGS: and grant unto thy servants, that with all boldness they may speak thy word, 30 By stretching forth thine hand to heal; and that signs and wonders may be done by the name of thy holy child Jesus.

These believers talked to *God*, not to the devil, even though the devil was behind the problem. And the main thing they asked God to do about their problem was to grant them boldness to preach *the Word* with signs and wonders following. They knew it was the Word that would change people and situations (John 8:32).

This prayer of the Early Church shows us the biblical way to pray as a church when we face the opposition of the powers of darkness. We're to pray to *God*. And we're to pray for boldness to proclaim the Word so *the Word* can set people free from Satan. And furthermore, notice they did not even ask God to do anything about the devil.

Then when the Early Church was scattered abroad because the persecution greatly increased, believers went everywhere preaching the Word — not directly fighting devils: *"Therefore they that were scattered abroad went every where PREACHING THE WORD"* (Acts 8:4). If any strongholds had to be pulled down, the Church trusted God and His Word to do that.

When Peter was in prison, the saints who were praying for him didn't try to fight against the religious devils over Jerusalem. They made their earnest entreaty to *God* in Peter's behalf.

ACTS 12:5
5 Peter therefore was kept in prison: but prayer was made without ceasing of the church UNTO GOD for him.

What about when the prophets and teachers gathered together in Antioch? Did they go into spiritual warfare and spend their time in spiritual combat before they sent out Paul and Barnabas for the work of the ministry?

ACTS 13:2
2   As THEY MINISTERED TO THE LORD, and fasted, the Holy Ghost said. . . .

No, they ministered to the Lord! They didn't fight devils. Too many times folks know nothing about ministering to the Lord; they spend all their time trying to fight a defeated foe.

It's when believers begin to minister to God, that things begin to happen. They create an atmosphere where the Holy Spirit can speak: *"As they ministered to the Lord . . . the HOLY GHOST SAID . . ."* (v. 2).

Also, in the Book of Revelation, Jesus talked to the Apostle John on the Isle of Patmos about a literal church that existed in the city of Pergamos at that time. The city of Pergamos was a stronghold of Satan, yet Jesus didn't say one thing about fighting satanic rulers over that city. Surely if it were scriptural to do spiritual warfare in the sense of fighting the devil and pulling down strongholds over cities, Jesus would have mentioned it here.

REVELATION 2:12,13
12   And to the angel of the church in Pergamos write; These things saith he which hath the sharp sword with two edges;
13   I know thy works, and where thou dwellest, even WHERE SATAN'S SEAT IS: and thou HOLDEST FAST MY NAME, AND HAST NOT DENIED MY FAITH, even in those days wherein Antipas was my faithful martyr, who was slain among you, WHERE SATAN DWELLETH.

Although Jesus said the church at Pergamos was "where Satan's seat is," notice that Jesus did not tell the believers there to do warfare against Satan. No, Jesus commended the believers for *holding fast to His Name* and for *not denying the faith* (v. 13). In other words, He was encouraging them to stay in faith!

Did the Disciples Try To War Against Devils Over Cities?

Let's look at some other passages in the New Testament to see what the disciples did as they traveled from city to city. These men were handpicked by Jesus. We can't find any Scriptures that say the disciples went around pulling down strongholds over the cities they went into. Neither can we find Scriptures where they taught others to do that.

In Jerusalem

When Peter and John went up to the temple, it was the Name of Jesus that healed a man who had been lame from birth.

ACTS 3:6,16
6 Then Peter said, Silver and gold have I none; but such as I have give I thee: IN THE NAME OF JESUS CHRIST OF NAZARETH rise up and walk. . . .
16 And HIS NAME through faith IN HIS NAME made this man strong. . . .

Notice that it was the Name of Jesus that was called into question and feared by the religious leaders of the day (Acts 4:10-12), because it is in that Name that believers have authority over the devil.

In other words, the disciples were teaching about the power and authority invested in the Name of Jesus (Acts 4:15-20). The Name represented all the authority of Jesus and all that He accomplished when He arose victorious over death, hell, and the grave.

ACTS 6:7
7 . . . the WORD OF GOD increased; and the number of the disciples MULTIPLIED in JERUSALEM greatly; and a great company of the priests were obedient to the faith.

It's interesting that when the Word of God *increased*, the number of disciples *multiplied*. If believers really want to do much damage to Satan's kingdom, they should get out and preach the Word.

It's the Word of God that has the power to set people free. Not once in the city of Jerusalem did the disciples talk about pulling down strongholds or ruling princes over cities through warring tongues or screaming at devils.

In fact, if you go through the Books of Acts and highlight what the disciples taught as they traveled from place to place, you will find that the disciples taught and preached the Word of God. They also taught about the Name of Jesus, and they taught and preached the gospel — salvation through Jesus Christ.

In every instance, receiving and acting on the Word was what brought people out from under the dominion of Satan's strongholds.

Did Paul Try To War With Strongholds Over Cities?

Let's see what the Apostle Paul did as he traveled and came into contact with strongholds in certain cities. After all, this great man of faith wrote much of the New Testament. If pulling down strongholds over cities through warring tongues or screaming at devils is a scriptural practice, surely Paul said something about it, or he practiced it in the cities where he went.

Paul in Damascus

Did Paul try to pull down strongholds over the city of Damascus? No, immediately after his conversion, Paul began to preach about *Jesus.* Jesus Christ was the focus of Paul's teaching, not the devil and not strongholds.

> **ACTS 9:20,22,27,29**
> **20 And straightway he PREACHED CHRIST in the synagogues, THAT HE IS THE SON OF GOD. . . .**
> **22 But Saul increased the more in strength, and confounded the Jews which dwelt at Damascus, PROVING THAT THIS IS VERY CHRIST. . . .**
> **27 But Barnabas took him [Paul], and brought him to the apostles, and declared unto them how he had seen the Lord in the way, and that he had spoken to him, and how he had PREACHED BOLDLY AT DAMASCUS IN THE NAME OF JESUS. . . .**
> **29 And he spake BOLDLY IN THE NAME OF THE LORD JESUS, and disputed against the Grecians. . . .**

Notice that Paul magnified and lifted up the Name of Jesus Christ. It's the Name of Jesus that breaks strongholds in people's thinking and in their lives. Paul taught people to exalt Jesus' power and majesty. But when believers teach others to concentrate on pulling down strongholds and warring against devils, the emphasis is on Satan and what he's doing. They are actually magnifying the devil, and that opens a door and gives him access. But when believers magnify *God*, they give *Him* access to their hearts and lives.

As we read the accounts of Paul traveling throughout the cities and villages of that day, the first thing we notice is that he established believers in *the faith*. We see no scripture where Paul made it a point of warring against the devil.

ACTS 16:4,5
4 And as they [Paul and Timothy] **went through the cities, they delivered them the decrees for to keep, that were ordained of the apostles and elders which were at Jerusalem.**
5 And so were the churches ESTABLISHED IN THE FAITH, and INCREASED IN NUMBER DAILY.

As believers were established in the faith, the Bible says their numbers increased daily. Wherever the Word is preached, there's an increase of souls into the Kingdom of God. That's how to scripturally "pull down" strongholds — the preaching of the Gospel pulls them down in people's lives by getting them saved.

Paul in Philippi

Did Paul try to pull down strongholds over Philippi? It was in Philippi where Paul had to deal with a demon that was stirring up trouble through a young damsel.

ACTS 16:16-18
16 And it came to pass, as we went to prayer, a certain damsel possessed with a spirit of divination met us, which brought her masters much gain by soothsaying:
17 The same followed Paul and us, and cried, saying, These men are the servants of the most high God, which shew unto us the way of salvation.
18 And this did she many days. But Paul, being grieved, turned and said to the spirit, I command thee in the name of Jesus Christ to come out of her. AND HE CAME OUT THE SAME HOUR.

An evil spirit was using this woman to hinder the disciples' ministry in this city. This woman had a spirit of divination or fortune telling, and the spirit in her knew who the disciples were.

But notice that Paul only dealt with *the spirit* that was causing this woman to continually cry out and cause a disturbance — he didn't deal with any strongholds over the city.

That woman followed the disciples many days, and the spirit in her proclaiming everywhere, *". . . These men are servants of the most high God, which shew unto us the way of salvation"* (v. 17). What she said was so, but who wants the devil testifying for him!

It was vexing to have the devil advertising for them, so why didn't Paul rebuke that foul spirit the very first day? Or the second day? The reason he didn't is that the gift of discerning of spirits didn't operate when *Paul* wanted it to operate; it operated as the *Holy Spirit* willed (1 Cor. 12:11). Until the operation of the gift of discerning of spirits came into manifestation, Paul was just as helpless as any of us would be to deal with that particular situation.

Paul waited until the Spirit of God gave him insight into the spiritual realm before he did anything about the evil spirit that was causing the disturbance. You see, Paul wasn't just binding the evil spirit in his operation against him and the work of the gospel — he was casting an evil spirit *out* of a person. Paul had to have the anointing and the gifts of the Holy Spirit in operation to get the woman *delivered* of that demon.

When the gift of discerning of spirits came into operation, Paul just spoke to the evil spirit operating through the woman: *". . . I command thee in the name of Jesus Christ to COME OUT OF HER . . . "* (Acts 16:18). And the Bible says, *". . . he came out THE SAME HOUR"* (v. 18).

It didn't take hours of yelling, screaming, and carrying on for Paul to cast that evil spirit out of her. And Paul didn't try to pull down the ruling spirit over Philippi because of that incident either. Paul merely spoke to the evil spirit in the Name of Jesus and commanded it to come out, and it came out in the *same hour*.

The key was that Paul waited until he had the insight of the Holy Spirit before he acted. In other words, he dealt with the evil spirit when he was *in the Spirit* — by the power and unction of the Holy Spirit — and the woman was delivered. We will have to rely on the Holy Spirit, just as Paul did.

In some Christian circles today, people are hollering and shouting and yelling at the devil, and not much is happening. That's because many people are trying to deal with the devil in the energy of the flesh.

It's the anointing or the power of the Holy Spirit that breaks the yoke of the devil's bondage (Isa. 10:27). The anointing is on the Word, so you're not going to have any anointing to deal with the devil unless you've taken time to sow the Word into your heart.

And you're not going to have the power of God operating in your life unless you're a *doer* of the Word.

Some Christians today are not in the Word. They haven't taken time to hide God's Word in their hearts by studying, reading, and meditating on it, so they try to fight the devil in the energy of the flesh. It won't work. You can't "fight" the devil in the flesh — shouting and carrying on. People who do that are just wearing themselves out.

The Bible says, *"That which is born of the flesh is flesh; and that which is born of the Spirit is spirit"* (John 3:6). The devil and his host of demons are spirit beings. That's why you can't deal with them in the energy of the flesh and win. The Body of Christ is going to have to realize they need to deal with things of the spirit realm *by the Spirit of God* with *the Word of God.*

Paul couldn't do any more than you or I can without the anointing! We are totally dependent upon the Word of God and the anointing of the Holy Spirit.

MARK 16:17,20
17 And these SIGNS shall follow them that believe; IN MY NAME SHALL THEY CAST OUT DEVILS. . . .
20 And they [the disciples] **went forth, and preached every where, THE LORD WORKING WITH THEM, and CONFIRMING THE WORD with signs following. Amen.**

What did *Jesus* tell the disciples about casting out devils? Did Jesus say He would confirm it with signs and wonders following when His disciples yelled at the devil in tongues? Or did Jesus say he would confirm it with signs and wonders when His disciples taught their spiritual experiences? Emphatically, no!

The Bible says Jesus *worked with* His disciples, confirming *the Word* they preached with signs following. He told them to preach the Word and the signs *would* follow (Mark 16:20).

Put the Word first and you won't have to worry about signs following — including casting out devils. One sign Jesus said would follow *the Word* is that believers would cast out devils (Mark 16:17-20).

Paul in Athens

The city of Athens was another major city where much wickedness prevailed. What did Paul teach people to do about the spiritual strongholds in that city?

ACTS 17:15,16

> **15** And they that conducted Paul brought him unto Athens: and receiving a commandment unto Silas and Timotheus for to come to him with all speed, they departed.
> **16** Now while Paul waited for them at Athens, HIS SPIRIT WAS STIRRED IN HIM, when he saw THE CITY WAS WHOLLY GIVEN TO IDOLATRY.

The Athenians had erected different images to various gods on Mars Hill. The Scriptures say that Paul perceived that the city of Athens was wholly given over to idolatry (v. 16). Paul's spirit was stirred because of the strongholds he saw in that city.

What did Paul do about the idolatry and the strongholds in that city? Did he wage spiritual warfare against the "spiritual prince" of Mars Hill in high places? No, the Bible tells us exactly what he did. He taught the people the gospel. He preached *the Word*.

> **ACTS 17:17,22,23**
> **17** Therefore disputed he in the synagogue with the Jews, and with the devout persons, and in the market daily with them that met with him. . . .
> **22** Then Paul stood in the midst of Mars' hill, and said, Ye men of Athens, I PERCEIVE THAT IN ALL THINGS YE ARE TOO SUPERSTITIOUS.
> **23** For as I passed by, and beheld your devotions, I found an altar with this inscription, TO THE UNKNOWN GOD. Whom therefore ye ignorantly worship, HIM DECLARE I UNTO YOU.

According to Acts Paul didn't attempt to pull down any demonic strongholds over the city even though he saw that there were many strongholds there in the city. He preached *the gospel*, and he preached about *Jesus* (Acts 17:31,32). No mention was even made about the devil in what Paul preached.

Those who believed what Paul said were saved. That's how Paul broke the strongholds over people's lives — he preached the Word so they could get saved! Then Satan no longer had legal dominion over them.

Paul in Ephesus

Acts chapter 19 shows us Paul's ministry in Ephesus. The people of Ephesus made images of the goddess Diana and sold them. When Paul came to town preaching Jesus Christ, they felt their livelihood was threatened, so they rose up against Paul to cause turmoil and to hinder him from preaching the Word.

Some kind of an evil spirit was surely ruling over that city caus-ing the people to come against Paul, wasn't it? But Paul didn't launch a spiritual militant attack to pull down the "Diana spirit."

It was Demetrius the silversmith who drew attention to the god-dess Diana, not Paul. Paul was busy drawing attention to Jesus. He was busy preaching the Word so people could come out from under Satan's control.

ACTS 19:1,8-10,20
1 ... Paul having passed through the upper coasts came to Ephesus....
8 And he went into the synagogue, and SPAKE BOLDLY for the space of three months, disputing and persuading THE THINGS CONCERNING THE KINGDOM OF GOD.
9 But when divers were hardened, and believed not, but spake evil of that way before the multitude, he departed from them, and separated the disciples, disputing daily in the school of one Tyrannus.
10 And this continued by the space of two years; so that all they which dwelt in Asia HEARD THE WORD OF THE LORD JESUS, both Jews and Greeks....
20 So mightily GREW THE WORD OF GOD and PRE-VAILED.

The city of Ephesus was taken over by the temple cult of Diana. Everywhere there were temples to Diana. She was the "goddess" that prevailed over that city, and there were other gods in other temples too. The city was given over to idol worship.

But Paul dealt with those demonic strongholds by preaching the Word! It took him about two years, but the Bible says the Word grew and prevailed. So many people believed the Word Paul preached that the *Word* began to prevail in their lives. The Word of God prevailed in that city as individual people accepted the gospel and made Jesus Christ their Lord.

On the Day of Pentecost, the Early Church started off with 120 people. Reading the Book of Acts, it's easy to see that the devil tried to keep the Early Church from growing. You talk about the devil's onslaught!

The devil attacked the Early Church on every side with persecu-tion, tests, and trials. Satan tried to destroy the Church in its infancy, but the believers overcame him with the Word. And because the Word prevailed, the Lord added daily to the Church such as should be saved (Acts 2:47).

Satan uses the same strategies today — tests and trials — that he used in the days of the Early Church. He is still trying to destroy the Church's effectiveness in spreading the gospel. But the Bible says the gates of hell shall not prevail against the Church (Matt. 16:18). Well, the Church today is equipped with the same armor the early believers used against the devil to successfully withstand his onslaughts and remain victorious over him.

We can overcome the enemy's strategies just as the Early Church did, not by focusing our attention on fighting a defeated foe or by trying to pull down demonic strongholds over cities, but by praying scripturally. We have authority to bind principalities and powers in their operations against us. And we can pray to God for people's hearts to be open to the gospel. Then we need to get out and preach the Word and tell people about their covenant rights in Christ so they can be set free.

Besides, have you ever been to those countries where people have supposedly pulled down demonic strongholds over them? It's interesting that after they've "pulled them down," they are still there! That's because it's only the Word that changes *people* and affects *nations* and brings people out from under Satan's dominion and bondage so they can learn how to stand against him.

'Tormenting' the Devil

As long as I'm talking about tactics against the devil that don't work and are harmful to the Body of Christ, there's another practice that's wreaking havoc in some churches today.

A pastor told me recently about a "school of deliverance" he had attended. I call them "schools of bondage." I've never seen one of them that didn't turn into a school of bondage because they teach people to be devil-conscious and to fear the devil. They're not new. I saw them crop up years ago.

The pastor later told me, "I thought it would be a school, and the ministers would teach on Bible subjects. But they never taught a thing. For more than four hours, all they did was holler and yell at the devil at the top of their voices. They said they were 'tormenting' the devil. I just sat there and never got a thing in the world out of it."

I don't mean to be unkind about it, but I call that ignorance gone to seed! The people at that "deliverance school" might as well have been twiddling their thumbs, saying, "Twinkle, twinkle little star. How I wonder what you are." Trying to torment a defeated foe by hollering at him is missing the real battle. The believer's primary "battle" is with his own unrenewed mind and is won as the believer stands in his authority in Christ.

Some believers seem to think yelling at the devil shows their authority over him. But the devil doesn't have to bow to the loudness of a person's voice. He isn't afraid of noise; he's afraid of the Name of Jesus! He fears the believer who stands in his authority in Christ.

The devil doesn't have to cease and desist in his operations against you based on how loud you can yell at him. But he *does* have to stop in every strategy against you when you exercise your authority in Christ. You just have to know your rights and privileges in Christ and enforce Jesus' victory over Satan with God's Word. We are not trying to win the victory over Satan. Jesus has already won that victory. We are simply enforcing Jesus' victory with the Word of God in our lives.

I heard a tape of a session that was supposedly "taught" at this "school." The minister said, "The Bible said that Jesus went into the synagogues and evil spirits would cry out, 'Have you come to torment us?' So we are going to torment the devil."

He was quoting from Mark 5:7 and Luke 8:28. But in Matthew 8:29 it says, ". . . *behold, they cried out, saying, What have we to do with thee, Jesus, thou Son of God? art thou come hither to torment us BEFORE THE TIME?*"

Jesus couldn't "torment" these evil spirits yet, and neither can we. Until Adam's lease runs out, demons and evil spirits are here on the earth. But, thank God, the day is coming when they will be cast into their eternal abode and be tormented (Rev. 20:1-3).

Think about it! Why would anyone want to torment the devil? Jesus has whipped him at the Cross. Because Satan is a defeated foe, I'm not overly concerned about him. I know what to do with him if he shows up, glory to God! I'm more interested in preaching about Jesus so that people can come out from under the devil's dominion and learn how to successfully take their stand against Satan in every test and trial.

Let's find out what the Bible says and base our strategy against the kingdom of darkness on scriptural grounds so we can win the lost in the world for Jesus!

Search the Scriptures for yourself. Again and again you will find that Jesus, the twelve disciples, and the Apostle Paul taught believers to preach the Word.

They taught about the Name of Jesus, and the authority believers have in that Name over all the powers of darkness. They taught believers to stand strong in faith in God's Word because it's the Word that dispels strongholds in people's lives and thinking. The anointing on the Word has the power to break any demonic bondage!

Chapter 10

Praying Scripturally To Thwart The Kingdom of Darkness

If believers are not to pull down strongholds in the sense of doing unscriptural things like warring in tongues in the heavenlies, then how *can* we pray so that our prayers will effect change in our cities and nations?

First and foremost, the Body of Christ needs to realize that it's only the Word of God that grows and prevails in people's lives. The Word of God will grow and prevail over any circumstance, any demon, or any force of the devil in any person's life or in any nation if it is planted in the ground prepared by prayer and watered by the Word and the Holy Spirit.

Producing a Crop Through the Word and Prayer

A great revivalist once said, "It is no more supernatural for believers to have a revival than it is for farmers to reap a crop." He meant that the same principles for sowing and reaping a crop apply in both the natural and the spiritual realms. A harvest doesn't just happen for no reason, and it doesn't happen overnight. The farmer prepares the ground and then plants the seed in the ground, and rain causes the crop to grow. Finally, the crops are ready to harvest.

The Bible calls people who are ready to receive the gospel a spiritual harvest (Matt. 9:38). And the Bible gives us instructions on how to pull people out of the kingdom of darkness and get a harvest of souls for the Kingdom of light. In the natural realm, a crop is produced from seed. But before the seeds can be planted, the ground has to be prepared. Then in order to produce a harvest, after the seed is planted, it also has to be watered. The same is true in the spiritual realm.

Spiritually, we prepare the ground of people's hearts through scriptural prayer and sowing the incorruptible seed of God's Word (1 Peter 1:23). The Word has to be sown in people's hearts through the preaching of the Word, because it's the Word that brings light and illumination to men's hearts to set them free from the dominion of the devil (Ps. 119:130).

The task of sowing the incorruptible Word and telling people about Jesus' victory over Satan is the responsibility of every believer, not just preachers because Jesus said, "Go YE therefore, and teach all nations . . ." (Matt. 28:19). The devil has been defeated and dethroned by Jesus from his place of dominion over believers, but now believers have to go tell people the good news.

Besides, in the Great Commission, Jesus instructed believers to preach and teach His Word in all nations. He didn't say, "Go ye therefore and pray to pull down demonic strongholds in all nations"!

If believers only prayed in regard to the harvest, but no one ever sowed the Word, there would never be a harvest of souls — no one would come out from Satan's dominion. A person can pray for a crop all year long, but if he doesn't get out and plant some seed in his garden, he will come up empty-handed at harvest time. And I don't care how good the seed is or how well-prepared the ground is — if there is no water or rain, there will be no crop and no increase. In the Bible, water is a type of both the Word and the Holy Spirit.

James 5:7 says the Husbandman has long patience for the precious fruit of the earth, until He receives the *early* and the *latter* *rain*. The rain mentioned in this verse is a type of the Holy Spirit. And in Zechariah 10:1, the Bible instructs us to *ask* the Lord to send the rain — the spiritual rain of the Holy Spirit: "*Ask ye of the Lord rain in the time of the latter rain. . . .*"

To prepare the ground for the seed of the Word to be planted, we can pray for an outpouring of the Holy Spirit upon all nations. But then someone will have to go preach the gospel in order to set people free because it is *the Word* that sets people free (John 8:32). That is the scriptural way to change nations.

You are not going to be able to deal with the devil in nations any other way than by *praying* according to God's Word and by *sowing* the incorruptible seed of God's Word.

Therefore, it is scriptural to ask for the rain — the Holy Spirit — to be poured out upon every nation to cause the seeds of the Word that have been planted in people's hearts to grow. Another way to pray scripturally to pull souls from the kingdom of darkness is to ask the Lord of the harvest to send forth laborers into the harvest (Matt. 9:38).

No matter how good the harvest is, if there are no laborers to reap the harvest, the precious fruit of the earth will not be gathered in. So just keep asking the Lord for the rain of the Holy Spirit, keep preaching the Word to people, and keeping praying for laborers to be sent forth. Then there *will* be a harvest of souls that will be brought into the Kingdom of God. That's how to scripturally change cities and nations, and because it's based solidly on God's Word, *God* will bring the increase (1 Cor. 3:6).

Preparing the Ground Through Prayer

Getting the Word to prevail in people's lives should be the primary goal of believers as they pray for the world. If believers would avoid praying in unbiblical ways and begin praying effectively according to the Word of God, Satan's strategies in cities and nations would be thwarted and God's purposes would be fulfilled to a greater measure on this earth.

Praying for revival effects change in our cities and nations by pushing back the darkness. The ministry of Charles Finney, the great revivalist, gives us insight into how to prepare the way for revival through prayer that is based firmly on the Word.

Finney had revivals in city after city. Sometimes almost entire cities would get saved when he came and preached there. That's invading the kingdom of darkness! Most students of church history would agree that Finney had the greatest success at soulwinning of anyone since the Apostle Paul. It's a historical fact that eighty percent of all Finney's converts remained faithful to God in their Christian walk. In most of the other great revivals in history, not even fifty percent of the converts continued to live for the Lord.

When asked the secret to his success in the ministry, Finney simply said, "The secret is prayer. I always get up at four o'clock every morning and I pray from four o'clock to eight o'clock in the morning. I've had some experiences in prayer that indeed alarmed me. I found myself saying, 'Lord, You don't think we're not going to have revival here, do You!' And then I found myself quoting scripture after scripture to the Lord, reminding Him of His promises."

When I read the account of how Finney prayed for revival, I realized Finney was practicing what God instructed us to do in the Book of Isaiah.

ISAIAH 43:26
26 PUT ME IN REMEMBRANCE: LET US PLEAD TOGETHER: declare thou, that thou mayest be justified.

You see, Finney pled his case with God for revival in the cities where he would be preaching *based on the promises in God's Word.* He put God in remembrance of what He had said in His Word. He prayed according to the *Word* for revival — for souls to come into the Kingdom of God. There isn't one account given that Finney ever pulled down demonic strongholds, prayed against devils, or dealt with ruling princes over cities, yet whole towns were won to the Lord where Finney preached.

Finney also talked about a man named Father Nash who supported Finney in prayer. Sometimes Father Nash would go ahead of Finney to the next city where Finney would be preaching to prepare the way in prayer for revival.

Once when Finney came to a particular city and began his meetings, a woman came to him and said, "About a week ago, Father Nash rented a room from me. After three days, I wondered why he didn't come out of his room, so I went up to his door and I could hear Father Nash groaning. I thought something was wrong with him, so I opened the door and peeked in. There he was, lying in the middle of the floor, groaning and praying."

Finney answered, "Don't worry about Father Nash, Sister. Just leave him alone. He just has the burden of intercession to pray for lost souls."

You see, Father Nash wasn't pulling down strongholds or fighting demons who were ruling over cities where Finney was going to be preaching. He was praying according to Romans 8:26, as the Holy Spirit helped him pray for lost souls with groanings that could not be uttered in articulate speech.

However, we need to realize that the Holy Spirit may lead a person to pray in private in ways that would be wrong in a public setting. For instance, many people, especially if unbelievers are present, wouldn't understand if a person suddenly got down on the floor at church and began groaning and carrying on in prayer.

But prayer that is in line with the Word prepares the ground of people's hearts so the Word can be planted and bear eternal fruit in people's lives. That is the scriptural way to change cities and nations — not by spending our time supposedly warring against spiritual forces ruling over cities and nations that have already been defeated by Jesus.

Thousands of souls were won to the Kingdom of God through Finney's ministry. Finney accomplished that by praying for souls — the precious fruit of the earth — and by preaching the Word.

Let me share an example of a woman I knew who prepared the way through prayer for many to be delivered out of the kingdom of darkness. We called her Mother Howard, and she was a strong woman of prayer.

When Mother Howard first moved to north-central Texas years earlier, there were no Full Gospel churches in any of the towns or cities in that entire region. But the Lord laid it on her heart to pray that a Full Gospel church be established in every town and city in that area.

So Mother Howard began praying, taking one town at a time and continuing to pray until a Full Gospel church was raised up in the town she was praying for. She'd pray from ten in the morning until mid-afternoon. Then after supper, she'd begin praying again and continue until midnight or later, depending on how the Holy Spirit led her.

In her prayers Mother Howard wasn't trying to pull down strongholds or trying to fight the devil. She wasn't basing her prayers on what the devil *was* or was *not* doing. Like Father Nash, she was praying for souls to be saved as the Holy Spirit helped her in prayer. She wasn't yelling at the devil, but she was certainly doing much damage to the kingdom of darkness. She was talking to *God* and asking for souls to be brought into the Kingdom of God.

Mother Howard was largely responsible for praying a church into every city and town in that region of Texas. She's a good example of how believers are to pray to help win cities for God by fervent, scriptural prayer and intercession.

'I Will Give You the City'

Biblical prayer and intercession prayed by the *power* and the *anointing* of the Holy Spirit effects change in cities and nations for the Kingdom of God. Let me illustrate this. I was preaching in a church once, and in the middle of my sermon, a spirit of prayer fell on the whole congregation and everyone just hit the floor praying. The Unseen One, the Holy Spirit, was directing the service. We all prayed for quite some time.

At the end of that time of prayer, the Lord said to me, "Tell these folks that if they will enter into intercession and travail for the lost in their city, I'll give them this city. I'll give it to them, but they will have to possess it. And the way they possess it is through intercessory prayer and soul travail for the lost."

You see, we can intercede on behalf of others with our understanding, as Finney did when he pled his case with God using the promises in God's Word. But we don't always know how to pray for folks as we ought. That is why we need to be sensitive to pray as the Holy Spirit leads us and as He takes hold together with us (1 Cor. 14:14; Rom. 8:26). Praying for the lost in this manner is a part of the scriptural way to win a city for God. To win a city, you must win souls.

Winning a city for God doesn't necessarily mean that *every* single person in that town would be saved, because people still have free choice. But prayers and intercession make it easier for people to yield to God and to desire to be saved. As a result of the believers praying for the lost, many came to the Lord.

In fact, when I went back to that town two years later, that church was the largest in town, and many, many souls had been prayed out of the kingdom of darkness and brought into the Kingdom of God. And the believers in that church never tried to pull down one stronghold! They just gave themselves to prayer that was based on the Word of God and the leading of the Holy Spirit.

'Mightily Grew the Word of God and Prevailed'

How does planting the incorruptible seed — preaching the Word — pull people out of darkness and bring increase for the Kingdom of God?

We saw that in Acts 19, Paul preached the Word of God in Ephesus and mighty miracles were wrought for God's glory. People were saved, believers were baptized in the Holy Spirit and spoke with tongues, the sick were healed, and those who were oppressed by evil spirits were delivered.

All of this happened as the result of Paul preaching the Word: *"So mightily grew THE WORD OF GOD and prevailed"* (Acts 19:20). It was the Word of God that grew and prevailed in the hearts and lives of the people of Ephesus and brought them out of the bondage of the kingdom of darkness.

If you want to see miracles happen, including people being set free from demonic oppression and influence, preach the Word. Put God's Word first, because God's Word never fails. When you emphasize or exalt anything other than the Word, you get off on doctrinal tangents and people aren't set free from the bondages of Satan. Exalting anything but the Word of God opens a door to the devil because it gets you sidetracked from God's purpose for the Church.

Preach *the Word!* Establish people in *the Word.* Then they will be able to stand in any test or trial Satan tries to bring their way because they have a solid foundation for their faith — *the Word of the living God.*

Acts 19:20 says it was the Word of God that prevailed in people's lives. The word "prevail" means *to gain ascendancy through strength or superiority; to TRIUMPH; to be or become effective or effectual; to predominate.*

When the Word gains ascendancy in people's hearts, it has the power to transform their lives and deliver them from every bondage of the devil. The Word prevailing in people's lives is the key to the triumphant Church prevailing over the powers of darkness on this earth. It is the scriptural way to change cities and nations for God.

I read the newsletter of a missionary who has ministered in the Philippines for many years. His report of ministering in the Philippines is an example of how preaching the Word can effect change in a nation.

His ministry team went to an island that had never been reached with the gospel, and the people on the island were in great bondage to Satan. These missionaries preached the Word to the people, and many were delivered out of the bondage of darkness.

Believers could have fasted and prayed for the people on that island for the rest of their lives, but no one would have been saved if someone hadn't gone to the island and preached the Word.

Believers could have commanded the devil to stop ruling on that island, but he would have gone right on ruling because without the knowledge of the Word, people would have consciously or unconsciously continued to yield to Satan.

Without the preaching and teaching of the Word, the people wouldn't have known they had authority over Satan themselves and that they no longer had to be defeated by the devil.

So effective, scriptural prayer was first made for those on the island who were in bondage to Satan. But then someone had to go and plant the incorruptible seed by preaching the Word to the people so that many, many people could be born again and delivered out of the kingdom of darkness.

The more believers get the Word to prevail, the more we will see cities and nations changed to the glory of God. That is the way to stand as the triumphant Church of the Lord Jesus Christ in the earth, reaching all nations with the gospel in these last days.

Why Pray?

Although the Bible doesn't teach believers to focus their praying on fighting demons or pulling down strongholds over cities or nations, we *are* instructed to pray in order to further the Kingdom of God on the earth.

Someone might say, "Let's back off from praying for our cities and nations altogether to avoid all the errors and extremes about pulling down strongholds and combating the devil in prayer. Let God do whatever He wants to do; there's no point in praying."

But we can not back off from praying for the lost. The world desperately needs prayer. And the Church needs prayer.

Some might even ask, "Why do we have to pray and intercede for others anyway? Since God is all-powerful, why doesn't He just save everyone today, since it's His will that all men be saved?" (1 Tim. 2:4).

I once read a statement by John Wesley that answers that question. Wesley said, "It seems that God is limited by our prayer life. He can do nothing for humanity unless someone asks Him."

The Word tells us why that is so.

JAMES 4:2
2   ... ye have not, because ye ASK not.

JOHN 16:23,24
23 And in that day ye shall ask me nothing. Verily, verily, I say unto you, Whatsoever ye shall ASK the Father in my name, he will give it you.
24 Hitherto have ye asked nothing in my name: ASK, and ye shall receive, that your joy may be full.

God waits for His children to ask Him to move in behalf of the lost. Asking based on God's Word is one way believers stand in their place of authority in Christ and enforce Satan's defeat on the earth.

Stand in the Gap

God can only move on this earth as His people ask Him to move. God is longing today for someone who will make up the hedge and stand in the gap before Him and intercede for souls in every nation. That's the scriptural way to win cities and nations for God.

EZEKIEL 22:30
30 And I sought for a man among them, that should make

up the hedge, and STAND IN THE GAP before me for the land, THAT I SHOULD NOT DESTROY IT: but I found none.

In these verses, God said He had to destroy the land because as a just God, He had to pronounce a penalty on sin. God's penalty for sin wasn't unjust because the people had brought judgment upon themselves by their own sin: *". . . THEIR OWN WAY have I recompensed upon their heads . . . "* (v. 31).

This scripture implies that if God could have found someone to stand in the gap and make up the hedge and intercede for the land, He wouldn't have had to bring judgment on the people.

That goes back to what John Wesley said, "It seems God can do nothing for humanity unless someone *asks* Him to do it."

If someone would just ask Him. Think about that! God didn't say we had to go out and try to fight Satan, a defeated foe. These verses say that if God's covenant children would just *ask* Him to move on the earth, He would hear and answer their prayers. Satan is no match for God!

The unsaved people of the world are dominated and ruled by the devil — not God. Therefore, they are destined to have "their own way recompensed upon their heads" unless they hear and receive the truth of the gospel and repent.

God looks for those who will boldly ask Him to hold back judgment and give the unsaved more time to repent and come to the knowledge of the truth.

Then it's our responsibility to preach the gospel so people can be saved and teach them their position of authority in Christ over the devil.

You see, these are the principles in God's Word on which we are to build doctrines for prayer and for taking cities and nations for God. God watches over His *Word* to perform it — not doctrines that are built on experiences or isolated texts taken to the extreme (Isa. 55:11; Mark 16:20).

Praying for Those in Authority

Another scriptural way to pray to win cities and nations for God is found in the Book of Timothy. We are instructed to pray for those in authority. It stands to reason that if people in positions of authority in a nation change to God's glory, then God has more liberty to move in that nation, so the devil's plans are thwarted and men are saved.

1 TIMOTHY 2:1,2,4
**1   I exhort therefore, that, FIRST OF ALL, supplications,
prayers, intercessions, and giving of thanks, be made for
ALL MEN;**
**2   For KINGS, and for ALL THAT ARE IN AUTHORITY;
that we may lead a quiet and peaceable life in all godliness
and honesty.**
**4   [God] Who will have all men to be saved and to come
unto the knowledge of the truth.**

Notice that Paul said in First Timothy 2:1, ". . . *FIRST OF
ALL*. . . ." That means we are to pray for all men and for all those
in authority *before* we pray for ourselves or our own families.

Praying according to the Word and putting first things first
always produces results. Praying according to the latest spiritual
"fad" that's not based firmly on the Word of God will never produce
lasting or eternal results.

As we pray for those in authority, the Bible says we will effect
changes in the nations of this world ". . . *that we may lead A
QUIET AND PEACEABLE LIFE . . .* " (1 Tim. 2:2).

Yes, there are ruling spirits over cities and nations that influence people who are in authority. Although we can't "pull down"
those demonic strongholds once and for all, as we pray for the leaders of nations, we can thwart and render inoperative the devil's
strategies on the earth and cause God's purposes to prevail.

But praying for those in authority doesn't mean we are to pray
that the politicians in our favorite political party will be voted into
office. We can't judge by political party alone which candidate is
best to fill the leadership positions in our nation.

In other words, we don't need to get involved with *personalities*
in praying for our government; we just need to pray that the right
candidate be elected to office. We may all have our *opinion* who is
the right one for office, but only *God* knows for sure. Therefore, we
just need to pray that God will have His way in the matter.

God wants us to pray for those in authority so there will be
peace in our nations. Then we can preach the gospel undisturbed.
As long as the devil has nations in an upheaval, we can't lead a
quiet and peaceable life and preach the gospel unhindered to the
ends of the earth.

2 THESSALONIANS 3:1,2
1   Finally, brethren, pray for us, that THE WORD OF THE

**LORD MAY HAVE FREE COURSE, and be glorified, even as
it is with you:
2   And that we may be DELIVERED FROM UNREASON-
ABLE AND WICKED MEN: for all men have not faith.**

When we pray, God will deliver us from "unreasonable and
wicked men" in every area and sector in our nation so the Word of
God will have free course.

So the most important reason God wants us to pray for the leaders of nations is so the gospel can be preached and people can be
delivered out of the kingdom of darkness. God's plan and purpose is
for the Church to preach the gospel to every nation: *"And this
gospel of the kingdom SHALL BE PREACHED in all the world for
a witness unto ALL NATIONS; and then shall the end come"* (Matt.
24:14). This is the scriptural way we render the devil's work inoperative upon the earth.

When the gospel has been preached to all nations, the Bible
says the end shall come. The devil doesn't want the end to come,
because he knows when the end comes, he's through! Therefore,
Satan is going to try to throw up every roadblock he can to prevent
the gospel from being preached in *all* the world (Mark 16:15). In
times of turmoil and war, it's more difficult to spread the gospel.
That's why the devil uses unbelievers, whose minds he has blinded
(2 Cor. 4:4), to stir up trouble. Satan wants to try to stop the work
of God from going forth.

However, it's up to Christians whether or not the devil succeeds
in his individual strategies against them. As we obey the Bible's
instruction to pray for those in authority and for the nations of the
world, we can help thwart Satan's plans and instead fulfill *God's*
purposes on the earth.

Christians have authority to pray in Jesus' Name and change
things in their country, no matter what country they are living in.
When we pray, we give God permission to move and rule in the situation instead of Satan, the god of this world, no matter what the
situation is. When Christians stand in their place of delegated
authority in prayer in Jesus' Name, God brings many into His Kingdom. We don't fight the devil to gain this authority. The authority
has already been given to us in the Name of Jesus (Matt. 28:18-20).
When we take our stand in prayer, we are simply exercising the
authority Jesus has obtained for us.

We've seen an example of the Word of God prevailing over the strongholds of Satan in the decline of Communism in the Eastern Bloc nations. In 1983, the Lord began to impress upon me to pray according to James 5:7: ". . . *the husbandman waiteth for the precious fruit of the EARTH . . . until he receive the early and latter rain."*

We were conducting a weekly prayer meeting here at RHEMA at that time, and I announced, "I believe we've missed it in how we've been praying for the Eastern Bloc nations. I think many of us have unconsciously marked off the Communist countries as unreachable for the gospel. We've prayed for the Christians there, but how many of us have prayed for the Communist leaders?

"But the Bible doesn't say the Lord is waiting for the precious fruit of the United States or the Free World. He is waiting for the precious fruit of the *earth,* and that includes the Communist countries. That means before Jesus comes again, there has to be a revival behind the Iron Curtain and the Bamboo Curtain, for the Bible says there will be a gathering of the harvest from the *whole earth."*

So week after week during our prayer meetings, we prayed for the Communist nations, as well as for the other nations of the world. We asked the Lord to send forth the rain — the outpouring of the Holy Spirit — upon those nations, according to Zechariah 10:1: *"Ask ye of the Lord rain in the time of the latter rain. . . ."* We prayed for the leaders of the Communist nations according to First Timothy 2:1 and 2. And we asked for the Lord of the harvest to send forth laborers (Matt. 9:38).

As we direct our prayers *to the Lord* of the harvest, we take our position on the earth as the triumphant Church of the Lord Jesus Christ, and Satan's dominion over the lives of the lost begins to be weakened. That's how we deliver people out of the bondage of the enemy. When we pray for those in authority in the cities and nations of the world, we weaken the effectiveness of Satan's kingdom in those cities and nations. When we pray, God can have His way in those countries instead of Satan.

I am well satisfied that the changes we have witnessed in the Eastern Bloc nations have occurred because many believers throughout the world prayed scripturally for these nations by the prompting of the Holy Spirit.

As Christians, we have the authority in Jesus' Name to bind the power of the devil over the political scene of a nation. We have the right to demand that Satan take his hands off the government and the economic and social scene of a nation. We can bind every foul spirit that is affecting these areas and command them to stop in their maneuvers and cease and desist in their actions against us (Matt. 18:18; John 14:13,14).

Satan's strategies against us on the earth can be stopped in every encounter, and God's purposes can be fulfilled, as Christians stand in their place of authority in Christ on behalf of the nations of the world by praying for those in authority.

Therefore, let's put first things first so God, not Satan, can have dominion in our city or nation. Before you pray for your family, pray first for those in authority, so that ". . . *we may lead a quiet and peaceable life in all godliness and honesty"* (1 Tim. 2:2). This is one way we can keep Satan from taking advantage of us, ". . . *for we are not ignorant of his devices"* (2 Cor. 2:11).

The reason we haven't been more effective over the powers of darkness is that we haven't taken our rightful place in Christ and we haven't based our prayers securely on the Word of God. And we haven't put first things first as much as we should have.

The Visions of the 'Frogs'

I had two very similar and unusual spiritual experiences, one in 1970 and the other in 1979, that showed me how real our responsibility is to pray for our nation and for the world. In both visions I saw three huge, black, frog-like creatures coming up out of the Atlantic Ocean. They looked like huge frogs except they were much larger — about the size of whales.

In the first vision in 1970, I saw these dark beings come up out of the Atlantic, and they seemed to leap all the way across the land. In the second vision in 1979, I again saw three frog-like creatures, and one of those creatures came up out of the water and looked like it was about to land on our shores.

You need to know how to interpret spiritual visions. Because these creatures came out of the ocean doesn't mean they came up out of a literal ocean. From Genesis to Revelation, "seas" or "waters" often symbolizes *a multitude of people.*

In the first vision, I knew that the three frog-like creatures leaping across our country meant that three strategies of the devil would arise out of the multitude of peoples against our nation. The first strategy of Satan would be riots and disturbances. The second, would be political upheaval (Watergate, as it turned out). And the third, problems in the economic sector of our nation.

These evil strategies from the enemy don't arise from the Christian population; they come from the masses of those walking in darkness because sinners are held bondage and dominated by the devil in the kingdom of darkness.

In the second vision in 1979, Jesus said to me, "If the Christians of this nation had done what I told them to do in My Word and had prayed for the leaders of their country, they could have kept those evil spirits you saw in 1970 from operating in this nation. None of those upheavals would have occurred in your nation. You would *not* have had the political, social, and economic disturbances in this nation, and the President never would have made the mistakes he made. In fact, I'm holding the Church responsible for the President's mistakes."

When I heard Jesus say that, I cried out, "My God!" and began to weep. Jesus continued, "Yes, the Church is responsible before God Almighty. I know when you tell that to some Christians, they will laugh. But you wait until they stand before My Judgment Seat and see if they laugh when they are the ones who will receive the judgment."

Jesus was saying that Christians could have stopped those evil strategies of the devil by taking their place in prayer based on the Word of God. Christians have authority on the earth in Jesus' Name, and if Christians had prayed for those in authority, America would not have had the riots or the political and economic upheavals we experienced in our nation in the 1970s.

In this vision in 1979, I saw those other frogs about to land on our shores again, and Jesus said to me, "You can see that three similar evil strategies of the devil are about to happen again in this nation. First, unless Christians pray, there will arise another time of riots and tumults and disturbances all across the nation, coming from different causes than the disturbances of the early 1970s.

"Second," He said, "something is about to happen to your President that should not happen and will *not* happen if Christians will pray, and take authority over the devil's strategies and bind his works in My Name. And third, unless Christians pray, there is something about to happen that will bring further trouble in the economic scene and in the financial structure of this nation."

Jesus concluded, "Once again, Christians can stop all three of these strategies of the devil against this nation. They can stop the upheaval through riots, tumults, and disturbances in the *social structure*. They can stop the upheaval and the activity of the devil in the *political scene* of their nation. And they can stop the devil from disrupting the *financial scene* of their nation."

Many Christians did pray and the plan of the enemy was greatly averted and thwarted. Because Christians stood in their place of authority in Jesus' Name and began to pray and exercise their authority over the devil, God intervened on our behalf.

Changing Nations Biblically

We're going to look at two men in the Old Testament who changed their nations through prayer. If you want to see how people of the Bible changed nations, study their prayer lives and see how they prayed. You'll find they prayed in line with the Word.

Abraham's intercession for Sodom and Gomorrah is an example of how God's covenant people can intercede and affect the course of events in this world so that God's purposes can be fulfilled — regardless of Satan's strongholds over cities and nations (Gen. 18:16-33).

How did Abraham effect change in his nation? Did he deal with demons and devils? Did he try to pull down demonic strongholds? No, Abraham pled his case with God (Gen. 18:16-33; Isa. 43:26). He talked to *God* about Sodom and Gomorrah.

Of course, there were wicked spirits in Sodom and Gomorrah; the judgment of God was about to come upon those cities because of the wickedness (Gen. 19:13). But Abraham didn't fight with the ruling spirits over the cities in his efforts to see the cities spared. Abraham made intercession to *the Lord* regarding the cities, and the Lord responded to Abraham by sparing the righteous.

Abraham's intercession teaches us that it doesn't take a great number of believers to effect changes on this earth through prayer. The Bible says, ". . . *if TWO of you shall agree on earth as touching any thing that they shall ask, IT SHALL BE DONE FOR THEM* . . . " (Matt. 18:19). And in Ezekiel 22:30 it says, ". . . *I sought for A man. . . .*" One person can make all the difference.

Besides, we are under an even better Covenant than Abraham was. Abraham didn't have authority over the devil, as we do under the New Covenant in Jesus' Name. If God moved according to Abraham's intercession under the Old Covenant, how much more under the New Covenant will God move in our cities and nations just because believers ask Him to — regardless of the strategies of Satan!

Christians could accomplish so much more for the Kingdom of God if they would only exercise the authority they have in the Name of Jesus and enforce the devil's defeat on this earth. The majority of Christians don't take advantage of the authority in prayer that belongs to them. If they did, much damage would be done to the kingdom of darkness and many souls would be won to God.

Christians can change the political, economic, and social scenes in cities and nations through scriptural prayer. Christians can hold back judgment on the unsaved, giving them more time to hear the gospel and repent. Whenever God's people take their place in prayer just as Abraham did for the nations of the world, they can change things on this earth to the glory of God and thwart the plans of the enemy in every encounter.

Daniel's Prayer Life:
Did Daniel Make 'War' on the Devil?

In Daniel's prayer life, we find another biblical example of a covenant man changing the course of events in a nation through prayer. If Daniel could change the entire course of the nation of Israel by his prayers regardless of satanic strongholds, then we need to see exactly how he prayed. We will find in every recorded instance that Daniel prayed to *God.* Not one time does the Bible say that Daniel 'warred' against the devil or that he ever dealt directly with principalities and powers.

The following passages show us Daniel's prayer life.

DANIEL 10:2,3,5,6,12-14
2   In those days I Daniel was mourning [fasting] **three full weeks.**
3   I ate no pleasant bread, neither came flesh nor wine in my mouth, neither did I anoint myself at all, till three whole weeks were fulfilled. . . .
5   Then I lifted up mine eyes, and looked, and behold, a certain man clothed in linen, whose loins were girded with fine gold of Uphaz:
6   His body also was like the beryl, and his face as the appearance of lightning, and his eyes as lamps of fire, and his arms and his feet like in colour to polished brass, and the voice of his words like the voice of a multitude. . . .
12   Then said he unto me, Fear not, Daniel: for FROM THE FIRST DAY that thou didst set thine heart to understand, and to chasten thyself before thy God, THY WORDS WERE HEARD, and I AM COME FOR THY WORDS.
13   But the PRINCE OF THE KINGDOM OF PERSIA [wicked spirits in the heavenlies] **withstood me one and twenty**

days: but, lo, Michael, one of the chief princes, came to help me; and I remained there with the kings of Persia.
14   Now I am come to make thee understand what shall befall thy people in the latter days: for yet the vision is for many days.

Both Ezekiel and Jeremiah had prophesied that God would deliver Israel out of Babylon. Daniel was one of the many Hebrew exiles held captive in Babylon at the time. One day Daniel read those prophecies about Israel's release from captivity, and he began seeking God about what God had promised.

It was the Word of God that stirred Daniel up to pray and seek God on behalf of his people. And as Daniel sought the Lord, God not only showed him what would happen in the immediate future, but He also showed Daniel certain kingdoms that would decline and other kingdoms that would arise in the future.

Daniel Prayed *to* God, Not *Against* the Devil

When you look at what the Word of God says, you see that Daniel did not personally deal with the prince that was ruling in the heavenlies in prayer. Daniel prayed *to God*.

On the other hand, there is a sense in which Daniel dealt with evil spirits indirectly in prayer because *when* Daniel *prayed*, God heard and answered him, and God's Kingdom was advanced and Satan's kingdom suffered a defeat. And as a *result* of Daniel's prayer to God there was fighting in the heavenlies. But Daniel wasn't doing the fighting.

You see, when the Body of Christ prays, there is much more going on in the heavenlies — the first and second heaven where demons operate — than we realize.

And it seems that whether or not the angels prevail in the heavenlies is up to us here on earth and the words and prayers we speak about the situation. Remember, the angel said to Daniel, ". . . *thy words were heard, and I AM COME FOR THY WORDS*" (Dan. 10:12).

When Daniel prayed, he was not trying to defeat the devil. Daniel was putting God in remembrance of His Word (Isa. 43:26). However, indirectly Daniel's prayers *affected* the principalities and powers and caused a battle that took place in the heavenlies as the forces of darkness tried to keep Daniel's answer from reaching him.

Daniel must have realized his answer was not getting through, so he continued to fast and seek God. What if Daniel had given up in prayer? The angel may not have prevailed in the heavenlies. But Daniel didn't give up in prayer, and as a result of answered prayer, situations were changed in that nation to the glory of God.

Because of Daniel's prayer *to God*, even though there was great wickedness and many strongholds of Satan prevailing in that nation, Israel was released from captivity in Babylon. But it was *God's Word* spoken by Daniel in prayer *to God* that moved and changed those circumstances. It wasn't Daniel's direct combat in prayer with spiritual wickedness in high places that changed things in that nation, because we don't see anywhere that Daniel prayed against evil spirits in high places.

'I Am Come for Thy Words'

This passage in Daniel 10 gives us insight about the power our words and prayer have in affecting the *spiritual realm* as God moves to answer our prayer in the *natural realm*. We can see this in what the angel said to Daniel: *". . . from the first day . . . THY WORDS WERE HEARD, and I AM COME FOR THY WORDS"* (Dan. 10:12).

That's a very interesting statement: "I am come for thy *words*." It was not words that were spoken in Heaven that sent the angel to Daniel or put the angel of God to work. It was words spoken *on earth* by someone praying in line with God's Word that put the angel to work against the powers of darkness (Ps. 103:20).

That tells us that whether or not the victory is experienced on earth has to do with God's children taking their rightful place of authority in Christ and praying in line with God's Word.

Also, under the Old Covenant, Daniel had no authority in Jesus' Name to stand against Satan or to bind the operations and strategies of principalities and powers because Jesus hadn't come yet and defeated Satan. Authority over demons hadn't been given yet, because Jesus hadn't died yet and risen from the dead and delegated His authority to the Church.

Therefore, Daniel couldn't take authority over the strategies of the devil as believers can under the New Covenant. Today under the New Covenant, we have a better covenant established upon better promises than Daniel did. We can take authority over Satan's strategies and render them inoperative in the earth. We don't fight to gain that authority, we simply take our stand in the authority Christ has already given us.

The Role of Prayer in Dealing With
The Kingdom of Darkness

As believers pray according to the Word, God will move on our behalf. And as we pray according to the Word, it seems as though our prayers actually push back the effects of the powers of darkness and allow the Word to prevail, so we can preach the gospel.

Let me share an example that shows the power of scriptural prayer to push back the kingdom of darkness and change the course of events in a nation. Several years ago the ambassador of an African nation visited RHEMA with a personal message of thanks from the prime minister of his nation.

A few months before that, a ministry team from RHEMA had visited that African country at a time when the nation was on the verge of a revolution. The RHEMA team met with the leaders of the nation and talked with them about the truth of Jesus Christ and were invited to a meeting of the Parliament to pray for a peaceful solution to the crisis in their nation.

God answered their prayers, and the crisis was resolved without bloodshed. The prime minister sent us the message, "The truth your people brought to our country about Jesus Christ saved our land from a blood bath." You see, the devil wanted to cause a bloody revolution. But when believers stood in their authority in the Name of Jesus, bound the works of the enemy, and then preached the gospel to the people, Satan's strategy was thwarted.

But the ambassador from that African nation told us, "We can certainly tell the difference when Christians pray for our country and its leaders. When they take their place in prayer it seems like the enemy's opposition is lifted. But if believers let up and stop praying, the effects of the forces of darkness just come creeping back in."

Praying for those in authority and for the nations of the world has to be a continual practice for believers. That's one way to cooperate with God's will so it can prevail in situations. Praying for those in authority is one way to dispel demonic hindrances that keep the Word from prevailing in people's lives.

We can't dispel the devil and his demons from the earth, or cast them into the abyss before their time of final judgment (Rev. 20:3). But through scriptural prayer we can keep the forces of darkness at bay, so to speak, so that the gospel can have free course and people's hearts will be receptive to the Word of God. The light keeps darkness pushed back and dispels the darkness so people will be receptive to the gospel. For example, when you enter into a dark room and you turn on the light switch, the light dispels the darkness. Darkness doesn't exist where there is light!

The Bible says that the devil tries to blind the minds of those who would believe: ". . . *the god of this world HATH BLINDED THE MINDS of them which believe not, lest the LIGHT of the glorious gospel of Christ, who is the image of God, should shine unto them*" (2 Cor. 4:4). By preaching the Word and praying for souls to come into the Kingdom of God, we push back and dispel the darkness so people can receive the gospel and get saved.

Binding the First Three Classes of Demons on Earth

Remember I told you that when Jesus appeared to me in the vision in 1952, He said, "You take authority over the first three classes of demons, and I'll take care of spiritual wickedness in high places."

Principalities, powers, and the rulers of the darkness of this world are the classes of demons which directly affect our personal lives because they rule in our domain, so to speak. Those are the ones we are to bind and take authority over on earth in the Name of Jesus. And if we exercise our authority in Christ, Jesus will deal with spiritual wickedness in high places.

In Matthew 18:18 when Jesus said, ". . . *Whatsoever ye shall bind on earth shall be bound in heaven . . . ,*" Jesus wasn't talking about binding a principality or a power up in God's Heaven, because there is nothing in God's realm that needs to be bound. No, Jesus was talking about the first heaven or the second heaven, because that's where these evil powers are at work.

Principalities and powers keep ruling in this realm on earth because they are able to operate through unbelievers or through ignorant and disobedient believers. But *believers* can stop principalities, powers, and the rulers of the darkness of this world in their operations in Jesus' Name as they exercise their authority in Christ.

Binding the devil in his operations against us is the scriptural way to deal with evil spirits ruling in the heavenlies.

Let me give you an illustration of scripturally dealing with evil spirits that occurred in my own life. I was preaching in one of our larger cities, and the Spirit of the Lord came upon me and directed me how to pray for this particular situation.

I spoke out by the unction and anointing of the Holy Spirit: "You foul spirit in the heavenlies that would come against our nation and government, cease and desist in your operations against us. You foul demons, all three of you that inhabit this city, I command you to cease and desist in your maneuvers in Jesus' Name. Take your hands off that man in political office. Take your hands off that group of men in authority. Stop now in the Name of Jesus. You *are* a defeated foe, and in the Name of Jesus, away you must go!"

I prayed that way according to the direction and unction of the Holy Spirit. I had no idea what was going on in that city at that time. But the Holy Spirit directed me, and shortly after this occurred, a major political leader in that city was removed from office because of corruption and vice.

And as a result of taking authority over the works of the devil in that city by the power of the Holy Spirit, soon afterwards judgment fell upon other corrupt political figures, and many in key positions in governmental offices were removed from office at that time.

I dealt scripturally by the unction of the Holy Spirit with these evil spirits that were ruling in the *unseen* realm. Then in the *seen* realm in that city, corrupt political leaders were exposed and removed from political office.

Limits to Our Authority

A person's authority in the natural realm and in the spiritual realm can only be exercised so far. For example, a believer has authority over the powers of darkness in his own home and for his own kinfolk (Acts 16:15,31; Matt. 8:1-13). But when a believer gets out beyond his own authority or jurisdiction as he prays for others, he'll have to get their permission in order to exercise any spiritual authority in their behalf.

That's the reason Jesus told us to pray in *agreement* (Matt. 18:19), and get both parties to agree together on God's Word. If we pray beyond our realm of authority for someone else, that person needs to be in agreement with us so our prayers can be effectual.

We also need to understand the limitations of our authority over Satan's kingdom if we are to deal effectively with the devil. For instance, we have the authority to break the power of the devil over people's lives in the Name of Jesus (Matt. 18:18,19; Phil. 2:9,10) and make it easier for them to accept Christ. But they still have free choice and can choose to accept Jesus or reject Him. By breaking the power of the devil over a person's life then that person is unhindered from Satan's influence so he can make a free decision for Christ.

But we do *not* have Scripture for breaking the power of the devil over an entire city once and for all time, because a city is composed of *people*. People have free choice, and they can choose who they will serve — Satan or God — and in every city many people *choose* to serve Satan and to continually yield to him. But we can push back the influence of darkness in prayer so that the Word has an opportunity to prevail in people's hearts and lives through the preaching of the gospel.

By the same principle, there are limitations to how the believer can exercise his authority in regard to demon activity. In other words, I can deal with the devil in my own life. But I can't necessarily deal with the devil in someone else's life unless that person gives me authority to do so. He may *want* the devil in his life; he may love the works of darkness and not want to come into the light. Every person has the right to choose whom he will serve, and you won't be able to violate his will.

We make a mistake when we try to take the rightful authority we have in our own lives in Jesus' Name and try to exercise it in someone else's life. We don't have that kind of authority. We *can* run the devil off from our own lives, but we can't always run the devil out of someone else's life. A person's will has a lot to do with his own deliverance.

Let me give you an example in the natural realm. I can handle my own finances, but I can't handle your finances unless you give me that authority. Well, spiritual things are just as real as natural things. But when it comes to spiritual things, it seems we think we can intrude into other people's lives without their consent. And sometimes people act like they are giving their consent, but their heart is not really in agreement. And unless people give their consent, you won't be able to get them delivered unless you have a supernatural move of God's Spirit as Paul did in Acts 16.

But as long as a person's own mentality and will are at work and he can control himself, he has a lot to do with his own deliverance. That's why we need to teach people their own responsibility in dealing with the devil, which is to stay full of the Word and full of the Holy Spirit and learn to stand against the devil for themselves. And if people do come to you for help, you need to teach them how to bind the devil and stand against him for themselves.

For example, when folks come to me for help, I can usually help them because by coming to me for help, they are giving me *permission* and *authority* to help them. And as long as they are in control enough mentally to give me that authority, I can help them. Otherwise, I'd need a supernatural gift of the Spirit in operation to set them free.

Smith Wigglesworth tells a story which helps illustrate the believer's realm of authority. Wigglesworth traveled by ship from the United States back to England, and a stranger occupied the same cabin with him. It was a young man, and he was sick in bed when Wigglesworth entered the cabin.

The man was just skin and bones, and he told Wigglesworth, "I'm going to England. My father has just died, and I've inherited his estate. But I'll just drink it up; I'll lose it all in gambling and drinking. I've drunk so much that I can't eat anything; I've got ulcers of the stomach."

Wigglesworth had never met this man before. But Wigglesworth said, "Just say the word, and I can get you delivered." The man said, "Yes, I want to be delivered." Wigglesworth laid hands on him and cast an evil spirit out of him, and the fellow was instantly healed. After that, the young man was totally set free and could eat every meal while he was on board that ship.

There's a scriptural principle involved here. Wigglesworth said to him, "Just say the word." You see, even though Wigglesworth had the *ability* in Jesus' Name to set the man free, he didn't have the *authority* to do anything for him until the young man gave him *permission* or *authority* to deal with the devil in his life. Until the man gave Wigglesworth permission, Wigglesworth couldn't help him.

You can't *make* people accept Christ or *make* anyone want to be delivered or to choose what God has for them, because people have free will. Yes, you can pray for them and bind the power of the devil over their lives, and it gives them an opportunity to make a choice unhindered by Satan's influence. But they still have free choice.

For example, a man brought his wife to one of my meetings for deliverance. He brought her up to the healing line, and when I prayed for her, I knew by the Spirit of God that an evil spirit had gotten ahold of her mind. I also knew that if she wanted to be delivered, she could be.

Then God revealed to me exactly what had made her lose her mind in the first place. She had heard a well-known preacher say that God had spoken to him in an audible voice. When she heard that, she began to seek voices — not *God*, but *voices* — until finally she became insane, and she had to be committed to an asylum.

God also revealed to me that her husband had brought her to several ministers for deliverance. But she hadn't been delivered, so her husband had gotten mad at every minister. I knew all that by the revelation of the Holy Ghost.

Then her husband brought her to my meeting. However, I knew that unless she wanted to get rid of that evil spirit and stop hearing those voices, I wouldn't be able to get her delivered either, and then her husband would get mad at me. So I didn't minister to her in the healing line; I waited until I'd had an opportunity to talk to both this woman and her husband after the service.

I told this couple exactly what the Lord revealed to me. This woman had been out of the asylum for a while, but her husband was going to take her back again because her mind had become confused again. However, the woman could understand what was said to her, so I told her, "Sister, as long as you want to hear those voices, you're going to hear them. But if you want to be delivered, you can be."

She replied, "No, I want to go on hearing these voices."

Now if her mind wasn't working properly, and someone in authority such as her husband gave me permission, I could have cast that evil spirit out of her mind. Or if the Holy Spirit moved supernaturally by a gift of the Spirit, I could have dealt with that evil spirit supernaturally.

But her mind was clear enough for her to make a rational choice, and she wanted to hear those voices, so there was nothing I could do. I couldn't violate her free will. God wouldn't violate her free will either. But anytime she wanted to be delivered, she could be through the power in the Name of Jesus.

There is a principle here that Christians need to realize about the limitation of our authority over the devil in other people's lives. The mind is the door to the heart.

If a person's mentality is such that you can communicate with him, and he gives you permission, you can deal with evil spirits in his life. But if the person doesn't give you permission, or if he wants to keep evil spirits, you won't be able to deal with the devil in his life.

If a person's mind is not functioning properly and he can't give you permission, then you can help him if the Lord gives you a supernatural operation of a gift of the Spirit to deal with the evil spirit that's harassing him. Or if the person can sit under the teaching of the Word for a period of time, he can be set free.

But the point I'm making is that there are limits to our authority in the spiritual realm when it comes to dealing with the devil in the lives of other people, just as there are limits to our authority in the natural realm when it comes to dealing with other people.

Some believers make the mistake of taking one scripture, "These signs shall follow them that believe — in My Name they'll cast out devils," and they try to cast the devil out of everyone they meet.

But you see, you cannot go around exercising authority over everyone you meet. Jesus didn't do that when He walked upon this earth. Neither did the apostles. Therefore, it couldn't be right for us to do it either. In fact, there's no pattern in the New Testament for trying to indiscriminately cast devils out of everyone we meet.

Many times when well-meaning Christians see the authority they possess in Jesus' Name, they get carried away in their excitement and start believing they can cast the devil out of everyone. They think, *I AM someone. I DO have power. I CAN work miracles* or *I CAN work in the supernatural realm.* No, they can't work the supernatural power of God on their own! No one can. The Holy Ghost is the Wonder Worker, not man. And we need to depend on Him to lead us in wisdom according to the Word in our dealings with the devil.

So, you see, there are limits to our authority in dealing with the devil in the lives of others. But what about in our own personal lives? For example, I've had believers ask me how much authority they have in keeping demons and devils off their own property. Believers do have authority over evil spirits that try to come on their property. In fact, despite limits to our authority, I'm convinced that the Church of the Lord Jesus Christ has more authority than most believers realize!

Let me share an incident that happened to Ernie Reb, a missionary to the Philippines, regarding devils on his property. Brother Reb had moved to an island that was supposed to be the very stronghold of Satan.

Brother Reb was building a home on the island, and during the construction, one of the carpenters started hollering. Brother Reb went to see what was wrong. The fellow was thrashing around like he was wrestling with something, yelling, "Get him off of me! Get him off of me!"

Brother Reb said, "I saw something rip his pants leg. Toothmarks appeared, and the wound started bleeding. All this time he was hollering, 'Get him off of me!' I realized it had to be a devil. I said, 'I command you in the Name of the Lord Jesus Christ to leave him! This is my property. You have no right on my property!'"

When Brother Reb told the demon to leave, it ran off. Brother Reb told me that He never did see the demon, but the other man saw it leave. After that, the other carpenters were afraid to work there. The witch doctor came, saying he wanted to sacrifice a pig and a chicken; their blood was supposed to appease the demons.

Brother Reb told the witch doctor, "No, you won't come on my property. You won't sacrifice anything on my property! There are no evil spirits here. I told them not to come back, and they won't return or set foot on my property. Tell that carpenter to come back to work. That won't happen again."

You see, those demons knew Brother Reb, and they recognized that he knew his authority in Christ. And if you are a believer, the demons know you. They'll run from you if you exercise your authority in Christ. But if you don't exercise your authority, they'll take advantage of you because they are out to kill, steal, and destroy (John 10:10).

The witch doctor told Brother Reb, "If that man comes back to work and the devil jumps on him and kills him, you'll be responsible. He has a wife and several children. If he's killed, you'll have to take care of them."

Brother Reb said, "Tell him to come back to work. Those devils won't attack him anymore. I have forbidden them to come on my property, just like I'm forbidding you to come on my property." The carpenter came back to work after his leg healed and was never attacked again.

Brother Reb's experience shows that we definitely do have authority over the devil when he tries to encroach or trespass on our property. When we boldly bind the devil's works, he has to cease and desist in his operations against us.

The devil has no right to trespass on God's property. But how much authority over the devil do we have when we are on Satan's territory? If you're on the devil's territory out of disobedience, ignorance, or curiosity, he's got a right to jump on you. If you are on his territory, you won't be able to keep the devil from attacking you.

Believers have authority over the devil on their own property, and they have authority when they are preaching the gospel on the devil's territory by the leading and direction of the Holy Spirit.

For example, missionaries are always invading the devil's territory with the good news of the gospel, and they have authority over him in the Name of Jesus. But if believers go on the devil's territory because they are walking in disobedience and against the light of God's Word, they give the devil a legal right to attack them.

Yes, we have to deal with the devil. He still rules in the darkness, and we can't stop him from ruling as the god of this *world*. But we can bind him in his operations *against us*.

And we can preach the truth to people to let them know they don't have to be dominated by the devil. Through biblical prayer and preaching the Word, we can help bring people out of the kingdom of darkness into the Kingdom of God. That's how we scripturally turn a city or nation upside down for God!

Chapter 11
Is the Deliverance Ministry Scriptural?

Many Christians today are being taken in by the devil's deception in the so-called "deliverance ministry." Much of what is happening today under the guise of "deliverance" is excess and error. Any kind of deliverance must have its foundation and practices firmly grounded in the Word of God — not in human experience. Much of what is going on today in deliverance ministries cannot be found in the Bible, but is based on human experience and excess.

Actually, the enemy is working through some in the so-called "deliverance ministry" in the Body of Christ to get many good people off track and diverted from what God desires to do in the world through His Church.

Deliverance Belongs to You

Despite the error that is being taught about deliverance and demonology, deliverance *is* scriptural. If you are a Christian, healing and deliverance *belong* to you. But you need to realize that the word "deliverance" doesn't just mean deliverance from demons. Actually, freedom from *anything* that would try to bind you is part of your redemptive rights in Christ. For that reason you should never allow *anything* from Satan to bring you into bondage, because your complete redemption from Satan's dominion has already been provided for you by our Lord Jesus Christ.

Jesus bought and paid for our redemption on the Cross of Calvary. For the believer, that redemption includes deliverance from *any* satanic bondage — spirit, soul, and body. Healing and deliverance are part of our covenant rights when we accept Jesus as our Savior (Matt. 8:17; Luke 10:19; 1 Peter 2:24).

Because deliverance is included in our redemption, it is scriptural to minister deliverance to those who are sick or oppressed by the devil. But in ministering deliverance, we should help people first and foremost by getting God's Word into them so faith will rise up in their own hearts. People can be healed and delivered just by acting on the Word for themselves. And if God wills, we can also minister to sick and oppressed people by supernatural manifestations of the Spirit of God.

But it is important to teach people what the Word of God says *first*, so they can receive their healing or deliverance for themselves and know how to *hold on* to what they receive from God. Their own faith plays a vital part in that; otherwise they won't know how to stand against the wiles of the devil for themselves when he tries to rob them of what they receive from the Lord.

God may choose to use supernatural manifestations of the Spirit to set people free, or He may not. But His Word always works when people know what the Word says and act on it for themselves (John 8:32). That's why you should teach people to rely on the *Word* to be set free from Satan's oppression and bondage — not on spiritual manifestations.

Errors and Extremes
In the 'Deliverance Ministry'

There are several areas in particular in the so-called "deliverance ministry" today that have no scriptural basis. For example, there's the erroneous teaching that most Christians have demons in them that need to be cast out. But you won't find even one example in the New Testament of the Early Church dealing with devils in Christians. All of the people the apostles and the Early Church cast devils out of were unbelievers. That ought to tell us something.

Although it's not possible for a Christian to be possessed by a devil in his *spirit*, a believer can be oppressed in *mind* or *body* by demons. Yet out of the vast numbers of Christians I have ministered to during more than fifty-five years in the ministry, only a small percentage of believers had a devil in their mind or body. But most of the so-called "deliverance ministries" today claim that the majority if not *all* Christians have devils that routinely need to be cast out. That is nonsense!

Even when I have dealt with demons in people, the only way I've known a demon was present was if the Holy Ghost revealed it to me *and* told me to do something about it. Otherwise, I just ministered to people by faith in God's Word and by the anointing of the Holy Spirit. Both ways are scriptural.

We can see a scriptural example of this in Acts 16 when Paul dealt with that evil spirit in the damsel. He didn't immediately just try to cast the devil out of her, even though that devil harassed him for many days. It was only when the Holy Ghost revealed to Paul what to do that he ministered to the girl and cast the devil out of her.

In other words, deliverance is not something we take upon ourselves. We don't just go out seeking devils to cast out of people or just decide to deliver someone. Deliverance should be done by the Holy Spirit's direction. Of course we can pray for someone who is being oppressed by the devil and stand with him in rebuking the devil. Ultimately, however, believers are going to have to learn how to stand against the devil for themselves.

But the point I am making is that you can't just look at a person and decide that since he is acting a certain way, he must have a demon. It isn't scriptural to try to categorize demons from your own *mental* understanding or to determine that certain demons always act in certain ways. A demon can affect the way a person acts, but the Holy Spirit would have to show you that a demon is involved, because it could just be the flesh too. You can't just figure it out in your mind; it has to be *spiritually* discerned.

In other words, true deliverance isn't just a matter of saying that a particular problem or illness, either mental or physical, is *always* caused by a demon. Be careful in trying to label certain patterns of behavior as demons, such as demons of jealousy, gluttony, greed, and so forth, when it may just be works of the flesh.

It's true that if people indulge in the works of the flesh, they can open a door to the enemy, but the Bible doesn't mention demons by those particular names. However, it does teach that those characteristics are works or evil tendencies of the flesh (Gal. 5:19-21).

It is too easy to blame problems of the flesh on a devil and remove the responsibility from ourselves to do something about our fleshly tendencies. Even when an evil spirit is involved, the kind of evil spirit influencing or affecting a person must be discerned or revealed by the Holy Spirit. Apart from the Holy Spirit, we wouldn't know what kind of evil spirit is involved.

Another excess in the so-called "deliverance ministry" is the idea that believers need to undergo repeated deliverances in order to be set free. There is not one example in the New Testament where Jesus or the Early Church ever ministered repeatedly to a person with a devil.

But to hear some people talk who are in the so-called "deliverance ministry" today, they are continually needing to minister deliverance to the same people over and over again. They also seek deliverance for themselves time and time again.

If that's the case, something is wrong! That is not scriptural. Notice in the Bible that when Jesus or one of the apostles dealt with a person who had demons, they spoke to the evil spirit and it left. They didn't spend hours, days, or weeks trying to get the devil to come out of a person.

When people spend hour upon hour trying to get rid of a demon in someone, it means they are trying to minister deliverance in the flesh. If deliverance is ministered by the Holy Spirit, under His power, unction, and direction, results are forthcoming, and the person doesn't need to have repeated deliverances.

If all of today's so-called "deliverance" is right and of God, why doesn't it work? Why do the same people keep having the same problems over and over again and need repeated deliverances? Or why do these people only get "partially delivered" and have to keep coming back for more deliverance sessions?

Deliverance Does Not Provide 'An Easy Way Out'

One reason most "deliverance" is not working is that people are trying to deal with demons when the problem is not a demon problem at all. It is a flesh problem or a soulish problem, and those kinds of problems can't be "cast out." How convenient if those problem *could* just be cast out! That would provide a trouble-free solution for us all.

The very reason "deliverance" has become so popular is that it is an easy way out. Everyone wants an easy way out — an instant cure and an instant answer. Crucifying the flesh may take a little longer and be more difficult to do, but most often that's the real answer — not casting out demons.

An entire chapter in this book has been devoted to discussing what the Bible *does* tell the Christian to do regarding his flesh and soul. The flesh must be presented to God as a living sacrifice (Rom. 12:1). A living sacrifice no longer does what it wants to do. A living sacrifice denies and crucifies self and the flesh in order to be able to do the will of God.

Learning to control the flesh will never be accomplished through "deliverance." That is an ongoing process of sanctification, and it is the Christian's responsibility for the rest of his life on this earth.

I have found over the many years of my ministry that most people's problems stem, not from demons, but from having unrenewed minds. Many Christians do not renew their minds to think in line with God's Word. They believe, think, and say the wrong things, and, therefore, they have emotional problems, mental problems, and bondages and are constantly inviting the attacks of the enemy because they have left the door wide open to him.

When I have been able to get across to people the importance of filling themselves with the Word of God, and when they have done just that, those same people have seen problems they've struggled to conquer for years just begin to fall away. People with traumatic pasts have begun to see themselves as God sees them, and they've learned how to live in the God-kind of life, which includes victory over the devil.

God's Word is powerful! Romans 1:16 says that the gospel is the *power* of God unto salvation. That word "salvation" in the Greek includes *healing, deliverance, protection, preservation,* and *wholeness* or *soundness*. All that power is in God and in His Word, if the Christian will only *believe* it, *appropriate* or receive it by faith, and *act* upon it. Very few Christians need deliverance in the sense of needing demons cast out of their bodies or souls. On the other hand, *every* Christian needs to accept the responsibility of renewing his own mind and presenting his body to God as a living sacrifice so he can stand strong against the enemy.

Wrong Focus Causes Error

Another major problem with the so-called "deliverance ministry" is that the people involved in it become so wrapped up in "delivering" one another and holding "deliverance meetings" that they lose sight of Jesus' primary command to evangelize the nations (Matt. 28:19; Mark 16:15).

In our day, you can see entire churches and ministries taken up with so-called deliverance. The result is that those churches and ministries haven't won souls as they used to since they began delving in to the "deliverance ministry"! That is proof they are off track. What fruit do they produce to the glory of God? Where is the fruit Jesus talked about in John 15:8: *"Herein is my Father glorified, that ye bear MUCH FRUIT . . ."*?

Also, much of the so-called "deliverance" of today gets people focusing more on the devil and what he is doing than on *God* and what *He* is doing. By this teaching, Christians see themselves as victims of any and every devil that desires to jump on them, instead of appropriating the all-powerful blood of Jesus Christ, Jesus' finished work on the Cross, and the power of the Word of God to keep them from the evil one.

If the devil can just jump on Christians at any time so that we all continually need deliverance, then the blood of Jesus is powerless and our redemption is not complete. That's not to say that Christians can't open the door to the devil themselves. Of course they can. But Christians who are walking in the light of the Word don't need to fear that evil spirits are going to be jumping on them all the time. If Christians are walking in the light and Satan does try to attack them, they have the authority to successfully withstand him.

No, the majority of Christians just need to spend quality time studying and feeding on God's Word in order to get their thoughts and flesh lined up with God's Word. The Word of God is anointed, and it can meet any need in their life. They need to stop trying to get quick-fixes through so-called "deliverance sessions."

Once the believer really sees who he is in Christ and the power that Christ has made available to those who are *in* Him, it won't be possible for any devil to get ahold of him, as long as he's obedient to the Word.

It is not God's plan that good Christian people get bogged down in practices that drain them of their spiritual effectiveness. They could be out getting people saved and healed, but instead they are constantly looking for devils that aren't there in themselves and in everyone else.

Actually, many of the current "deliverance teachers" are little more than novices in the ministry, having been in the ministry less than ten to fifteen years. I have been in the ministry for almost sixty years. Just by virtue of being in the ministry a while, I've seen certain patterns reoccurring from time to time in the Body of Christ.

For example, the current "deliverance" teaching is not a new doctrine or a special revelation for the last days, as some of these "deliverance" teachers would have you believe. I have seen the so-called "deliverance" ministry come and go, even when I was a young minister back in the 1930s and 1940s. It seems to rise up about every fifteen to twenty years, and it draws a certain segment of Christians into it.

When some Christians are sufficiently off track and caught up in excess, others begin to see the error in doctrine, and it begins to wane. Then the devil causes some other "wind of doctrine" to surface and draws others off into excesses in another area. The Bible says we are not to be ignorant of the devil's *wiles* — his *methods to deceive.*

True Deliverance From Anything That Binds

Yes, there is a true deliverance, but it is not the deliverance that is built on human experience, as so many are teaching today. It is deliverance based solidly on the written, anointed Word of God, and it is accomplished by the direction and power of the Holy Spirit.

It does not matter what kind of experiences "deliverance" ministers claim to have had. If their experiences aren't rooted in God's Word, they are being deceived. God's Word is the only standard for judging any *doctrine* or *practice.*

Actually, the word "deliverance" has been overemphasized and overplayed in the Body of Christ. By overemphasizing deliverance, some well-meaning Christians have left the impression that "deliverance" just means deliverance from demons.

Deliverance does include deliverance from demons, but it actually covers a much wider range than just demons, because our *redemption* covers a far broader range than just deliverance from demons. Thank God, we are delivered from sin, sickness, bad habits, bondages, and the like. Thank God, through Jesus Christ we can be delivered from *anything* that tries to bind us by the power of the Word and the Holy Spirit.

We will have problems anytime we overemphasize a scriptural truth. Yes, we are delivered from demons, but that is not all we are delivered from. Actually, whenever we preach the gospel and people are born again, they are delivered because they are delivered from the power of darkness and translated into the Kingdom of light (Col. 1:13).

Some folks think deliverance is just going through some kind of ritual, screaming at demons and trying to get free, but it isn't. True deliverance already belongs to you. And you don't need to run to a "deliverance" minister to get it either! Just appropriate the power of God's Word for yourself.

I believe some folks who have gone to the extreme on the so-called deliverance ministry are thoroughly honest and sincere people. They have many good characteristics. But I believe they are sincerely wrong. How can I say that? Because I have been in the same boat, so to speak, that they are in now, and that's how I've learned some of the things I know.

My Early 'Deliverance Meetings'

I received the baptism of the Holy Ghost in 1937. I began pastoring a little Full Gospel church in 1938 where I met my lovely wife, Oretha.

After we were married, we accepted the pastorate of a larger Full Gospel church in a little country town. More than half of my congregation were farmers in the backlands of Texas. Cotton was "king" in those days.

I'd been pastoring that church about two and a half years, and as a Baptist boy preacher, I'd learned a lot from the Pentecostals. They had every kind of service you'd want to mention. They had deliverance meetings, loosening services, getting-free services, double-anointing services, and anything else you could think of.

So I began to announce in my services that we would start having deliverance meetings every Saturday night. Well, the meetings started off fine. We laid hands on people, and they supposedly got delivered. We had every kind of manifestation and physical demonstration you've ever seen, and some you wished you hadn't seen! You may think these physical manifestations and demonstrations that are going on today in deliverance are new, but they're not. We had similar occurrences and demonstrations back then too.

We had a high-heel time in the Lord in these deliverance services. But after about ninety days of Saturday night deliverance meetings, the novelty began to wane. So I announced that the next Saturday we were going to start having "loosening" services. Everyone who got delivered in the deliverance services started coming to be loosened in the loosening services! In these loosening services, we also had every kind of a manifestation and every kind of a physical demonstration you could ever think to mention and some you wouldn't want to mention.

Then the novelty of those loosening services began to play out and wane too. So I announced that we were going to start having "getting-free" services. Every Saturday night was going to be a "get-free" service. Everyone who had come four, five, or six months before to get *delivered* and then to be *loosened* started coming to *get free*. So we went along in those "getting free" services for a while, and then the novelty of those services began to wear off too.

I may be slow to catch on, but I finally said to myself, *This is not working. These people are not free.* I knew these people weren't any more set free than they had been before any of these services began. I lived among these people. I was their pastor. I visited them in their homes; I knew they weren't set free.

I would go out to their farms, and I'd help the farmers pick a little cotton as we walked up and down the rows talking. We would walk along the corn rows together talking as we threw the ears of corn into the wagon. And I could tell that these people hadn't been set free from anything. They still had the same problems and bondages they had before.

I would also visit them in the evenings in their homes, and I could see that the people were no more delivered, no more loosened, no more set free than they were before we began all those meetings. *And yet we had all those physical demonstrations!* In fact, we had just about every kind of physical manifestation you could think of.

I began to fast and pray and seek the Lord about it. I said, "Lord, why didn't this work?" I'd held these kinds of meetings because others were doing it, but I'd done it in all sincerity and honesty. This is one way I learned that you don't do things just because others are doing them and that you don't build on physical manifestations or demonstrations. The Word of God is our guide and standard, not what other people are doing, no matter how popular it is or how much it's the "fad" doctrine of the day. I said, "Lord, where did I miss it?"

The Anointed Word Sets People Free

The Lord answered me. He said, "You are trying to do through prayer and laying on of hands *what only My Word will do.*" Then He gave me John 8:32, *"Ye shall know the truth, and the truth shall make you free."* Actually, you could say it like this and not do any injustice to that verse: "You shall know the *Word,* and the Word will make you free."

Actually, it's *knowing* and *acting* on the Word that sets you free. When the Lord said that to me, I saw that I'd have to get the Word into people, so their knowledge of the Word could begin setting them free. And that's when I realized that people can get into trouble when they try to get "delivered" from things that are works of the flesh, because that opens a door to the devil.

When the Lord told me that, I began to teach people the Word. You see, Jesus said the words He spoke are *spirit* and *life* (John 6:63). The Word of God is God-breathed and God-inspired (2 Tim. 3:16). That means the Word is anointed, and it is the anointing that breaks the yoke of satanic bondage (Isa. 10:27). So when a person teaches or preaches the Word under the anointing or the power of the Holy Spirit, the Word will deliver those who *believe* and *act* on the Word they hear.

So I began putting the teaching and preaching of the Word first. I wasn't so interested in physical manifestations. In the course of time as I taught people what the Word said, every single one of those people was delivered and set free from bondages and problems. You see, it was the truth they were hearing and acting on that was setting them free. After I left that church and went out on the road, I went back to visit that church some years later, and those same people were still free. Bondages didn't have a hold on them because they knew the Word.

Whenever the Word is put first, it will work.

Stick With the Word

The Body of Christ needs to stay scripturally based on the deliverance issue and not get off in a ditch on either side of the road. Just stick with what the Word says about healing and deliverance. Yes, demons are real, and we have to deal with them. And in some cases, demons do have to be cast out of a believer's body or soul. But as I've said, in all my years of ministry very few Christians have needed deliverance in the sense of needing a devil cast out of their body or soul, except in some cases of sickness and disease. Remember, the Bible calls *sickness* satanic *oppression* (Acts 10:38).

But on the other hand, you don't go casting demons out of everyone you encounter who is sick either. You don't go casting demons out of someone unless you first have the revelation from the Holy Spirit that it's a demon causing the sickness in his body. You don't cast demons out of people just because someone else did or because you *think* you should. You need to be led and directed by the Holy Spirit. And, of course, believers can stand against the devil for themselves too.

I sometimes tell about the fellow who came by our offices years ago when my son-in-law, Buddy Harrison, worked for us. Buddy asked the man, "Well, how are you doing today?" This Full Gospel preacher answered, "Oh, just fine. I've already cast seventeen demons out of myself this morning!"

That's pushing the demon issue too far! You see, with some of these folks, *everything* that's wrong is directly caused by a devil or demon. They forget about dealing with the flesh. They forget about the power in the Word of God. They talk more about the devil than they do about God, and they magnify the devil more than they do Jesus and the finished work of the Cross. That's how they get into the ditch on one side of the road and give Satan access to them.

None of these excesses are new. I've been in the ministry many years, and I have observed that these errors run in cycles. Back in the late '40s and '50s in the days of *The Voice of Healing,* we had an outbreak of this same excessive deliverance teaching we have today. Then we had another outbreak of extremes and excesses in the deliverance ministry in the '70s.

And now I am seeing the third outbreak of it since I began my ministry almost sixty years ago. This teaching will surface every so often and then die out because it isn't scriptural and it doesn't work. I'm against extreme teaching and extreme practices in any area.

'Deliverance' in the Days of The Voice of Healing

There was a powerful healing revival in America from 1947 through 1958. Then the healing revival began to wane. During that revival, some people got off into extremes in this area of deliverance.

In fact, because some people got into extremes on the deliverance issue, I quit using the word "deliverance" in my meetings, and I stopped ministering along the lines of deliverance or teaching on that subject. I just backed off that issue altogether because I didn't want to be classed with those who were doctrinally off track and in error.

I've never gotten sick in the last fifty-six years unless I missed it. But when I backed off the demon issue completely, I got sick. I began to make all the faith confessions and stand on the Word of God for my healing, but nothing happened.

We ought to have enough sense to know that when we confess the Word and pray and stand on the Word over a period of time and nothing works, something is wrong.

We might as well check up on ourselves and find out what the problem is because it can't be with God; He never changes (Mal. 3:6; Heb. 13:8).

So when I wasn't healed by standing on the Word, I knew I wasn't making my connection with God, so I finally said to the Lord, "Lord, where did I miss it?" The minute I asked Him that, the Lord began to talk to me. He told me exactly where I missed it.

Jesus said to me, "You missed it by backing off of deliverance and from dealing with devils because of people who are extreme in their teaching on deliverance."

Jesus said, "These folks who are extreme in this demon issue by teaching that everyone has a devil in him and that everyone has to vomit and cough up a devil have gotten over in the ditch in fanaticism and excess. You tried to pull away from that, and by doing so, you got in a ditch on the other side by not dealing with devils at all. That got you in trouble."

When Jesus said this to me, I repented, and I was instantly healed. Then I began preaching what *the Word* says about demons and deliverance.

You see, some of the same extremes that are being taught today were taught in the days of *The Voice of Healing* too. For example, one healing evangelist carried a frog around in a jar and told everyone, "This was a demon that jumped out of a woman's mouth when I cast a devil out of her." I don't believe that anymore than I believe you landed on Mars yesterday! You can't put a demon — a spirit being — in a jar!

But right on the other hand, when the gift of discerning of spirits is in manifestation and a person sees into the realm of the spirit, demons will sometimes take on different forms and appearances. You need to understand that. However, you don't go around building a doctrine on what you see in the spirit realm. Just say what *the Word* says about demons and deliverance. You see, sometimes there is just a fine line between what's genuine — and fanaticism and excess.

Extreme Teachings Cause Harm
To the Body of Christ

The excesses and extremes in the deliverance ministry as it's taught today always produce negative results. Often this extreme teaching either offends people and they back off from even biblical teaching, or it makes fanatics out of them they find "devils" in everything and everyone. In either case, the Body of Christ is hindered and hurt.

One extreme is that demons don't exist. For example, I knew a pastor who had an experience involving an evil spirit. But his experience was discounted and condemned by many Christians because they didn't believe that evil spirits even exist.

The pastor had been under pressure for a long time because his wife had been seriously ill and had finally died. He decided to go on a trip, and he stopped at Denver, Colorado. On Sunday he walked around downtown.

The pastor told me, "I saw a sign in front of a theater that said, 'Services here tonight at 7:30.' I thought, *A Full Gospel or Pentecostal church must be holding services in this theater.* So I decided to come back for the evening service. I went back that night, and I got the last seat in the theater."

The pastor said, "On the platform was a grand piano. Almost immediately the lights went out in the theater, and a spotlight focused on a woman wearing a low-cut evening gown. I knew then that it wasn't a Pentecostal service! She sat down at the piano and began to play 'Rock of Ages.'

"As she was singing," he continued, "another spotlight came on, and a man wearing a tuxedo and a high-topped silk hat began singing a verse of 'Rock of Ages.' He had a beautiful voice. One spotlight was on him, and another spotlight was on the woman at the piano. The stage was well lit up.

"All of a sudden," the pastor related, "the woman just disappeared! The man just kept singing, and the piano kept on playing, even though the woman had disappeared. The man finished singing, walked off the platform, and walked down the aisle to the back where I was sitting. The spotlights followed him down the aisle."

The pastor said, "The man walked right up to me and said, 'Sir, your wife died thirty days ago, and she is here now. I have a message for you from her.'"

The pastor said to me, "I answered the man by saying, 'Sir, my wife did die thirty days ago, but she was a Christian, and she's with Jesus. She's not here.' The man in the tuxedo acted like I didn't even say anything. In fact, he acted sort of like he was in a trance or in some other world."

Two more times the man in the tuxedo repeated, "Sir, your wife died thirty days ago, and she is here. I have a message for you from her." Both times the pastor responded, "Sir, my wife did die thirty days ago. But she was a Christian, and she's not here. She's in Heaven with Jesus."

Finally the man in the tuxedo said, "Then you refuse to accept the message?"

The pastor said, "I emphatically do," and the pastor left the building.

If that pastor had responded to this man and received that message, the man in the tuxedo would have told the pastor something no one but the pastor and his wife knew. You see how people can be deceived? It would have been supernatural all right, but it was the work of a familiar spirit. And if the pastor had allowed that familiar spirit to operate by receiving the man's message, that pastor could have opened the door to satanic influences in his life.

That man in the tuxedo wasn't getting his information from the pastor's wife. She was in Heaven, for the Bible says when a believer dies, he goes to be with Jesus in Heaven (2 Cor. 5:8). This information was from the wrong source; it was a familiar spirit in operation. We are not to be ignorant of Satan's devices (2 Cor. 2:11).

God can top anything the devil can do. We're not supposed to go to the devil to hear what he has to say. We're not supposed to go to fortune tellers, soothsayers, astrologers, or anyone else for that matter. We have the Word of God and the Holy Spirit, and God will reveal to us what He wants us to know.

This incident happened in the days of *The Voice of Healing*, and this pastor personally told me about it. The pastor's account circulated in Full Gospel, Pentecostal circles, and preachers of that day talked about it. But some denied that it even happened. They went to the extreme by denying the existence of demons and evil spirits. We're not supposed to hide our heads in the sand and pretend that evil spirits and demons don't exist. But we're not supposed to get in a ditch on the other side of the road and see demons in *everything* and everyone either.

People make a mistake by putting too much emphasis on the devil and by spending all their time dealing with the devil. When people think only about the devil and what he is doing, they become devil-conscious and actually give place to the devil. You see, when people become devil-conscious, the devil accommodates them and manifests himself.

But when God is glorified and His Word is lifted up, the Spirit of God manifests *Himself*. If people yield to the Holy Spirit, He will demonstrate Himself and God will be glorified.

Physical Manifestations Are Not Necessary in Deliverance

Another extreme deliverance teaching in our day is that the devil has to manifest himself in order to be cast out. Some people are always wanting to see manifestations. Some believers seem to be more interested in *demonic* manifestations than they are in *Holy Ghost* manifestations!

Some ministers teach as *doctrine* that people must cough or vomit or have some other kind of physical manifestation in order to get rid of a demon. People think that's new, but we had an outbreak of that in the days of *The Voice of Healing* too. As I said, these errors and deceptions seem to run in cycles because Satan is the same old deceiver he's always been.

Don't misunderstand me. There may be occasions when a demon will manifest itself when it leaves someone. For example, the Bible says a demon manifested itself as it came out of a child who had a dumb spirit: *"And the spirit cried, and rent him sore, and came out of him . . ."* (Mark 9:26).

However, when Jesus appeared to me in the vision in 1952, He specifically said to me, "In dealing with the devil, don't ever tell anyone to cough or vomit up a demon. Expelling a demon through coughing or vomiting may happen occasionally. If it does, fine. But don't you ever tell anyone to put on any kind of a physical manifestation in order to get delivered of an evil spirit. If you tell people that some physical manifestation is to come forth, they'll try to put on a physical manifestation, and instead of *getting rid* of a demon, they'll *get* one."

You see, here's where folks are missing it. Just because some kind of physical manifestation occurs *one time* when a demon leaves someone's body or mind, some people think, *Evidently that's the way it's supposed to happen every time.* So they begin telling people to start vomiting or coughing to get rid of evil spirits. I have seen ministers do this. For instance, I was in a certain meeting, and one of the ministers announced to the entire audience, "Everyone bring a paper sack to the next meeting." He wanted people to bring a paper bag so they could vomit up evil spirits!

But you can't build a doctrine on a manifestation or on an experience and expect it to happen that same way every time. In studying the New Testament, you won't find even one *example* of anyone vomiting or coughing up evil spirits. And you won't be able to find any scriptural *principles* or *doctrine* to support such a *practice*.

Believers who go around seeing devils in other believers are creating havoc in the local church body. I've actually dealt with people who became so devil-conscious because of extreme teaching in this area that they actually got an evil spirit when they didn't have one before. When people are taught that believers have devils which routinely need to be cast out and there always has to be a physical manifestation when the devil departs, it actually opens a door to the devil.

You see, Satan is the god of this world (2 Cor. 4:4), so he can manifest himself in the physical realm. He can work in the realm of the flesh through what people experience with their five physical senses. In other words, Satan's realm is based on what people can *see*, *feel*, and *experience* in the natural realm.

But *faith isn't based on what you can see. Faith is based on what the Word says.* The Bible says that Jesus cast out evil spirits with His *Word* (Matt. 3:16).

Therefore, if you tell people they are going to have some kind of physical manifestation in order to get rid of an evil spirit, you are really teaching them how to yield to the devil, because the devil operates in the physical realm.

Instead of trying to create fleshly demonstrations to get rid of evil spirits, teach people what the Word says so they can learn how to yield to the Holy Ghost. When people yield to the *Holy Ghost, He* will manifest *Himself.* Let's just get back in the middle of the road on the demon issue, and stick with the Word of God!

Extreme Practices: Watch Where You Go

Let me share something that happened to someone to show you how dangerous it is to go to meetings where extreme deliverance teachings are taught. My wife and I were holding a meeting in a certain city, and a woman asked if she could talk to us.

She told us her story. She said, "I went to a certain place where some ministers were holding a 'deliverance meeting' and were casting devils out of people. I never had any problem before, but these ministers told me, 'You've got a devil. Let us cast it out of you.'

"Then they told me to begin to cough and vomit up that devil; they said it would come out of me that way. I started trying to cough and vomit. All of a sudden white froth started coming out of my mouth. They told me it was a manifestation of an evil spirit. They said, 'That devil is out of you now.'"

You see, these ministers taught this woman to do something that is unscriptural and something Jesus told me not to do. They told her to try to put on some kind of a physical manifestation in the flesh, and that opened the door for a demon to come in and accommodate her.

She told my wife and me, "It's been months since I went to that deliverance meeting, but this white foam never stops flowing out of my mouth. I stayed there several days and tried to get them to help me. But they just told me, 'We can't do anything about it.' Brother Hagin, can you help me?"

I had noticed this woman holding a tissue to her mouth during the entire service. She must have gone through a whole box of tissues just during that one service alone. She told us that she had to hold tissues to her mouth wherever she went because that white foam continually came out of her mouth.

When she asked if I could help her, I said, "Sure I can. That *is* a manifestation of a devil. But you didn't have a devil to begin with. You got one because you went to the wrong place and got on Satan's territory, and you let folks who weren't scriptural in their teaching or practices minister to you. They told you to do something that wasn't scriptural, and they actually told you how to yield to the devil. By doing that, you opened the door to the devil, and he accommodated you."

Never submit to anyone's teaching, I don't care who they are or who they claim to be, unless they can prove that what they are *teaching, preaching,* and *practicing* is in the Bible. Nowhere in the Gospels did Jesus ever tell anyone to try to have a physical manifestation in order to get rid of an evil spirit. And you won't see that practiced anywhere in the New Testament either!

So I said to this woman, "Yes, certainly I can help you. But I'm not going to do a thing about it unless *you* will do something."

"What?" she asked.

"Don't ever go to a 'deliverance school' or a 'deliverance meeting' again. Stay away from places where extreme doctrine is taught. Avoid extreme doctrines and extreme practices like you would poison, because you'll get devils instead of being delivered from them."

She said, "I'll never go to one of those meetings again." Then she asked me, "When you rebuke this evil spirit, will there be any manifestation?"

I said, "No, none at all, except that the white froth running out of your mouth will stop instantly the minute I rebuke the evil spirit that's causing it."

She asked, "Am I supposed to *do* anything?"

I said, "No, you don't need to do a thing. Just sit there."

My wife and I were sitting on one side of the room, and the woman was sitting in front of us. We didn't even get up. All I did was point my finger toward the woman and calmly speak to that demon, saying, "You foul spirit, in the Name of Jesus, come out of her." And as quickly as you'd snap your finger, that froth stopped. It had been running out of her mouth continually for three or four months, but it stopped instantly the moment I commanded it to in the Name of Jesus. She never had any more trouble with that demon again.

This woman wasn't demon possessed, because she was a Christian. But she had yielded to an evil spirit, and that demon accommodated her and was manifesting itself through her flesh. Because she accepted this extreme doctrine that every believer has demons, she'd become *demon-conscious* and had opened a door for the devil to manifest himself through her body.

When this woman was delivered, she was so grateful. She came back to our services later, and she was still completely delivered.

Here's something else I want you to see. To get that woman delivered, I didn't have to yell at the devil for hours. You won't find any scripture in the Bible where Jesus yelled at the devil for hours, or where it took Him days to cast the devil out of anyone. He cast out demons with His Word. *His Word!*

You need to be careful where you go to be ministered to. Don't get involved in meetings where people want to see the devil manifesting himself through physical demonstrations. And don't go to places where ministers teach that every Christian has a devil that needs to be cast out.

I don't care who the minister is, if he tells you that you have to carry on and demonstrate in the flesh in order to get delivered, don't listen to him! If you start putting on a physical demonstration by coughing and vomiting to try to get delivered, you might get a devil!

Don't Build Doctrine on Experiences

Actually, in all my years of ministry, only three times has there ever been a physical manifestation like vomiting or coughing when a demon left a person. One time I was praying for people in a prayer line, and I knew by the word of knowledge that a certain woman had a demon in her body.

In this woman's case, I knew in my spirit that there would be a physical manifestation as the evil spirit left her, so I asked my wife to take her to the restroom. And that woman did expel the evil spirit by vomiting. But, you see, *in that instance*, the Holy Spirit directed me to deal with the evil spirit in that way, and the demon was expelled privately where it wouldn't create confusion among the congregation.

A minister needs to use wisdom in dealing publicly with evil spirits in someone. Even if a believer is afflicted in body or soul by an evil spirit, you don't necessarily cast it out in public where there are baby Christians and people who wouldn't understand, or where it could cause fear or panic to come upon a congregation.

Two other times a similar situation occurred in my ministry when I knew by the Holy Spirit that there would be a physical manifestation and the person would vomit up an evil spirit. But that has been the *exception*, not the *rule*.

You see, we can't make ironclad rules about these things. Why would we need the Holy Spirit if we could go by a set of rules or formulas? *These things have to be spiritually discerned.* You have to rely on the Holy Spirit. You can't just use *human reasoning*.

Receiving 'Words' From the Lord

There is another extreme practice pertaining to deliverance in the Body of Christ today. Some believers are always giving out personal "words" of prophecy, telling others what demons they have.

A pastor of a church told me an incident that illustrates how dangerous these "personal words" of prophecy can be. The pastor said that a guest speaker came to his church and would call certain people out of the audience to minister to them.

The pastor told me, "We took these people into a side room to minister to them. The guest speaker laid hands on one particular woman, and said, 'The Lord shows me that you have a spirit of homosexuality. He shows me that you have had encounters with other women before you were married and even since you were married.' Then that minister wanted to cast the evil spirit out of her!"

This woman had been happily married for many years and had two children. She'd never been involved in homosexuality in her life!

But after this guest minister said this to her, she began to be tormented with the thoughts, *Maybe way down deep inside me there is something evil lurking in me that I don't know about. After all, this is a man of God and he said 'Thus saith the Lord.'*

The pastor told me, "This poor woman virtually lost her mind over what this minister said to her because it opened a door for the devil to torment her. She told me, 'I've never in my life had any sexual relations with anyone except my husband. And I have never had any desire for a relationship with anyone else, much less a *homosexual* relationship!'"

I don't care who the minister claims to be, if what he says doesn't line up with the Word of God and if it doesn't bear witness with your own spirit, forget it.

You see, the devil tries to torment people, and he can get away with it when believers are ignorant of their rights and privileges in Christ, and when they aren't familiar with the whole counsel of God's Word. This woman was devastated by this so-called "word from the Lord," thinking she had to accept it as the truth.

People who aren't well grounded in the Word of God can misuse and abuse spiritual gifts and create havoc in the Body of Christ. Some believers who try to operate in spiritual gifts act like children playing with toys.

Misguided people can misuse and abuse the operation of the gifts of the Spirit and just talk out of their own minds. Or even worse, they can yield to familiar spirits. This hurts innocent people and allows the devil to take advantage of them.

It's through erroneous teachings and practices like this that many people have become afraid of evil spirits and the devil. If believers would receive solid scriptural teaching in this area, that wouldn't happen.

Believers aren't to fear Satan, because Jesus already defeated him on the Cross of Calvary. The Body of Christ isn't a defeated Church — always running away from Satan in fear. We are seated with Christ in heavenly places, and we are to exercise our position of authority in Jesus' Name. We are the Church triumphant!

Chapter 12

Scriptural Ways
To Minister Deliverance

What does the *Bible* say about ministering deliverance to people? We know deliverance is scriptural because everywhere Jesus went in His earthly ministry, He ministered deliverance to the sick and the oppressed. Jesus is our Example. We are to follow in His footsteps in what He taught and practiced (1 Peter 2:21; 1 John 2:6). So how did Jesus minister deliverance to people?

Jesus' Deliverance Ministry

Keep in mind that even in Jesus' deliverance ministry, He didn't minister here on this earth as the Son of God. The Bible says He stripped Himself of His mighty power and glory when He came into this world and became as a human being (Phil. 2:7).

It's true that Jesus had the Spirit of God *without* measure (John 3:34), and believers only have the Spirit *in a* measure (Rom. 12:3). But in His earth walk, Jesus ministered as any person would who was anointed by the Holy Spirit. Jesus Himself said He had to be *anointed* to minister deliverance to the captives (Luke 4:18,19). In other words, He didn't minister deliverance just because He was the Son of God. He was anointed by the Holy Spirit to minister, just as we have to be.

The Word always came first with Jesus even in ministering deliverance. Jesus said He was *anointed* by the Holy Ghost to *preach* deliverance to the captives and to *heal* the sick and oppressed. Jesus *preached* deliverance. That means He preached the gospel. Jesus always put the Word first, and He was anointed by the Holy Spirit.

Just as Jesus did, we'll also have to put the Word first and rely on the *anointing* of the Holy Spirit to preach and minister healing and deliverance.

ACTS 10:38
38 ... God anointed Jesus of Nazareth with the Holy Ghost and with power: who went about doing good, and HEALING all that were OPPRESSED OF THE DEVIL. ...

The Bible calls sickness *satanic* oppression. Therefore, we know that all sickness and disease is directly or indirectly a result of satanic oppression.

And according to the Bible, there sometimes seems to be a relationship between healing the sick and casting out devils. In other words, the Bible gives us some instances where evil spirits had to be dealt with before people's diseased bodies could be healed.

In the following scriptures, we can readily see a relationship between healing the sick and casting out devils.

LUKE 4:40,41
40 Now when the sun was setting, all they that had any SICK WITH DIVERS DISEASES brought them unto him [Jesus]; and he laid his hands on every one of them, and HEALED them.
41 And DEVILS also came out of many, crying out, and saying, Thou art Christ the Son of God. And he REBUKING THEM suffered them not to speak: for they knew that he was Christ.

LUKE 6:17,18
17 And he came down with them, and stood in the plain, and the company of his disciples, and a great multitude of people out of all Judaea and Jerusalem, and from the sea coast of Tyre and Sidon, which came to hear him, and to be HEALED of their DISEASES;
18 And they that were VEXED WITH UNCLEAN SPIRITS: and THEY WERE HEALED.

LUKE 7:21
21 And in that same hour he CURED MANY OF THEIR INFIRMITIES and PLAGUES, and of EVIL SPIRITS; and unto many that were blind he gave sight.

In all these scriptures, casting out evil spirits and healing the sick seem to be linked together.

But in studying Jesus' deliverance ministry, you'll also see that the Bible often *differentiates* between *healing the sick* and *casting out devils.*

In other words, Jesus didn't always cast out devils to get the sick healed because not every sick person had demons in him causing the sickness.

What this means to us is that there are no ironclad rules; you'll have to follow the Holy Spirit in ministering to the sick and oppressed, just as Jesus did.

Study the Gospels for yourself and see how Jesus dealt with evil spirits. You'll find that at times Jesus dealt with evil spirits in order to heal sickness and disease.

At other times Jesus merely healed the person using a variety of methods (Matt. 8:16; 9:22,29). Jesus also used various methods in dealing with demons and evil spirits. He didn't always cast them out. He dealt with them by other methods too.

Let's look at an example in Jesus' ministry where we see a connection between evil spirits and sickness. One method Jesus used to minister deliverance was by the anointing of the Holy Spirit through the laying on of hands.

> **LUKE 13:11-13,16**
> **11 And, behold, there was a woman which had a SPIRIT OF INFIRMITY eighteen years, and was bowed together, and could in no wise lift up herself.**
> **12 And when Jesus saw her, he called her to him, and said unto her, WOMAN, THOU ART LOOSED FROM THINE INFIRMITY.**
> **13 And he LAID HIS HANDS ON HER: and immediately she was made straight, and glorified God. . . .**
> **16 And ought not this woman, being a daughter of Abraham, WHOM SATAN HATH BOUND, lo, these eighteen years, be loosed from this bond on the sabbath day?**

The Bible says this woman's affliction was caused by an evil spirit — "a spirit of infirmity" (v. 11). Jesus said it was Satan who had bound her (v. 16).

In this case, an evil spirit of infirmity was present in the woman's body causing and enforcing this physical condition.

But notice how Jesus dealt with the evil spirit in this case. He didn't cast it out. He laid hands on the woman and gave the command of faith, ". . . *Woman, thou art loosed from thine infirmity*" (v. 12). And the woman was delivered.

You see, when the anointing or power of the Holy Spirit came upon this woman, she was instantly "loosed" or set free from an evil spirit of infirmity.

So demons *can* be directly involved in physical ailments. But Jesus didn't *cast out* that spirit of infirmity; He laid hands on her, and the anointing broke the yoke of satanic bondage.

In other situations, Jesus did cast evil spirits out of some people. How did He do it? With His Word!

MATTHEW 8:16
16 When the even was come, they brought unto him [Jesus]
many that were POSSESSED with devils: and he CAST OUT
THE SPIRITS with HIS WORD, and HEALED all that were
SICK.

In some cases of sickness, the sickness or disease is a result of natural causes, but *indirectly* it's still satanic oppression. If sickness is the result of natural causes, the person needs to be healed — he doesn't need evil spirits cast out of him.

On the other hand, sometimes an evil spirit is present enforcing a disease or infirmity. You'll only know by the Holy Spirit.

If the Holy Spirit doesn't reveal the presence of an evil spirit, you can help people get healed by teaching them faith in God's Word. But I am thoroughly convinced that a number of different ailments can be dealt with *only* by dealing with evil spirits.

And in those cases, unless the evil spirit is dealt with by the power and direction of the Holy Spirit, you can anoint people with oil and lay hands on them until you've worn every hair off their heads, but you still won't get results.

Those kinds of sicknesses don't respond to the usual biblical methods of ministering healing. In those cases, the evil spirit has to be dealt with by the unction and leading of the Holy Spirit.

That's the reason some cases of sicknesses don't respond to medical treatment. Sicknesses that are caused by the actual presence of an evil spirit can't be treated with natural remedies.

But if an evil spirit is *directly* causing the sickness and disease, and the believer is standing on the Word in faith, he can depend on God to deliver him. However, the evil spirit will have to be dealt with by the power of the Holy Spirit and the Word of God.

In Mark 9:17-29, we see another example of Jesus dealing with an evil spirit, this time in the lunatic boy. How did Jesus deal with that evil spirit? He *rebuked* it and *cast it out* of the boy.

But Jesus did that by the same *anointing* of the Holy Spirit that was upon Him when He touched and loosed the woman bound by the spirit of infirmity.

Sickness and disease is not always the result of the presence of a demon. For instance, in Mark 7:32-37 Jesus dealt with a man who was deaf and had a speech impediment.

Evidently, an evil spirit wasn't involved in this infirmity because Jesus just put his finger in the man's ears and said, "Be opened," and the man spoke plainly. Jesus didn't deal with an evil spirit at all. Evidently the man's deafness resulted from natural causes, so he just needed to be healed.

But in another instance, Jesus ministered to a man who was "dumb" or couldn't speak. This time, before Jesus could get the man healed, He had to cast out an evil spirit.

> **MATTHEW 9:32,33**
> **32 ... they brought to him a dumb man POSSESSED WITH A DEVIL.**
> **33 And WHEN THE DEVIL WAS CAST OUT, THE DUMB SPAKE: and the multitudes marvelled, saying, It was never so seen in Israel.**

But the point I'm trying to make is that Jesus didn't set a pattern as he dealt with devils and evil spirits. Even in his deliverance ministry, Jesus followed the leading of the Holy Spirit and ministered by the power and direction of the Holy Spirit.

Deliverance By the Anointing

It was the Word that Jesus taught and the *anointing* that brought deliverance to those who were afflicted by demons. Today we will also have to minister deliverance by the Word and the anointing — the power of the Holy Spirit.

> **LUKE 6:17-19**
> **17 And he came down with them, and stood in the plain, and the company of his disciples, and a great multitude of people out of all Judaea and Jerusalem, and from the sea coast of Tyre and Sidon, which came to HEAR him, and to be HEALED of their diseases:**
> **18 And they that were VEXED WITH UNCLEAN SPIRITS: and THEY WERE HEALED.**
> **19 And the whole multitude SOUGHT TO TOUCH HIM for there WENT VIRTUE [the Greek word is "dynamin" or power] OUT OF HIM, and healed them all.**

Notice in verse 17 that the people came to *hear* Jesus and to be healed. It was the anointing on the Word that set people free. Faith comes by hearing the Word of God, and it is by faith that we receive the promises of God, including deliverance from any kind of bondage.

Faith in the Word of God is the key that opens Heaven and activates the power of God to work in a person's life no matter what kind of demonic activity or influence is involved. When Jesus taught the people the Word of God — preached deliverance to the captives — and the people believed the Word, they were healed and delivered.

The multitude who sought to touch Jesus were people who were diseased and oppressed or "vexed" by unclean spirits. The word "healed" in verse 18 means the people were made *whole* or *delivered*.

In this passage, not one evil spirit was cast out of anyone. As far as we know, not one evil spirit was even discerned, yet when those who were vexed with unclean spirits heard what Jesus taught, they were delivered. What delivered them? It was the Word that Jesus taught and the power of the Holy Spirit.

The same power that heals a person will run the devil out no matter what kind of demonic influence is involved — if the person will act on God's anointed Word in faith.

Studying the Gospels, we can see that Jesus ministered healing and deliverance by a variety of methods. But no matter how Jesus ministered deliverance, the delivering power of God was always present to heal people and set them free when activated by the person's faith. The same is true today. The delivering power of God is always available to set people free.

Also, Jesus didn't have prolonged and repeated 'deliverance' sessions to get people free from satanic bondages. Regardless of the method He used, the person's healing or deliverance was always forthcoming.

Ministering deliverance is scriptural, but we can't go beyond the Word and the leading of the Holy Spirit. That is how people have gotten into error and excesses in the deliverance ministry and have caused harm to the Body of Christ. Let's just stick with the Word and follow Jesus' example of ministering deliverance to the sick and oppressed.

In my own ministry, many times I've seen that people who had the same type of sickness or disease were healed or delivered by various methods, as the Holy Spirit directed.

Epilepsy:
Healing vs. Deliverance

Because Satan is the god of this world (2 Cor. 4:4), there are cruel tormenting spirits of fear, unclean spirits, dumb, blind, and deaf spirits, spirits of infirmity, and other evil spirits here on the earth.

You'll notice that every one of those spirits is mentioned in the Bible. On our own, we can't tell whether the cause of a person's physical infirmity is an evil spirit or a natural cause. However, the Holy Spirit knows all things. He will lead us into all truth and show us how to minister to a person.

For example, I've laid hands on some people who had epilepsy, and they were healed because the epilepsy was caused from a physical disorder. No demon was involved. But right on the other hand, I've also laid hands on people with epilepsy, and the Holy Spirit showed me that a demon *was* involved that was causing the epilepsy.

I was preaching in a meeting once and many people came forward for healing, so I just laid hands on the people. The next year we were in the same area, and a woman came forward to give us a testimony about her son who had been healed in that first meeting. He was twelve years old, and he'd had epilepsy all his life.

She related, "When you prayed for my son, the healing power of God came upon him and he fell under the power of God. He's never had another seizure."

You see, in that case of epilepsy, the boy only needed healing; he didn't need an evil spirit cast out of his body. If an evil spirit had been present, the Lord would have shown me by the Holy Spirit.

But in another case of epilepsy, the Holy Spirit showed me that an evil spirit was present causing the infirmity. A young man came forward for healing in one of my meetings who had suffered from epileptic seizures since high school. When I laid hands on him, I knew by the word of knowledge that an evil spirit was involved in his epileptic seizures and that I would have to cast it out of his body before he could be set free. So I did. A few days later we closed the meeting and left that area.

A year later I held a meeting in the same town, and I saw that same young man. When I looked at him, the Spirit of God said to me, "When you were here last year, you cast an evil spirit out of him, and for twelve months, he didn't have one single epileptic seizure. But in the last two weeks, he's had three epileptic seizures."

The Holy Spirit said, "When he had these seizures before, he never had them in the nighttime when he was sleeping. But in these last two weeks, he's been awakened in the nighttime with seizures. And the reason he had those seizures is that he went to sleep afraid. So before you begin preaching, call him up here and cast that evil spirit out of him again."

You see, in that instance, the Lord not only told me that an evil spirit was involved causing the man's seizures, but He also told me how the man had let the evil spirit back in. Sometimes you need to know if there's a *cause* — if the person has opened a door to Satan that let the sickness and disease in — before you can minister effectively to people.

So before I began preaching, I called the young man forward. I said to him, "When I was here last year, I ministered to you, and you were delivered from epileptic seizures. For twelve months you did not have one single epileptic seizure."

He said, "That's right, but . . ."

I said, "Wait a minute. Don't say anything. Let me tell you what happened so you'll know God is moving supernaturally on your behalf. If I miss it, just speak up and say, 'You missed it.' After all, I'm human. I can miss it. Anyone can. In the last two weeks, you've had three seizures that have awakened you out of sleep. When you had epileptic seizures before, you were never awakened with a seizure in the middle of the night."

His eyes got big and he said, "Why, that's exactly right. You must be a mind reader or a fortune teller!"

Isn't it strange that Christians would think that mind readers or fortune tellers could reveal something like that, but poor ole God has lost all His revelation ability!

I asked him, "Do you know why you began to be awakened with seizures in the night?"

He said, "No, do you?"

I said, "I sure do. You went to sleep afraid, and the fear opened a door to the devil."

He said, "Now I know you're a mind reader. That's exactly what happened."

I said, "I'm not reading your mind. And I didn't get that out of *my mind* either. In fact, my mind doesn't have a thing in the world to do with it."

Moving in the realm of the Spirit is not a *mental* experience. If we could follow the Spirit of God and the Word of God without human reasoning getting in the way, we'd be better off! God operates through the recreated spirit of man; he doesn't operate through man's mind because it hasn't been born again.

This young man said, "I usually dealt with that fear before I went to sleep. But those particular nights when I had the epileptic seizures, I didn't get rid of fear before I went to sleep."

Fear can open the door to the enemy. For example, if you went to bed tonight and left the door in your home open, there's no telling who or what would come in. A burglar could come in and rob or kill you. It's just better to keep your door shut and your house secured! It's the same way in the spiritual realm. You'd better keep the door shut to Satan.

Fear is a spirit. But God didn't give us the spirit of fear (2 Tim. 1:7), so that means you have authority over it. Since it doesn't come from God, you have no business with it. So if fear is troubling you, get rid of it in Jesus' Name.

I told this young man, "I'm going to cast the evil spirit out of you again, and I'm going to show you how to keep the door shut on the devil." In the Name of Jesus, I cast out the evil spirit that was causing the epilepsy. Then I spent forty-five minutes teaching him how to resist Satan and maintain his healing and keep the door shut on the devil. Many years have passed since that man was healed, and he's never had another seizure.

The Anointing Breaks the Yoke of Bondage

We saw that in Jesus' healing ministry, many people were delivered from evil spirits just by the anointing of the Holy Spirit. In other words, evil spirits don't always have to be *cast out*; the anointing of the Holy Spirit can drive them out too. I've seen that in my own ministry too. I could tell you testimony after testimony of people who were delivered from demonic oppression just from the anointing — the power of God coming upon them.

For example, several months after we had held a meeting in Detroit, a woman wrote me telling her testimony. In the letter she said, "Brother Hagin, I had a stomach disorder, so I came to your crusade to receive my healing. You laid hands on me and prayed for me. The anointing came on me, and I fell on the floor under the power of God. After all these months, I am still healed."

She continued, "I've been saved about eight years. Before I got saved, I was in the occult. But after I was saved and filled with the Holy Spirit, I still had problems with demons manifesting in my presence. In the nighttime I still heard voices and rappings on the wall and other demonic manifestations.

"But since the power of God came on me so strongly when you

laid hands on me," she wrote, "I've never heard another voice, and there's never been another demonic manifestation in my home."

Cancer:
Deliverance by a Manifestation of the Holy Spirit

I want to show you that God has a variety of methods of delivering His people. I'm going to relate several instances of dealing with people who had cancer and the various ways the Holy Spirit led me to deal with each of them. I want you to see that you will have to be led by the Holy Spirit — you cannot formulate ironclad rules about ministering to people.

In 1952, I held a revival in Texas. One of the ministers told me about his niece who was dying of cancer of the lungs. She was twenty-three years old and had two small children. During the first week of my meetings, she was brought to a service, and I prayed for her. The second week, I laid hands on her two different times and prayed for her.

During the third week, the young woman was brought to the service again. I no more expected what happened than anything in the world. When I laid my hand on her this time, suddenly a white cloud of the Holy Spirit came down and enveloped me. The altar disappeared and it seemed like the young woman and I were the only ones standing there in that cloud of glory. No one else could see what I saw, nor hear what I heard, but they could all hear me talking.

Enveloped in that white cloud, I saw into the realm of the spirit, and I saw a little creature — a demon — hanging on the outside of this woman's body. It looked like a little monkey hanging on to a tree limb. This woman was saved, so she wasn't demon possessed, but her body was being oppressed from the outside by a demon. That little monkey-like creature was hanging on to her body over her left lung; that's where the cancer had started.

I just spoke to the demon and said, "In Jesus' Name, you're going to have to leave her."

That little creature answered me, but no one else heard it because I was seeing and hearing in the spirit realm. That's the gift of discerning of spirits in operation.

That little monkey-like demon said to me, "I know I have to go if you tell me to, but I don't want to."

I said, "I command you to leave her in the Name of the Lord Jesus Christ." That little demon fell off of her body and landed on the floor. He lay there on the floor and whimpered and whined and shook, just like a little pup that had been whipped.

I said, "Not only leave her body, but you leave these premises in the Name of Jesus." When I said that, the demon got up and ran down the aisle and out the door.

This woman had been saved since she was eight years old, but she had never been filled with the Holy Spirit. She immediately lifted both hands and began speaking in tongues. That same week, she went back to the cancer clinic and the doctors told her, "Your lungs are completely clear. There's not a thing in the world wrong with them. What happened?"

She told them exactly what had happened. She told them what I had seen and done. The doctors said, "Well, whoever the fellow is, our hat is off to him! Evidently he's got the answer. We don't. But we'll give you a signed affidavit that you had cancer of both lungs and that now you're free of it."

God has the answer, not me. If a manifestation of the Holy Spirit doesn't come, I always just teach, preach, and minister the Word of God to people, because I can't operate gifts of the Holy Spirit at will (1 Cor. 12:11).

What I want to get you to see is this. Until I was *in the Spirit,* I didn't know an evil spirit was afflicting this woman's body. You can't guess at these things. Certainly, I ministered to people according to faith in God's Word, and people were getting saved, healed, and filled with the Holy Spirit. But when I was in the Spirit, God revealed that it was an evil spirit causing this woman's lung cancer, and God supernaturally equipped me to deal with the demon that was enforcing the disease in her body.

Also, if it were just me operating a gift of the Spirit, I would have dealt with that spirit the very first night the woman came to the meeting. If the Holy Spirit doesn't operate through me, I'm helpless. God has His own ways of doing things, and it's best just to let Him do what He wants to do. I don't have supernatural manifestations in every meeting because no one can produce a manifestation of the Spirit himself. A person can't work something up and try to make something happen. If he tries to, he will open himself up to evil spirits and get off into error.

And just because I had that particular manifestation in one meeting, if I'd tried to produce the same manifestation at the next meeting, I would have gotten off track and opened the door to the devil.

You and *I* don't operate spiritual gifts. If *you* try to operate them, the devil will accommodate you, and you'll open the door for satanic deception. Spiritual gifts operate as the *Holy Spirit* wills.

You see, you don't necessarily deal with every cancer case the same way every time or any other kind of disease the same way in every case. But you always tell people what the Word says. Just because you had one experience that resulted in a person's deliverance, you don't build a doctrine on that and try to minister to every person the same way.

You follow the leading of the Holy Spirit, and if a gift of the Holy Spirit is manifested to minister to the person, that's fine. Then you can follow the leading of the Holy Spirit and minister to the person by the power and unction of the Spirit of God.

If the Holy Spirit doesn't choose to manifest Himself in spiritual gifts, just keep teaching people how to stand against sickness and disease with the Word of God. The Word always works.

Bedfast With Cancer

I remember another instance of ministering to a woman with cancer. My wife and I went with another pastor to pray for a pastor's wife who was bedfast with terminal cancer. The cancer had started in her left breast and had spread to her lymph glands. By the time she got to the doctor, he told her, "It's too late. We can't do anything for you." By the time we went to pray for her, she was bedfast. The doctor said, "She ought to be dead already. We can't understand how she's lived this long."

As we gathered to pray for this woman, we waited on God in prayer and sought His direction. We were there in that parsonage praying almost continually for her for two days and two nights. We slept four hours each night. The rest of the time we prayed and sought God.

The Sending End or the Receiving End?

Finally, at four o'clock in the morning on the third night, I said to the pastor, "In fifteen years of ministry, I've never prayed to God this long about anything without getting the answer. We must be missing it somewhere. We don't have to pray this long for something that has already been promised to us in the Word. I think this is where we're missing it. We're working on the *sending* end, '*God*, heal this woman!'

"But, actually," I said, "we've gotten nowhere because as far as God is concerned, He has already healed her. He laid her sickness on Jesus at the Cross. When we pray for her in the morning, let's work on the *receiving* end instead of the sending end."

Here's where a lot of folks miss it. When they don't make their connection in prayer, they don't stop to listen to the Spirit of God and find out why they haven't. They just go on without checking with God. Many times if we aren't making our connection in prayer, we need to inquire of the Lord and find out why. Then we need to let the Holy Spirit correct us if we need correction. And if we've taken the wrong turn, so to speak, we need to back up and take the right turn.

So we gathered in that room the next morning at eight o'clock — the pastor and his wife, my wife and me, the sick woman's husband who was also a pastor, and the woman with cancer. I told them what the Lord had shown me.

We all knelt down by the bed to pray again. We sought God to see what the Holy Spirit would say about this woman's situation. We all prayed in the Spirit in other tongues, seeking God's direction.

Suddenly something on the inside of me said, "Go stand at the foot of the bed." I stopped praying in tongues and got back in the mental realm. I thought, *What good would it do to go stand at the foot of the bed?* So I just dismissed the thought. This was all new to me. I didn't know the Voice of the Holy Spirit then like I do now.

I went back to praying again, and I heard these words again, "Go stand at the foot of the bed!" I got back into mental reasoning. I thought, *Standing at the foot of the bed won't get this woman healed.*

But did you ever stop to think about it? Jesus spit in the dirt and made mud and put that mud in a fellow's blind eyes and said, "Go wash it off in the Pool of Siloam" (John 9:7).

Well, in the natural, what good would mud do to heal that man? But, you see, it's faith and obedience that counts with God. It's just best to follow the leading of the Holy Spirit and do what He tells you to do. That always brings results! The Holy Spirit will always lead you in line with God's Word, and what *He* tells you to do will always work.

The Holy Spirit said that same thing to me the third time. This time I went and stood at the foot of the bed and continued praying in tongues. Suddenly my wife stood up, and still praying in other tongues, came and stood at the foot of the bed with me. She never did open her eyes. She told me later that she didn't know I was there.

Suddenly, as my wife was praying in tongues, the tongues changed. She began speaking out what we call a message in tongues. But I heard what she said as though she spoke to me in English.

The Holy Spirit said through her, "Go stand at the head of the bed and say, 'Come out, you spirits of doubt and fear in the Name of Jesus.'" So I just moved up to the head of the bed and said, "Come out, you spirits of doubt and fear in the Name of Jesus."

I had my eyes open, watching. The moment I said that, it looked to me like a great big black bat, twice as big as a man's hand, just rose up from that dying woman's left breast and flew out the window. The pastor who was standing on that side of the bed told me later, "Something went right by me and flew out the window. I didn't see anything, but it flew by me like a bird in flight."

The woman instantly rose up completely healed and praised God and danced all over the house. That afternoon she ate watermelon with us in the backyard, totally delivered and set free.

Now here's something I want to get across to you. We didn't do "warfare" with the devil to get that woman healed. We just prayed in faith to God, and expected Him to give us direction.

This woman was healed by a manifestation of a gift of the Spirit in operation. Yet even though you may have an experience of the Holy Spirit that's based on the Word of God, you can't go out and build a doctrine on an experience — even if it is in line with the Word.

And you can't go out and teach other people to try to have the same experience or even the same manifestation. You have to let God manifest Himself as He wills, not as you will.

This is where people miss it. They try to put on a manifestation of the Holy Spirit, or they minister and try to work up something in the flesh. Both are dangerous, and will lead people into error.

Just teach people the Word, and let God do the rest. God will make His Word good in people's lives if they'll dare to stand by it. Of course, if people don't stand by God's Word, He doesn't have anything to make good in their lives.

But an experience like this one may never happen again in ministering to someone. *Experiences may come and go, but the Word always works.* If we could do everything by a pat formula, we wouldn't need the Holy Spirit. Build your life and ministry on the Word, not on experiences and manifestations.

I would have gotten people in a mess and my own ministry in a mess if I had gone out and taught that *experience* as doctrine. I saw this when I was young and coming up in the ministry. So many ministers who came up in my day failed in the ministry because they didn't have a foundation in the Word; they built their ministries on spiritual gifts. They were marvelous people and had marvelous gifts of the Holy Spirit operating in their lives. But they didn't have a foundation of the Word in them, so one by one they eventually got into error and deception and fell by the wayside.

I told some of them, "When you've come and gone, I'll still be out there preaching and teaching because I'm building my ministry on the Word of God, not on spiritual gifts."

You can't built your life or ministry on the gifts of the Spirit and succeed. No, build both your life and ministry on the Word of God. Let manifestations and operations come as the Spirit of God wills. But just be faithful to put the Word first, and base everything you do on the Word, not on experiences.

Healed by the Anointing

I'll share about another cancer healing where I didn't deal with an evil spirit at all. A young man came to one of my meetings, and he also had cancer of the lungs.

The doctors had given him six months to live. I prayed for him twice, but I knew in my spirit that we hadn't made our faith connection. Many times you can lay hands on folks and it's like getting ahold of a live wire; you know they are in faith and are believing God. But you can lay hands on other people and it's like laying hands on a doorknob. Somehow or another, the power of God is short-circuited, because God is always willing to heal.

At one of the services, the spirit of prayer fell on us, and everyone just hit the floor praying. This young man with cancer knelt at the altar praying. I just walked back and forth praying.

Suddenly an unction of the Holy Spirit came upon me, and I went over to this young man. It was as if an unseen hand picked up my hand and placed it on his head. But instead of praying, I found myself saying, "You are now healed of cancer. Be filled with the Holy Spirit. I have a place for you in ministry in My vineyard." Instantly, that young man started speaking in tongues.

Afterwards, this young man went back to the hospital and the doctors asked him, "Can you stay for a few days? We don't understand it, but the cancer is all gone." They kept him for five days, running every kind of test on him. They never did find out why the cancer had left him. But, praise God, we know why it left! God healed him by the power of the Holy Spirit.

You see, that time I didn't even pray for this young man. I didn't cast anything out of him. In fact, I didn't even deal with an evil spirit, yet he was totally delivered and healed of cancer. The doctors said, "We wouldn't believe he ever had cancer if we didn't have the records to prove it."

Folks make a mistake when they think they've got to cast a devil out of every sick person just because they dealt with an evil spirit one time in a particular situation. That's how they get things in a mess.

Years later, the pastor told me that this young man had been pastoring a church for the last five years. God had said to him, "I have a place for you in My vineyard."

Healed by Faith in God's Word

I ministered to another person with cancer, in which the Lord healed in an entirely different way than He did in these other cancer cases.

I was holding a tent meeting for a Full Gospel church. Months later I got a letter from the pastor, telling me about a woman in his church who had terminal cancer. She had attended one of my meetings, but I wasn't even aware of it.

This woman had been to one of the largest clinics in our nation for treatment. The doctors there said she had six months to live and had sent her home to die. Nearly every healing evangelist in America at that time had prayed for her healing. I'd laid hands on her twice, but she didn't receive her healing.

The pastor related to me, "She was so sick that she had to be brought to your meetings in an ambulance every day. There was a side room with a speaker in there, so she just lay in that room and heard you teach the Word."

No one ever knew the woman was there. I never knew it and never prayed for her. We ran this meeting two weeks, so this woman went to ten meetings and heard ten Bible lessons on faith. *She put those lessons into practice, and she was totally healed.*

The pastor told me, "Brother Hagin, she's completely well. She's been back to the cancer clinic, and they've run every test on her, and they can't find a trace of the cancer."

There was no discerning of spirits that took place in this

woman's deliverance. She wasn't prayed for. She just received deliverance through her own faith in the Word of God.

You won't be able to minister to people through the gifts of the Spirit unless the Holy Spirit chooses to manifest Himself in that way. But you can always minister to people by teaching them what the Word says.

Just by sitting under the anointing of the Word and by *applying* the Word to their lives, people can be set free from *any* force of the enemy that's trying to bind them and hold them in bondage. Once people hear the Word of God, they need to act on it for themselves because the Bible says it's the *doer* of the Word who is blessed (James 1:22,25).

However, the Spirit of God can also operate through various other gifts of the Spirit such as prophecy or the word of knowledge or discerning of spirits in order to set people free. Let's rejoice in what God is doing. That's what counts. And let's just let God be God and let Him move any way *He* wants to move!

I have related here various cancer cases. Each one of these people were delivered by different methods by the direction of the Holy Spirit. But each one of them got delivered.

Keep preaching the Word. If the manifestation of the gifts of the Spirit come, fine! If they don't, keep preaching the Word anyway. Keep putting the Word out. It's the holy, incorruptible seed of God's Word that produces the results, and it endures forever (1 Peter 1:23-25).

And the Word always works because the Bible says God watches over His *Word* to perform it, and His Word doesn't return to Him without producing results (Jer. 1:12; Isa. 55:11).

Eventually, if you are faithful to teach people what the Word says, it will produce a bumper crop in their lives. The Bible says, *"He sent HIS WORD, and healed them, and delivered them from their destructions"* (Ps. 107:20). It doesn't say, "He sent spiritual gifts and healed them and delivered them from their destructions," although God may choose to move that way in some instances.

Dealing With the Insane

Now I want to relate to you several cases of dealing with insanity and show you that the same principle applies. I've noticed particularly in dealing with insane people, if they are still mentally coherent and you can get through to them by preaching the Word, they can receive it and be delivered. But if their minds aren't functioning, you'll need to have a manifestation of the Holy Ghost or you won't be able to help them. And you can't produce that manifestation yourself.

A Christian woman brought an insane woman to one of my meetings. The insane woman was just waiting for the authorities to come and institutionalize her. She sat in the service and acted like a little child, constantly shuffling and moving around and fidgeting. Right in the middle of my Bible lesson, she'd stand up and say, "I have to go to the bathroom!" or "I want a drink of water!" The woman with her would make her sit down again.

In that first service, the insane woman didn't pay any attention to the Bible lesson. In the second meeting, she began acting the same way — moving around and fidgeting like a little child. But before the service was over, I noticed that her eyes were fastened on me. She was listening intently. The third day she brought her Bible with her, and during the Bible lesson, she opened her Bible and followed me.

On the fourth day, she had a little notebook with her and was taking notes. Before the ten days of the meeting were over, she was saved, baptized in the Holy Ghost, speaking in tongues, and her mind was completely restored. She was totally delivered!

I think sometimes we underestimate something Paul said. He said, ". . . *I am not ashamed of the GOSPEL OF CHRIST: for IT is the POWER of God . . .*" (Rom. 1:16). The gospel of the Lord Jesus Christ — this living Word of God — is the power of God, and it is the power of God unto *salvation*. Salvation from what? Salvation for anything you need to be saved from!

That woman never did have to be committed to the mental institution. Five years later when I went back to the same church, the woman and her husband were still in that church and they were both on fire for God. But the point I want to make is, I never did pray for her, lay hands on her, or cast any devil out of her. What delivered the woman? The gospel of our Lord Jesus Christ. The Word of God is the power of God unto salvation, deliverance, healing, and victory! The Word of God did it all.

I've also seen people come to my meetings whose minds were completely incapacitated because of drugs. But the Word of God got in them and it registered on their spirits, and their minds were completely restored. Today those people are just as sane as anyone else.

There's power in the Word. And teaching the Word is one way

you're going to help people who are insane and mentally incoherent. It doesn't matter whether their mental state is due directly or indirectly to demonic influence — the Word still works.

I received a letter from a woman who said, "Brother Hagin, I'm thirty-eight years old. I've spent more than half of my life in a mental institution. Then someone gave me your book, *Right and Wrong Thinking.* I began to order more of your books and read them, and my mind has been completely restored."

That woman never did have a demon cast out of her. The same doctors who said she would always need institutional care pronounced her well and dismissed her. She went on to devote her life to helping those in mental institutions.

If people will mix faith with the Word of God and believe it, the Word of God will work for them no matter what they need deliverance from. In the case of insanity, teach the Word to those people whose minds are coherent. Get the Word into them. If they will stand in the place of victory in the Word, they will be delivered. How do they stand in the place of victory? By faith. By believing the Word. The Word is the power of God. Teach them to put the power of God to work for them by believing God's Word and acting on it.

If people's minds are completely taken over by an evil spirit, and they are totally incoherent or incapable of sitting under the teaching of the Word of God, then you will have to rely on the Holy Spirit to show you what to do. But in every case, there is deliverance in the Lord Jesus Christ.

Gift of Special Faith

Let me give you an example of an insane person whose mind was *not* coherent, but she was delivered by a manifestation of the gifts of the Spirit.

This woman wasn't born again. She'd lost her mind, but it was more or less from a physical ailment. She really wasn't that old, but she didn't know God. Sometimes people seem to age faster without the life of God working in them (Rom. 8:11). She had become senile at a young age. One doctor said she had the mind of a two-year-old child.

My wife and I prayed for this woman for about two hours. We weren't combating the devil or coming against satanic powers or strongholds. We were talking to *God.* We were just praying and worshipping God, and waiting on Him to see if the Holy Spirit would manifest Himself and show us what was wrong with her and how to deal with her situation.

The Holy Spirit didn't show us anything, so finally the woman's daughter said to her, "Come on, Momma, we've got to go now." The daughter got her mother up and put her coat on her. My wife, Oretha, began to talk to the daughter, so the insane woman sat back down on the couch. I sat down beside her, and she muttered and made strange sounds. She had a wild look in her eyes, like she was having some sort of a spell.

As I sat there watching her, such great compassion rose up in me that with tears, I said, "Lord, why can't I help this dear soul? Why can't I help her? If I can't get through to her and help her to accept You, she'll go to hell!"

About that time, my wife and the woman's daughter finished their conversation. The daughter turned around and took her mother by the shoulders and sort of shook her to bring her out of that spell she'd fallen into.

The daughter said, "Come on, Momma, we've got to go." Suddenly, her mother blinked her eyes, turned her head, and looked directly at me. The entire time she'd been in our house, probably two to three hours, she had not recognized anyone or said one sensible word. But she suddenly turned to me and said very distinctly, "Will I ever be any better?"

When she said that, it was just like an electrical charge struck me on the top of the head and went through me. I knew exactly what it was; it was the manifestation of the gift of special faith. The Holy Ghost dropped the gift of special faith down in my spirit to minister to this insane woman (1 Cor. 12:9). It wasn't ordinary faith, or general faith, the faith that is common to all of us (Rom. 10:17). It was a manifestation of one of the gifts of the Spirit, the gift of faith.

That's where we miss it so many times. You see, in a case like this, you could yell and scream and holler at the devil all day long with ordinary faith, and nothing would happen. Or if you yelled and screamed at the devil in the natural, you could actually give place to the devil, and he would accommodate you.

In some cases, it takes the gift of special faith — an operation of the Holy Spirit — to bring about deliverance. Otherwise, you could say to an insane person, "Be healed! Be healed! Mind, work normally!" all you wanted, and the person would be just as insane as before.

But the minute that gift of faith dropped down in me, I answered the woman by the unction of the Holy Spirit, "Yes! You will, in the Name of Jesus!" I couldn't have doubted that she would be delivered if I had tried. I knew it was as good as done. That's all I said, just as calmly, as simply as can be. There was no other manifestation whatsoever. The daughter bundled her mother up and took her home.

About two years later, the woman's daughter came to visit us. One of the first questions we asked her was, "Whatever happened to your mother?"

"Well," she said, "I took Momma home, and the next day and the day after that there was still no change. But on the third day at three o'clock in the afternoon, as quickly as you could snap your fingers, her mind was totally restored."

The daughter explained, "I'd talked to her about Jesus before she lost her mind, and she'd always say to me, 'I don't believe in things like that. If you want to believe it, fine. But just don't ever talk to your father and me about Jesus or the Bible.'

"So I just prayed for them," the daughter continued, "but I never said another word to them about Jesus. But that day, the minute her mind was restored, she got down on her knees and gave her heart to the Lord. Daddy came into the room and saw Momma repenting and accepting Jesus, and he got on his knees and said, 'Pray for me too. I want to be saved too.' And he gave his heart to Jesus!"

I didn't cast a devil out of this woman. I didn't lay hands on her. All I did was to follow the leading of the Holy Spirit and speak under the unction of the Spirit of God. Actually, it was the gift of special faith in operation. I obeyed God. I didn't try to operate something by myself in the flesh.

I've given these examples from my own ministry to demonstrate that God heals and sets people free by various methods, all of which are in line with His Word. I've also used these examples from my own ministry to show you that *we* can't operate the gifts of the Holy Spirit ourselves. We must be totally dependent on the Holy Spirit for everything we do. If we try to minister by set formulas, we'll be in the flesh. Not only will we fail, but we can even open a door to the devil.

By ministering in the flesh, you can also eventually go into deception because Satan operates in the realm of the flesh — in the sense realm. Just stay with the Word of God and be led by the Holy Spirit. The Holy Spirit will always lead you in line with the Word of God.

Base everything you do on the Word, not on supernatural manifestations. If you operate according to God's principles — according
to Scripture — great deliverances can be wrought because ultimately
it's the knowledge of the truth of God's Word that makes us free.

We Are the Church Triumphant!

And whether you are ministering deliverance, praying for the
sick, or just taking a stand against the devil in your own life —
keep in mind that Satan is a defeated foe. If you are a believer, you
are seated with Christ in heavenly places *now*. *Jesus'* victory over
the devil is *your* victory because you are in Him.

Wherein does the authority of darkness lie? In Satan. But we've
been delivered from the authority of Satan! And we need to remember that he's been defeated and dethroned!

That's why I'm not going to fight the devil! I just going to walk
on over him and put him in his place because I'm part of the triumphant Church!

After all, just stop and think about it. Can anything exert
authority over your body without exerting authority over your head?
No, it can't. Whatever belongs to your Head belongs to your Body.

Well, since Jesus Christ, the Head of the Church triumphed
over demons, evil spirits, and Satan himself, we did too, because
we're His Body. His triumph is our triumph! That's why we should
call ourselves the triumphant Church. That's who we are now —
not when we get to Heaven — but *right now*.

Since we've been delivered from the authority of Satan, he has
no authority over the Body of Christ in any way, shape, form, or
fashion. But *we* have authority over *him* in Christ! Jesus made an
open show of Satan and put his defeat on display by triumphing
over him in the Cross!

Yes, we have to deal with evil forces, but we've got authority
over them. They're dethroned powers! We're a triumphant Church,
enjoying the victory that Jesus already provided for us. We don't
need to make war on the devil. All we have to do is stand our
ground against him and put him on the run with the Word.

Instead of these dethroned powers ruling over you — you rule
over them! In fact, if you not looking down when you're dealing with
the devil — you're not high enough! Come on up and sit in heavenly
places in Christ where you belong — as the triumphant Church!

ABOUT THE AUTHOR

The ministry of Kenneth E. Hagin has spanned more than 60 years since God miraculously healed him of a deformed heart and incurable blood disease at the age of 17. Today the scope of Kenneth Hagin Ministries is worldwide. The ministry's radio program, "Faith Seminar of the Air," is heard coast to coast in the U. S. and reaches more than 100 nations. Other outreaches include: *The Word of Faith*, a free monthly magazine; crusades, conducted nationwide; RHEMA Correspondence Bible School; RHEMA Bible Training Center; RHEMA Alumni Association and RHEMA Ministerial Association International; and a prison ministry.